StARTing With...

Third Edition

Kit Grauer, Rita L. Irwin & Michael J. Emme

Editors

Canadian Society for Education through Art
Victoria, British Columbia

Kit Grauer or Rita L. Irwin
Department of Curriculum Studies
University of British Columbia
2125 Main Mall
Vancouver, B. C. V6T 1Z4 Canada

Michael J. Emme
Department of Curriculum & Instruction
Faculty of Education
University Of Victoria
P.O. Box 3010, STN CSC
Victoria, BC V8W 3N4 Canada

To purchase this or any other CSEA material contact:
CSEA National Office
www.csea-scea.ca
or
P.O. Box 3010, STN CSC
Department of Curriculum & Instruction
Faculty of Education
Victoria, BC V8W 3N4 Canada
office.csea@gmail.com
Phone: (250) 721-7896

Cover: Tita do Rêgo Silva, *Kindheitserzählungen* or *Contos de
infância* or Tales from childhood, woodcut, 1997.

We wish to thank Tita do rêgo Silva for giving us copyright
permission to use her woodcuts for the cover and throughout the book

StARTing With...

Third Edition

Kit Grauer, Rita L. Irwin & Michael J. Emme

Editors

nd creativity and be the kind of teacher that brings
nd adventure to learning. I want my students to drea
magine, draw, paint, sculpt, build, create and invent.

nd diversity in the world and learn to see things
ew ways and explore new perspectives. I want to find o
ow art can open worlds and ways of seeing. I want
ind ways of teaching art that are engaging and imag
ative and touch children's lives in meaningful way

Contents

Introduction

StARTing with… is an introduction to the art of art teaching in Canadian schools. It was designed and written by art teacher educators from across Canada who wanted to provide a stARTing point for those interested in teaching art to think about their beliefs and values toward art education. With this in mind, we want you to be actively engaged with the ideas presented in the next hundred plus pages so you become a co-author making connections with the ideas you have about art in the education of children, reflecting on how the ideas fit within your conceptions of yourself as a teacher of art, and especially, imagining, (in image or in text) how you will use this information in your own teaching repertoire. We want you to push the boundaries of this book at all levels - questioning the assumptions, exploring some of the possibilities, and researching what lies beyond, as you consider your own personal experiences and the literature in the field of art education. What follows are some suggestions on how you might use the text as a working resource.

No resource book can provide all the inspiration, knowledge, pedagogical strategies and techniques necessary to make a great art teacher. This book introduces you to the key roles, values and issues concerning teachers of art at the elementary level while also asking you to move beyond the pages into the realm of the possible. Many of you will be using this text in conjunction with your elementary art education methods classes, and as such, will have the opportunity to explore the ideas within a community of beginning teachers representing a range of understandings about the place of art in schools. We hope you will take advantage of this opportunity to listen carefully to the stories of others as you make sense of your own beliefs and practices. We firmly believe the process of becoming a teacher is a process of starting from your experience, while exploring new ideas and conceptions, as you build a basis for making the best decisions possible in the classrooms you will teach. This process is a life long journey as a teacher. We hope you will take the initiative to go beyond what is within these pages in order to search out what is meaningful to you in your memories and experiences, as well as in art galleries, museums, community centers and cultural events, and even media sources such as books, articles, magazines, film, video and the internet.

One of the important places to start this search is from your own art experiences in school: have your own experiences shaped what you believe to be possible? Deborah Smith-Shank (1993) uses the metaphor of Dragon teachers - teachers of art, who like dragons, inflict injury on their students – who teach unreflectively and in so doing, often make art classrooms a site for anxiety and angst rather than a place of transformation. No one intentionally, we hope, becomes a dragon teacher. By starting with your own experiences and continuing to critically reflect on them as you move through theory and practice, we hope you become aware of, and critically examine, your underlying assumptions with the view toward positively transforming children's learning through art experiences.

What are some of the ways that you can reflect on your experiences with art in school? One possibility is to create a visual metaphor of yourself as a teacher of art. Select a metaphorical image, either from a found source, an existing artwork, or an image of your own creation, and use it to discuss your beliefs around art in children's lives and your place within that vision. Visual metaphors are open to interpretations that may not be obvious at the time of choosing. They also open up sites of emotion and ambiguity as well as reasoned argument. Comparing visual metaphors during your teacher education program, or during your ongoing development as a teacher, may help you articulate or visualize your changing perceptions of your role as a teacher. Other possibilities might include personal written narratives of your experiences with art that are in turn shared with others. Some of these stories may have inspired, nurtured, confused or destroyed your own encounters with art. Use these narratives as springboards for journal writing, drawing or collaging in the open spaces within each chapter layout. Record your thoughts and beliefs as you encounter each new chapter and consider how they fit or do not fit into your own worldview. These types of reflections are designed to build a connection between your personal and professional experiences, as you highlight what experiences may help or hinder the place of art in the lives of children. It is surprising how differently we may wish to teach once we recall our experiences as children. We hope you will start with some form of reflective process as you begin this journey of becoming an art teacher. Do the Dragons of your experience stop you from the possibilities or do they make you more steadfast in your quest?

Moving from your own beliefs and experience, we also ask you to venture out into the world around you and observe children in the process of making and responding to art. Watch a group of two or more children draw. Bring the drawings back into class and use them as springboards for discussion as you consider theories of children's drawing development or what young children do or say. You might ask yourself some questions such as: What surprises you or adds to your knowledge? What differences did you observe between the engagement of individual children and children of various ages? In your continuing quest you could interview adults and children about their definitions of art (and learning in art) and consider their conceptions alongside your own growing definition of art and learning in and through art before asking yourself even more questions. What art activities bring joy to you or challenge your values and assumptions? When is it appropriate to teach skills and what skills need to be taught? How should we endeavor to balance art making with responding to art, and how do we choose whose art to study? It is instructive to learn from others as you position your own beliefs within the field.

There are a plethora of resources available to teachers in books, magazines, and on the internet, that give lesson and unit ideas for art in elementary schools. Start collecting sample lessons or units on various topics. You might want to start with some of the ideas presented within this resource to see how the topics are played out in other contexts. You will be amazed at how many resources are available to teachers and how many will need to be modified or discarded. Choose those that fit with your beliefs about how art should be taught - share them with your class mates and be prepared to reflect critically on why they should be taught. Debating what might work and why is an important characteristic of excellent teachers. Curriculum guides and instructional resources are just that - guides and resources. It is up to you as a teacher to make the pedagogical choices that bring ideas to life in your classroom. Question how your art lesson may or may not be integrated in a thoughtful way with other curriculum areas. Collect copies of how teachers evaluate student's artistic learning and question whether the evaluation values the learning. What are the criteria used for making judgments? How are students a part of the process or recipients of judgments? What does this information tell you about the conceptions of art education being employed?

Investigate the resources you have as a teacher in your area: you might be pleasantly surprised to find an artist in your neighbourhood or you might expand your definition of art, who makes art, and what art is for through your interactions with local venues such as galleries. Think about how we incorporate experiences with art and artists as we give children a chance to connect to the world outside of school. Furthermore, consider how we display the art works of children as a site for conversations around teaching and learning in art.

Many of the chapters will ask you questions as a way to help you make connections with your own experiences and the experiences of others. This book is of particular benefit to educators interested in the changing Canadian context. It is situated in the collective experience of the authors as art teacher educators working alongside beginning art teachers over many decades. This current edition adds many new voices and to update the changing field of art education. . Belidson Dias, the art educator who took on the initial design of the book, deserves the credit for developing a visual feast to echo the content. In this third edition, Mike Emme has expanded that vision and produced what we hope is an inspiring and visually rich document. Please make this book a resource for you as you question and shape your identity as the teacher of art you envision.

Reference

Smith-Shank, D.L.(1993) Beyond this point there be dragons: pre-service elementary teachers' stories of art and education. 46 (5), 45-51.

CHAPTER 1

Learning

In,
Through,
and
From
Art

Rita L. Irwin

When I visit galleries, museums, or concert halls, I know I will have particular kinds of experiences. These venues are designed and maintained in ways that inspire particular qualities of experience: we enter each place knowing we are going to pay attention to something. I know when I venture into one of these environments I am bringing my unique set of attitudes, beliefs and knowledge with me as I experience the features of the event or object. I enter these environments also knowing, perhaps expecting, to be enriched. Once inside, my senses are recharged, my imagination is ignited, my emotions are revealed, and my soul often finds meaning in unexpected ways.

Whereas venues for the arts call us to experience the fullness of our humanity, schools are often limited to, or defined by, reaching the cognitive potential of students at the expense of realizing our full potential as human beings. Unfortunately, less attention is often given to knowing through our bodies, emotions, and spirits than the attention given to our minds where testing and rankings are used to measure intellectual rigour, competencies, and ultimately, one's abilities in narrowly defined ways.

As I reflect upon my learning experiences in each of the earlier mentioned venues I am struck by a fairly obvious revelation, one that so many of us know but gradually disregard under societal pressures. Being in environments rich with artistic activity, whether as a spectator or creator, calls me into experiencing the world in holistic ways. I am instantly transported into a space and time that causes me to feel, to perceive, to move, and to contemplate. I am thrust into the wholeness of my being. I am no longer objectifying knowledge rather I am experiencing knowing. For instance, why is it that most of us cannot retain facts we have memorized for an exam? I suspect it is because we did not experience that knowledge (see Dewey, 1934). When I have allowed myself to experience meaning-making through movement, emotional response, and soulful attachments, as well as perceptual engagement, I have always retained my new found knowing. It stays with me. It means something to me. I understand it in very concrete ways. Schools, and the curriculum found within our schools, have something to learn from the arts and from venues that celebrate and challenge the arts. Holistic learning is essential for learning (see for instance Hocking, Haskell, & Linds, 2001; Miller, 1988; Nava, 2001) and the easiest way to ensure that learning is holistic is to embrace learning in and through the arts (see for instance Burnaford, Aprill, & Weiss, 2001; Grauer, Irwin, de Cosson & Wilson, 2002; Krug & Cohen-Evron, 1999).

11

feeling • meaning • vision • touch • learning

A number of the authors in this volume talk about the importance of the arts to the rest of the curriculum. Recent research shows when students are involved in learning activities that include the arts, their mathematics achievement scores increase (Upitis & Smithrim, 2003). This is but one small reminder that a holistic education that includes the arts is not provided at the expense of mathematics. In fact, more mathematics instruction does not necessarily yield higher mathematics scores. Research suggests the opposite: a balanced curriculum, which includes the arts, actually strengthens *all* learning. Students should be engaged with their own learning, find their own passion, and create their own minds (Eisner, 2002).

What can we learn from the arts? A number of educators have written extensively on the importance of the arts (e.g. Chalmers 1996; Eisner 2002; Greene, 1995; Lankford 1992; McFee & Degge, 1980). If you were to read their work you would see that people value the arts for a wide range of reasons. For instance, the arts provide pleasurable, sentimental, inspirational, informative, and surprising experiences; the arts provide economic, social and political influences; and the arts provide insight into society through skilful accomplishments, historical interpretations, and cultural characterizations. Art communicates by generating, recording and transmitting ideas. Art acts as a cultural source and resource by helping people form identities and recognize accomplishments while also destabilizing practices that are problematic. Art enhances our lives by making the ineffable tangible. In very general terms, the arts contribute to our personal efficacy as well as our interconnectedness with all living and spiritual entities.

Photo by: Julia Freeman-Woolpert

Learning in Art provides a rich base from which to explore ideas, sensory qualities, penetrating questions, and personal feelings

Learning in art provides a rich base from which to explore ideas, sensory qualities, penetrating questions, and personal feelings through the use of materials, in the case of studio-based art, or through the use of texts (highlighting art history, criticism, or aesthetics), in the case of discourse-based art. Nothing can replace learning in art. Just as I recognize learning to play the piano offers me greater scope in appreciating the work of great pianists, so too does my learning in art offer me greater understanding of the work of those who spend their lives committed to the discipline of their art. As I paint, I understand the work of painters even more. I appreciate the work of artists whose ideas and styles are similar to, yet different from, my own. Recently, I experienced an artist-in-residence program in which an African drummer visited a school. He created simple drums for his students and together they played impressive rhythms. Excited to keep their new skills, students requested drums for their holiday gifts later in the year. Drumming became an important expressive and creative activity for his students.

While the arts are important for many reasons, one might wonder what principles should guide educators as they design curricula. Eisner (2002), a foremost art educator and curriculum specialist, articulates five principles that can guide our practices. He states: "In justifying its case, art education should give pride of place to what is distinctive about the arts … foster the growth of artistic intelligence … help students learn how to create satisfying visual images … help students recognize what is personal, distinctive, and even unique about themselves and their work … [and] make special efforts to enable students to secure aesthetic forms of experience in everyday life (pp. 42-45)." Keeping these principles for designing curricula in mind, several authors in this volume elaborate upon how a teacher might go about planning for quality art instruction. **Boyd White** discusses how human values are central to art education: to do so, he emphasizes values, feelings, and visual distinction as the basis for aesthetic response. **Patti Pente** provides an overview of child development research and argues for a holistic approach to working with children. **Robert Kelly** invites teachers and students to consider the virtues of living life with a disposition to creativity. **Miriam Cooley** explores creativity and what it means to be an art teacher or a teacher of art, and provides a range of strategies for teaching art in K-12 settings. **Kit Grauer** draws our attention to how art making and writing share similar yet different processes. By understanding this teachers may be able to strengthen their planning practices in both language arts and art instruction. **Harold Pearse** illustrates cross-curricular connections through his daily drawing practice and provides an example for how teachers may develop similar experiences. **Fiona Blaikie** discusses art assessment practices in BC, Ontario and Nova Scotia. Though many practices are similar a few differences exist. This comparison should help teachers analyze the best assessment practices for their classroom. While many authors help us consider how to plan for art teaching and learning, **Anita Sinner** takes us one step further and details how an ecologically-aware art classroom is one in which art educators are informed by legislation, safety, and a holistic teaching philosophy.

Learning through Art

stresses a holistic education by infusing the arts throughout intended learning experiences

Learning through art stresses a holistic education by infusing the arts throughout intended learning experiences. The arts force us to address learning in a holistic manner. *Learning through art* provides the basis for experiential learning to take place: learning that is durable in and through time. Many authors in this volume explore *learning through art*. For instance, **Michael Emme** and **Karen Taylor** discuss, and illustrate, how arts educators can use sequential art as way to develop literacy across the curriculum. **Mary Blatherwick** elaborates on how student art exhibitions are an important part of an art education curriculum as those involved learn to talk about art, appreciate it and learn from it in ways that are only accomplished through the display of ongoing art making experiences. **Stephen Elliott** guides teachers through discussions on the nature of art and details how one might help students talk about art using notions of art criticism. **Sharon McCoubrey** continues along this same line by providing in-depth examples of image development sources, strategies, and skills as well as a rich array of image development activities. These chapters have helped us understand how to make image development both personally and socially meaningful. **Heather Pastro** outlines the elements of design in great detail, not only for their basic properties, but also for their use within a range of studio-based activities. This listing of ideas should serve to introduce the design elements to teachers in very practical ways. **Aileen Pugliese Castro** and **Juan Carlos Castro** help us understand how to rethink celebrating holidays so that art lessons are meaningful, for all students, despite cultural, religious, orientations. **Kit Grauer** provides an illustrated description of visual journals, helping all art educators to consider the importance of regular visual journaling in and across the curriculum. **Jennifer Eiserman** takes us into the realm of visual literacy and illustrates how teachers can access art in galleries and museums. Several models are described and Eiserman outlines how each can be integrated into one process. For those teachers who are unable to take advantage of galleries and museums, one might be able to create a school art museum for all students, teachers and community members to enjoy.

forest • tree • leaf • pattern • learning

Photo by: Michal Zacharzewski

Painting by: Rita Irwin

Learning in · through · and from Art

Learning in art and *learning through art* are both important to a vital educational program for all students. Yet there is one more twist of phrase to be considered. *Learning from art.* What can art teach us about learning that will inspire a love affair with learning itself? **Dónal O'Donoghue** provides a detailed analysis on how the work of contemporary artists can be used as a basis for reconsidering how we teach art. His seven commitments call us to re-examine how and what we teach. Most importantly, he asks us to move away from how we have traditionally taught, and allow the work of contemporary artists to guide our practices. **Graeme Chalmers** takes *learning from art* to another dimension when he attempts to have us look critically at *why* we teach art. He posits that teachers and students alike need to recognize that all art is political and even elementary students can make visual statements about injustice. **Bill Zuk** and **Robert Dalton** guide us through understanding how to include First Nations art and culture in an art curriculum. They place much emphasis on tradition and innovation, showing how both are important to understanding First Nations cultures today. **Lorrie Blair** describes the benefits and challenges of teaching a visual culture based curriculum, pointing us to again reposition our practices so that we examine the visual nature of our world and how that impacts students today. **Joanna Black** believes teaching technology in visual art without meaningful art content is meaningless. By engaging students in planning to videotape a subject within one's everyday experience, students become creators in a study of historical and contemporary culture. Related to visual culture is the idea of design education. **Michelle Wiebe** details how students might begin to think of themselves as designers of logos, packages, and poster designs, among other possibilities. **Hilary Inwood** describes the need for place-based education – one that is community-based. In doing so, we would create strong bonds between students and their communities while nurturing a sensibility of sustainability.

self · family · community · questions · learning

...are essential to a rich art education experience. Art is critical because art transforms our consciousness.

We understand our selves, our cultures, and our histories, through our sensory and aesthetic experiences.

Learning in, *through* and *from* are essential to a rich art education experience. Art is critical because art transforms our consciousness. We understand our selves, our cultures, and our histories, through our sensory and aesthetic experiences. "Work in the arts is not only a way of creating performances and products; it is a way of creating our lives by expanding our consciousness, shaping our dispositions, satisfying our quest for meaning, establishing contact with others, and sharing our culture" (Eisner, 2002, p. 3). **Harold Pearse** has done this within his own life. In this volume he illustrates how making cross-curricular connections through thematic daily drawing experiences opened up opportunities for learning with and through art in richly stimulating ways. Focusing on his dog, he *learned from art* (by studying art works with dogs he was able to learn about dogs) and he *learned through art* (by expressing his feelings toward his dog through his art making, he came to appreciate his relationship with his dog even more). Yet it was his *learning in art*, or his drawing experiences, that allowed him to explore a wide array of ideas. Making connections *in through* and *from* art became powerful learning experiences for Pearse to explore his relationship with his dog. It is here that all art educators need to aspire.

As I reflect upon treasured experiences in my studio, my many long walks in nature, or my lingering visits with works of art, I am struck by the ways the arts have caused me to keep learning out of the sheer joy and excitement I feel for learning. The arts have taught me there isn't one right answer; how something is communicated is just as important as what is communicated; imagination transforms my understanding in unique and surprising ways; aesthetic sensibilities define my quality of life; being purposefully flexible enhances my work and life; and lingering in an experience is vital to appreciating the inherently rich qualities I initially sought from the experience (see Eisner 2002). As I have reflected upon these ideas over my career, I have attempted to consider my teaching as an art form. At times this means paying attention to the rhythms of the day and the lesson while being careful to attend to patterns of interactions, to spatial relationships between individuals as well as between individuals and objects, to the colours in the classroom as well as tonal qualities in other sensory experiences, and to the storytelling nature of learning. These qualities have often sparked my attention to the ineffable, to that quality of experience that is difficult to talk about yet is easily recognizable by all who experience it. Performing teaching as an art form, calls teachers into a space of artistic work many seldom consider. Teachers who attend to their practice as an art form are often viewed as the teachers we remember years later, those teachers whose practices/processes make just as much difference, if not more, than the actual products of learning. People follow passion. Everyone wants to love what he or she does and who he or she is. When we experience teachers who are passionate about their own learning and their work, as learners we find ourselves motivated to learn for we want what our teachers have!

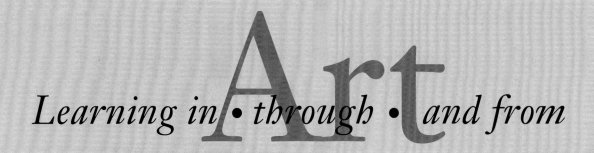

Learning in • through • and from **Art**

are each important to the design
of curriculum experiences in any learning
environment at any age level.
Possibilities for learning are endless
if one considers the magnitude
of these ways of learning.

References

Burnaford, G., Aprill, A., & Weiss, C. (2001). *Renaissance in the classroom.* Mahwah, NJ: Lawrence Erlbaum.

Chalmers, F. G. (1996). *Celebrating pluralism: Art, education and cultural diversity.* Los Angeles, CA: The J. Paul Getty Trust.

Dewey, J. (1934). *Art as experience.* New York: Minton, Balch.

Eisner, E. W. (2002). *The arts and the creation of mind.* New Haven, CT: Yale.

Grauer, K., Irwin R. L., de Cosson, A., & Wilson, S. (2001). Images for understanding: Snapshots of learning through the arts. *International Journal of Education & the Arts,* http://ijea.asu.edu/v2n9/

Greene, M. (1995). *Releasing the imagination: Essays on education, the arts, and social change.* San Francisco, CA: Jossey-Bass.

Hocking, B., Haskell, J., & Linds, W. (Eds.). (2001). *Unfolding bodymind: Exploring possibility through education.* Brandon, VT: Foundation for Educational Renewal.

Krug, D. & Cohen-Evron, N. (1999). Curriculum integration: Positions and practices in art education. *Studies in Art Education: A Journal of Issues and Research in Art Education, 41*(3), 258-275.

Lankford, E. L. (1992). *Aesthetics: Issues and inquiry.* Reston, VA: National Art Education Association.

McFee, J. K., & Degge, R. M. (1980). *Art, culture and environment: A catalyst for teaching.* Dubuque, IA: Kendall Hunt.

Miller, J. P. (1988). *The holistic curriculum.* Toronto, ON: OISE Press.

Nava, R. G. (2001). *Holistic education: Pedagogy of universal love.* Brandon, VT: Foundation for Educational Renewal.

Upitis, R. & Smithrim, K. (2003). *Learning through the arts national assessment.* Toronto, ON: Royal Conservatory of Music.

Photo by: Valeer Vandenbosch Digital Illustration by Michael J Emme

CONNECTIONS, REFLECTIONS AND CREATIONS

CHAPTER 2

Art Education and Human Values

Boyd White

Introduction

A generation ago the late Louis Arnaud Reid (1976) stated, "… the arts have as one chief source of their importance their endlessly new revelation of new values and new relationships of values, each art having its own reservoir of resources" (p. 21). This chapter looks at Reid's assertion and its applicability to the aesthetic response component of art education. In the process I will also say a few words about the role of the elements and principles of design within aesthetic response.

My students are pre-service elementary generalist teachers, but their experiences echo what I have tried with children. Some things are consistent, no matter what our ages. So let me begin with a little anecdote about a university class exercise. Afterwards I will put the exercise into context through a discussion about its various components and their theoretical underpinnings.

An Example

At the beginning of term I often show a reproduction of a painting, give students about a minute to look at the work and write down a word or phrase that the work suggests to them. I tell them that I am not looking for a factual term such as green, or dark. Rather, I want to know their response to that colour, setting, or whatever has captured their attention. When I ask the students to share their responses inevitably we find that there is substantial correspondence, although the wording might be slightly different. For example, one painting I use frequently is called The Gift, by Martha Teles.[1] It features, centrally in the composition, a young girl seated on a large chair. Her feet dangle well above the floor. She has on a white dress, and there are flowers entwined around the back of her chair. Behind, and therefore unseen by the child, is an open doorway, a balcony, and a suggestion of sea beyond. By one leg of the chair, well out of the reach of the child, is a small rectangular package, with a ribbon around it, apparently the gift to which the title refers.

Along with the sense of material comfort that the work portrays is a certain dissonance: The separateness between indoor and out, the colour contrast between the child and the darkness of the room's interior, the distance between the child and the gift. There are a number of other odd juxtapositions, too numerous to mention here.

Responses to the work result in terms such as lonely, sad, oppressive, frightening, bizarre, trapped, waiting. As the students volunteer their words and phrases I ask them to point to something in the image that contributed to their response. It is at this point that they begin to identify specific features of the dissonance.

What quickly becomes apparent to the class is that each word means something a little, or occasionally, a lot different from the others. But even when one student's response is quite different, the class is usually able to see why the individual responded in that way. For example, one word that is suggested occasionally is "spoiled". This response is so at odds with the others that the class is usually quite disconcerted. But when I ask the student to point to the features that prompted her response, she offers the signs of material prosperity—impeccable clothing, a somewhat overweight child, flowers; even the dominant eggplant-like colour suggests a richness. So this student can defend her choice of word. But the students also quickly realize that each term, by itself, is an over-simplification of the work; that is, when they see the combination of words they begin to grasp the potential of the image to provide multiple but related responses that coalesce into a larger, though ambiguous, meaning. This is what Swanger (1990) suggests by the phrase "open form". The work "… affords a variety of interpretations, even ones that may contradict each other, and resists unequivocal judgment" (p.95).

The Gift   Martha Teles   1980
oil on canvas, 46.5cm x 38.2cm

The next step is to get my students to understand that their responses, their spontaneous feelings about the work, are symptomatic of underlying values that they already hold. With the painting in the above example I simply ask them if this is the kind of celebration they would organize for a child of their own. Invariably the answer is, "No". As the students explain the reasons for their answer they talk about appropriate ways to treat others, especially children. Quickly they realize that they are discussing human values. Underlying and contributing to the designation of sadness, for example, is an awareness of a stance that each student takes in relation to how children should be treated.

Despite our different backgrounds, family histories and so forth, the students see that the painting enables us to share certain values; and the sharing is fairly easy because, as we have seen, the students can point to specific features of the work to back up their statements. But, keeping Reid's statement about new values in mind, one of the most intriguing outcomes of the exercise is dawning student awareness that the apparently simple image presents conflicting ideas simultaneously—material wellbeing together with social deprivation, for example. In fact, the image portrays layers of complex yet complementary relationships. To grasp these is to enlarge, however, slightly, one's world of values. In other words, heightened perception may lead to increased values awareness.

Aesthetics – Setting the Stage

Why do I do this exercise? What's the point of a focus on values? The questions seem justified since there is relatively little in the art education literature that addresses the issue of values explicitly. Those that do address the topic tend to fall into one of two groups. First, there are those whose writings are devoted to social issues such as multiculturalism and feminism, to name but two inter-related foci. See, for example, Chalmers (1996), Clark (1996), Gude (2000, 2004, 2007), and Neperud (1995). This is the larger group.

Then there are those who address the topic from the standpoint of aesthetics. See, for example, Bai, (1997), Curtler (2000), Maynell (1986), Portelli and Bailin (1993), Shusterman (2000), and White (1993, 2009). This chapter belongs with this latter group. This is not to say that specific social issues cannot emerge from an aesthetic orientation, as the above anecdote suggests, but such issues are not the initial focus, which is on the individual respondent. That is, if a focus on aesthetic response initially draws one's attention to the particularities of one's response, subsequent reflection may lead to awareness of the connectedness of that response to the encompassing social context and hence, to social issues.

For my interpretation of "aesthetic" I go back to ancient Greek usage of the term. In doing so, I reject, in large measure, concepts of aesthetics developed in the eighteenth century by Baumgarten (1750/1758/1961) and Kant (1790/1957) that have garnered much of the attention over the past couple of centuries.[2] As Buck-Morss (1992, p. 6) reminds us:

Aisthetikos, is the ancient Greek word for that which is 'perceptive by feeling'. *Aisthisis* is the sensory experience of perception…It is a form of cognition, achieved through taste, touch, hearing, seeing and smell—the whole corporeal sensorium.

To grasp the full sense of Buck-Morss' emphasis it may be helpful to think of modern surgical practice. Anaesthetic is used to induce a deprivation of the senses, and cognition, during surgery. Aesthetic experience, then, is just the opposite, that is, an emphasis on perception.

The aesthetic is not exclusively sensuous, however. Where Buck-Morss emphasizes the corporeality of perception, Nussbaum (1990), without rejecting that component, adds further considerations. She observes that a specifically Aristotelian conception of perception is a combination of intellect, imagination and feeling. Thus the term 'aesthetic' might be considered a form of astuteness in terms of the senses aided by intellectual, imaginative and feeling-filled acts. In other words, aesthetically oriented acts are not just acts of seeing; they come with a full complement of associated mental acts. As Husserl (1977) notes, every perceived form contains a mentality "intrinsically blended in" (p. 85). Or as Nelson Goodman (1968) has said, "There is no innocent eye" (p. 7).

These contemporary interpretations of aesthetic experience are useful insofar as they provide an understanding of the holistic nature of our interactions with our visual world, especially the world of art, how values are connected to those interactions, and why these are educationally valuable exercises.

Values, Feelings and Visual Distinction-Making

(a) Values

(i) Why should values be a primary concern in art education? In order to answer the question we have to look more closely at what values are and how they operate. Rader and Jessup (1976) provide some helpful scaffolding on which to build an understanding of the nature of values. They state, "Value can be analyzed into three components, I-R-O, in which "I" is the interest of the subject, "O" is the object of the interest, and "R" is the relation between them" (p.10). Let us examine each of the components in turn. Their relation to aesthetic experience will become apparent.

The "I" in the equation suggests that values emerge only if there is interest in the object or event in question. As Frondizi (1971) has pointed out, interest is not limited to curiosity. Will, desire, aversion, in short, a "…disposition in favour of or against something…" signifies "interest" (p. 45).

Let us move on to the "O" in the I-R-O equation. It represents the object or event that is the focus of a valuational exercise. Such an apparently straightforward designation is, however, an over-simplification. Values are not simply the product of a self-centred and self-contained world (typified by the "I know what I like" attitude). Rather, values emerge as we focus on something exterior to ourselves. Values require what Frondizi (1971) calls a "carrier"; that is, if they are not entirely subjective, values are not independent entities either. Values are attached to our external world but they need human perception in order to emerge. We can see this in the example of the Teles painting and my class' interactions with it. The painting is the value carrier, but the value, loneliness for example, is neither exclusively in the painting nor in the students looking at it. It is a quality that we distinguish as we interact with the work.

This suggests that when the term "object" is used in relation to values, it should be understood to mean "object-as-experienced". For example, when we stand before a painting or watch a movie we do not limit ourselves to the empirical presentation—the number of dots and colours on the screen, and so forth. Rather, we attempt to get beyond, or transcend, the empirical. In other words, the physical object supplies part of, but certainly not the whole meaning of the work. At best, it provides occasion to establish, spontaneously, a general categorization. (This is a painting of an apple; that on the table is a real apple.) As useful as this ability is to our everyday existence, it does not fulfill the real purpose of looking with valuational intent. That purpose is to grasp the object-as-experienced; such action, in turn, entails an imaginative grasp, an Aristotelian awareness of the personal significance of the moment in all its singularity.

The term "singularity" brings us to the final letter, "R"—for *relation*—in the I-R-O equation. The concept is an elaboration on what I introduced in regard to meaning making in the previous paragraph. That is, personal meanings, replete with values, are established for us in our daily interactions with our world, on the basis of the particularities of our individual histories.

Meanings are evolutionary, albeit share-able. They are the product of an ongoing, lifelong process of experiencing and synthesizing, new experiences adding layers of meaning on top of, enriching, and sometimes replacing, older ones. So when Rader and Jessup speak of Relations between Interest and Object we should keep in mind that such relationships are dependent upon the kind of lives we lead, and how

experientially rich or poor they are. Suffice to say that if one's life experiences have a narrow horizon, his/her relations with the world will not be as richly layered, significant, or valuable as those of someone more broadly experienced.

(ii) Local and regional properties: an application of values. As I mentioned earlier, students are able to point to specific properties of the Teles painting—the colours, proportion of child in relation to chair, distortions in perspective, and so forth. Curtler (2000) notes that these descriptors are called "local properties". All students can see them. They are fact-based entities.

In concert with the local properties are regional properties. It is these that, according to Curtler, define the value. The dissonance I mentioned earlier is an example of a regional quality. Unlike a local quality it cannot be pointed to directly, but the designation can be justified through reference to the local properties. As Curtler says, local properties "anchor" regional ones (p.11). This is a reciprocal relationship in which each property, local and regional, helps to support, clarify, and define the other.

The terms my students used to describe the painting—sad, oppressive, and so forth—denote the regional qualities. Curtler is correct in pointing out that valuations, as feelings, are not values; and words like "sad" do suggest a feeling. But it is important to keep in mind that the viewing of the image did not make my students sad. They just recognised the value quality—sadness. Sadness was a dormant quality, awaiting recognition brought about through the interaction (relation) between viewer and image.

While Curtler argues that the regional properties are the values, we can go one step further. When my students point to sadness, oppression, loneliness in the painting, I agree that they have identified a human quality. But I also suggest that these initial values point to others. The reason that the image depicts oppression or loneliness is that it also suggests what is not there, but should be—human sociability, justice and related values. Curtler insists that values must be experienced, not inferred (p.11). But the power of artworks often rests in our ability to experience what is not there as well as what is.[3]

In such instances the local features, the value-carriers, provide a dormant value-field, the potentiality for value awareness. The regional features emerge when we bring our world contexts (our understanding of, for example, loneliness) to bear on the local features. At that moment the value-field becomes no longer dormant; the field actively contains a value of which we are conscious. But it is not simply a matter of saying, for example, "The work is about loneliness." Underlying that recognition is a simultaneous acknowledgement that one values sociability. The need for human contact is the value counterpart of the value "solitude". So in our example, the student must not only empathize with the girl in the painting; the student must also be able to see the image as a metaphor—for desirable sociability, justice for children, the importance of human attention relative to material goods, or some such comparable interpretation. The ability to form the metaphor is a fundamentally imaginative and, as Swanger suggests, reciprocal act that requires input from both the individual participant and, in this case, the painting. *The Gift* is the title of the painting, but the real subject matter is the metaphoric interpretation. And it is the value.

We can summarize this section now with the following definition: Values are qualities that acknowledge, describe, and correspond to the regional properties of objects and events. In turn, these regional properties may be metaphors for larger issues. The regional properties correspond to the local properties of the thing/event itself.

(b) Feelings

Now let us look at the relation of feelings to values, and the educational implications of that relationship. Feelings are not values, but feelings are symptomatic of values. Their existence indicates values that one already holds. For example, if my students have empathy for the girl in the painting, this is the result of their value judgements, that this is not an appropriate way to treat a child. Each judgement is a result of values already formed by prior experiences that we bring to bear on the current moment in a spontaneous, that is, non-volitional, act of comparison. Such acts of comparison result in the simultaneous experience of a particular feeling. In short, feelings are values-laden responses to a given situation.

It is for this reason that Reid (1976) can make the claim: "It is when we come to the world of values that the vital importance not only of feeling but of its cultivation and education is seen" (p.15). Reid then, not only draws attention to the essential connections between values and the arts, he also emphasizes the direct contribution of feelings to the educational equation.

We find this emphasis on feeling in other writings too. Efland (1990) makes the point clearly: "The arts make a virtue of affective engagement and participatory learning, celebrating the life of feeling and imagination" (p. 263). I will return to the essential role of imagination later. For now let us look more closely at a justification for an emphasis on feelings in education. Within the general curriculum, it is mainly within the arts that personal, particularized feelings are cultivated. Otherwise, curricular emphasis is on fact, not feeling.

It is tempting to suggest that the emphasis on feeling within art has made the discipline suspect in the eyes of many. In other words, it is not clear to many non-art and art teachers alike, not to mention students, parents and school administrators, what the educational benefits are of an emphasis on feeling. It is also obvious that an expensive school system isn't necessary to the production of feelings. Pre-school children regularly show evidence of feelings after all. What then is an educational justification for such an emphasis?

(c) Visual Distinction-making

That justification may be found in the relations between our ability to make subtle distinctions in our visual world, and the shades of feelings those distinctions engender. In other words, we are not talking about simple categories of feelings. Any pre-schooler can experience those. But our capacity for subtle nuances of feeling extend beyond our usual verbal vocabulary, even adult vocabulary, and the ability to tease out those nuances is directly proportional to our ability to make visual distinctions. This is a unique contribution that art education can make to general education; that is, a distinction-making ability, based on concrete experiences of visual stimuli, is essential to the development of an extended capacity for feeling.

In turn, as authors such as Nussbaum (1990) and Bailin (1993) have argued, this capacity is crucial to the development of practical reason and education in general, including education in regard to values.

Sokolowski (1979, p. 653-654) argues that such abilities are frequently ignored in those parts of education that have garnered the most attention and prestige. He states:

> The bias of education and general opinion now is clearly toward explanation by decipherment rather than explanation by distinction. Astronomy, physics, economics…have inclined us to interpret what we directly experience in terms we do not directly encounter, like nuclear particles,…genes, concealed laws of money. …such hidden things are taken as the truth of what appears…This … is a bias; it overlooks a fact—that things described or constructed in science are dependent on distinctions and identifications made in the world in which we live.

Sokolowski's cautionary words seem as relevant today as when they were first written; for, reliance upon abstraction to describe the world seems, if anything, to be on the increase. I am not advocating an abandonment of abstract thinking in education, however; it has earned its place. On the other hand,

our task in art education is one of balancing such a focus with an equal emphasis on concrete experience, in the form of visual distinction-making, together with an awareness of how we feel about such distinctions; that is, what difference do the distinctions make to us as individuals experiencing them? As Sokolowski suggests, this first-hand, subjective experience provides a foundation for subsequent ideas, together with an important sense of participation and ownership. Without such a foundation, ideas remain the realm of others, and if one accepts them, one must do so on the basis of faith that those who have done the work are correct. This is a passive model of education; these days emphasis across the curriculum is inclined toward active models.

To sum up this section, visual distinction-making is a form of understanding, one that is essential to refinement of our feelings, and ultimately, expansion of our values. When we apply this idea to art education we may say that careful, distinction-making interactions with art can be identified and compared with moments in one's everyday world and can result in value recognition and enlargement. The identification becomes part of our ongoing growth as individuals.

Elements of Design, Principles of Organization

It is perhaps useful at this point to touch briefly on the topic of elements *of design* and principles *of organization*. Art educator Arthur Wesley Dow introduced these terms in the early twentieth century as a means to interpreting the visual world (Gude, 2004). Dow considered the elements and principles to be the building blocks or scaffolding upon which we construct our visual thinking. At the time, the concept was an appropriate strategy for understanding emerging modernist art. Over the past century art teachers gradually conflated the terms into the elements and principles *of art*. As Gude (2004) and others have pointed out, this conflation implies universality, one that the diversity of art forms across cultures and eras does not support. Still, for some people, attention to an element such as line, or an organizational feature such as rhythm might provide an initial toehold upon which to build an interaction with certain works (not all works). We might also argue they are what make up the local properties of which Curtler speaks. But as we have seen, for students to arrive at a value designation such as loneliness or injustice, they must synthesize the impact of a number of these local properties. So, yes, students must recognize a colour or line and how and why it is used. More importantly, they must see how such features are inter-related holistically into the meaning of the work. Meaning is seldom, if ever, dependent upon a single feature acting alone. To focus on one design element or organizational strategy would be to fall into the formalist trap and forego possibilities of meaning making.

This does not mean that a teacher can't show a Van Gogh drawing for the sake of its line; but if she talks only about the line as line, without discussing how it contributes to the feeling of the landscape, then the teacher misses the point as to why we find the work significant. That is, it's not just about line as an example of line, but about a particular landscape and Van Gogh's interpretation of it, as well as about a tradition of European drawing, Van Gogh's participation in that tradition and extension of it. In other words, Van Gogh's drawing is an encapsulation of western culture to that time, as distilled through the artist's personal life and temperament. Then too, our capacity for engagement with the drawing depends on our own history that we bring to bear on the moment—our familiarity with the work, comparisons to other works, our own attempts at drawing, and a host of other influences, many of which we are likely not even aware.

In short, preoccupation with physical properties alone cannot provide an aesthetic experience. What such preoccupation provides is size, shape, manner of execution, and the like. It might even provide an awareness of the unity of the whole. But without attention to feeling, context (one's own and that of the work at the time of its making), synthesis, and potential for meaning, then we lose the significance of the work to us. We lose the value.

So it is that current art educators such as Gude (2004, 2007), Duncum (2010) and others have taken the phrase,

elements and principles, and turned it on its postmodern head. If Dow's focus was appropriate to the beginnings of the twentieth century, we must acknowledge that the world has changed since then. Therefore it seems reasonable that the foci of art education should reflect those changes. Gude (2004) notes: "A basic tenet of all postmodern theory is a suspicion of totalizing discourses and grand narratives—the belief that there is one right way to organize and understand things" (p. 13). So, in place of Dow's elements and principles, Gude suggests we adopt more postmodern concerns that she has noted in contemporary art practice. In her 2004 article she consolidates these practices into eight categories, or 'principles', for example, appropriation and juxtaposition. To that list Gude (2007) has more recently added "principles of possibility", to address "…from the students' point of view, imagining what important ideas about the uses and making of art we want the students to remember as significant" (p.2). She suggests, among other considerations, playing, encountering difference, and forming the self.

Like Gude, Duncum (2010) is anxious to move educators away from a reliance on the modernist elements and principles. Thus, in his turn, Duncum has proposed his own list of seven principles, influenced by his focus on visual culture. The first of these is power.

> Power is the key principle because most of the other principles intersect with issues of power… all images involve an assertion of ideas, values, and beliefs that serve the interests of those for whom they are made—political, social, and economic— and audiences, in their turn, exercise the power of interpretation. (p. 6)

Duncum then fills in his list with what he considers to be starting points for others to build on—ideology, seduction, representation, and so forth.

What Gude and Duncum have in common, apart from their rejection of the modernist elements and principles, is a reliance on attention to context in the development of alternative perspectives. It is clear that the concept of elements and principles has taken on new roles, perspectives and possibilities for art education.

Summary

My main argument has been that human values— individual, cultural and societal—may be, and should be, a central focus of art education. I have said that attention to values is an appropriate and timely concern in education today, and that art education is ideally suited to address the issues. The reasons I have cited have to do with the nature of value itself, the interconnectedness between people and things, (fundamentally an imaginative, empathic act), associated feelings, the essentiality of concrete distinction-making to current educational practice, and the importance of taking context into consideration. I have suggested that all of these features can be addressed efficiently in art education, especially in that part of it that deals specifically with aesthetic response.

References

Bai, H. (1997). Ethics and aesthetics are one: The case of Zen aesthetics. *Canadian Review of Art Education, 24* (2), 37 -52.

Bailin, S. (1993). The bad and the beautiful: On moral and aesthetic appreciation. In Portelli, J. P. & Bailin, S. (Eds.) *Reason and value: New essays in philosophy of education* (pp. 93-103). Edmonton, Alberta: Detselig.

Baumgarten, A. G. (1750/1758/1961). *Aesthetica*. Hildesheim: G. Olms.

Buck-Morss, S. (1992). Aesthetics and anesthetics: Walter Benjamin's artwork essay reconsidered. *October, 62*, 3 – 41.

Chalmers, F. G. (1996). *Celebrating pluralism: Art education and cultural diversity*. Santa Monica, CA: Getty Center for Education in the Arts.

Clark, R. (1996). *Art education: Issues in postmodern pedagogy*. Reston, VA: National Art Education Association.

Curtler, H. M. (2000). In defense of values in the fine arts. *Journal of Aesthetic Education, 34*, (1), 7 – 17.

Duncum, Paul (2010). Seven principles for visual art education. *Art Education, 63*, 1, 6 – 10.

Efland, A. (1990). *A history of art education: Intellectual and social currents in teaching the visual arts*. New York: Teachers College, Columbia University.

Frondizi, R. (1971). *What is value? An introduction to axiology* (2nd edition). Lasalle, Ill.: Open Court Publishing.

Goodman, N. (1968). *Languages of art*. Indianapolis: Bobs-Merrill.

Gude, O. (2000). Investigating the culture of curriculum. In Fehr, E., Fehr, K., & and Keifer-Boyd, K. (Eds.), *Real-world readings in art education: Things your professor never told you* (pp.75-81). New York: Palmer Press.

Gude, O. (2004). Postmodern principles: In search of a twenty-first century art education. *Art Education, 53*, 1, 6 – 14.

Gude, O. (2007). Principles of possibility: Considerations for a twenty-first century art and culture curriculum. *Art Education, 60*, 1, 6 – 18.

Husserl, E. (1977). *Phenomenological psychology: Lectures, summer semester, 1925*. (John Scalon, Trans.). The Hague: Martinus Nijhoff.

Kant, I. (1790/1957). *The critique of judgement*. (J. C. Meredith, Trans.). Oxford: Claredon Press.

Leader, D. (2002). *Stealing the Mona Lisa*. New York; Counterpoint.

Maynell, H. A. (1986). *The nature of aesthetic value*. New York: State University of New York Press.

Neperud, R. W. (Ed.) (1995). *Context, content, and community in art education: beyond postmodernism*. New York: Teachers College Press.

Nussbaum, M. (1990). *Love's knowledge: Essays on philosophy and literature*. New York/Oxford: Oxford University Press.

Portelli, J.P. & Bailin, S. (Eds.) (1993). *Reason and values: New essays in philosophy of education*. Edmonton, Alberta: Detselig Enterprises.

Rader, M. & Jessup, B. (1976). *Art and human values*. Englewood Cliffs, NJ: Prentice-Hall.

Reid, L.A. (1976). Feelings and aesthetic knowing. *Journal of Aesthetic Education, 10*, (3 -4), 11 - 28.

Shusterman, R. (2000). *Pragmatist aesthetics: Living beauty, rethinking art*. (2nd edition). New York: Rowman & Littlefield.

Sokolowski, R. (1979). Making distinctions. *The Review of Metaphysics, 32*, 4, 639 - 676.

Swanger, D. (1990). *Essays in aesthetic education*. San Francisco, CA: Mellon Research University Press.

White, B. (1993). Aesthetic judgements as a basis for value judgements. *Canadian Review of Art Education, 20* (2), 99 - 116.

White, B. (2009). *Aesthetics*. New York: Peter Lang.

Notes

[1] The reproduction is from a grade one portfolio, part of a series entitled L'image de L'art, produced in Montreal, Quebec by Le Centre de Documentation Yvan Boulerice Inc.

[2] Baumgarten, in his unfinished text *Aesthetica* (1750, 1758) departed from the Greek usage of the term "aesthetic" so that it became a judgement according to the senses—emphasis on *judgement*. Ultimately this orientation led to a focus on taste and implied standards of taste. But preferences in taste are culture-bound, and art teachers have no mandate to dictate taste. Baumgarten's point of view is understandable insofar as his conceived world was smaller than ours is today, and Euro-centered. Our world is increasingly pluralistic and complex. To insist on a more correct taste is to place on a lower rung of the cultural-hierarchy ladder those who choose otherwise. There would appear to be little justification or need for such a stance in a democratic, pluralistic society. Amore profitable line of inquiry, from an educational perspective, is to search out the distinguishable features.

Similarly, Kant's (1790/1957) bias in favour of mind over body led him away from the early Greek orientation. Perhaps Kant's most controversial idea is his notion of a disinterested interaction with art, that is, an interaction devoid of the features discussed by Buck-Morss and Nussbaum and reliant solely on rationality. Most art educators today would argue that this notion does not conform to our experiences with art.

[3] Darian Leader (2002), in his text, *Stealing the Mona Lisa*, reinforces this point with his anecdote about the crowds who came to see where the Mona Lisa used to hang after it was stolen in 1911.

CHAPTER 3

Child Development in Art
What do You Need to Know?

Patti Pente

What is the most important information about the ways children make art, and what is the ideal way to help student teachers understand this complex topic?

I often contemplate these questions when my students come to me and ask,

"What kind of art does a grade two child make?"

The short (and long) answer to this legitimate student-teacher question is that the level of sophistication of children's learning in art will correlate to the level of sophistication present in their lessons. Children can be surprising with their thoughtful, insightful comments and actions about how, and why they – and artists - make art. Student teachers need to know how to frame projects and ask questions to facilitate the kind of learning that is engaging and deeply reflective of the contemporary world. They can instill inspiring, sensitive approaches to children's art making processes by thoroughly understanding the sensory world in which they – and children – live, under the domination of a culturally specific visual culture; and by creating opportunities to explore ideas using a great range of art materials over time. In order to be successful, student teachers must reflect upon their positions in the world as co-constructors of knowledge by carefully listening to children.

As I continue to expand upon this complex and important answer to my student teachers' questions about how to provide excellent teaching for children at different ages, the slightly glazed look entering their eyes gives me pause and then stops me completely, as I remember my own nervousness as a student teacher who was preparing to enter into the teaching profession. I begin again.... "I know you would like a formula for what to teach in each grade. However, you know more than you think you do if you allow yourself to listen to and observe carefully what children actually say and do when they are making art." Although this answer may not be as specific as some student teachers might like, it is the awareness gleaned from experiential knowledge in tandem with theoretical knowledge that will guide new teachers. This chapter therefore, provides a historical grounding in what art educators have concluded about child art making, offers an expanded view of contemporary issues about child art, and concludes with strategies to help student teachers build their understanding of children's artistic processes.

Historical Grounding of Child Development in Art

Historically, understanding the kinds of art children make at different ages has been situated in the developmental or stage theories in cognitive psychology, following education theorists such as Jean Piaget. From the earliest scribbles made by a toddler to sequentially more detailed and realistic depictions, the "stage-by-age" theories influenced art education for much of the twentieth century. Under this linear model, the child is seen to gradually and progressively move from one level of drawing or mark-making to the next, until, as Jessica Davis (1997) suggests, the child either gives up due to an inability to represent the world realistically, or she/he feels successful at this endeavour and continues to pursue art in adulthood. The most common developmental models of children's art making are found in the work of Viktor Lowenfeld, along with W. Lambert Brittain (1987), and Rhonda Kellogg (1969). Kellogg classified the scribbles of very young children into groups that indicated stages of symbolic development. Lowenfeld and Brittain (1987) described stages of development from early scribbles passing through the tadpole stage to the emergence of realism in adolescence.

Later, Howard Gardner (1983) proposed an alternative developmental model to account for children's learning in art making. His theory of multiple intelligences includes divisions of cognition into separate areas, but with much overlap and flow from one area into another. Art educators point out that Gardner does not dedicate a separate category to artist intelligence, which suggests the holistic nature of artistic activity where student artists use a variety of cognitive and affective abilities (Kindler, 2004; Pariser & Zimmerman 2004). Indeed, Gardner (2006) recommends that curriculum resemble a spiral metaphor so that students revisit concepts with increasingly greater levels of depth to offset the linearity of stages. The MUSE project (museums united with schools in education), which emerged from under his influence and in collaboration with Davis (1996), advises that children be invited into discussions and explorations with and about art in a variety of ways. The key components of this approach include inquiry, access, and reflection (MUSE, nd). This position parallels constructivist learning theories where new information is built upon the child's previous knowledge so that ideally, student teachers become attuned to individual learning styles and will frame curriculum to offer a variety of approaches. Anna Kindler and Bernard Darras (1997), concluded that growth in children's art was more closely aligned to a map-like model, with art making heavily influenced by social interactions. This model is grounded in Vygotsky's (1978) theory of proximal development so that child development in art is understood as a communicative activity that is heavily influenced by social interactions and context (Kindler & Darras, 1997). In a slightly later interpretation of child development in art, Duncum (1999) theorized that there exist multiple end-points in the progressions of children's artistic development.

Regardless of what developmental theory proposed, Brent Wilson (2004) raises an important point that all developmental views assume that children move from simple to complex depictions of their worlds based upon social-cultural or psychobiological influences. This, in itself, is a culturally and historically bound interpretation that is based upon assumptions about definitions of child art. It is important, therefore, to analyze the specific context under which curriculum is produced (Wilson, 2004).

For student teachers, these developmental models are useful places to begin to understand the ways that children make art, and to understand the broad differences among various ages. This general knowledge can avoid circumstances where a novice teacher misinterprets a pupil's art. Christine Marme-Thompson (2005) recounts how a new teacher gently reprimanded a student for colouring hair non-realistically and yet, had that teacher understood the general developmental level of the child, she would have understood that realism was not the child's intention. This is an example of the benefit of understanding general guidelines found within stage theories. However, to leave the conversation at this point is detrimental for new teachers as well as for their future pupils.

Photo By: Shannon Pifko

Many student teachers' confidence levels and abilities to create age-appropriate lessons increased greatly when developmental theories were strongly supported by field experiences in art education (Luehrman & Unrath, 2006). Ultimately, developmental theories are interesting as historical data that help student teachers to loosely ground child art at a starting position, but the lived experience of teachers and pupils in an art classroom often bear little resemblance to separate stages. Thus, many experienced art educators working in the field consider the stage-by-age approach outdated and flawed (Freedman & Stuhr, 2004; Kindler, 2004; Marme-Thompson, 2009; Pavlou, 2009). There are important limitations in developmental stage theories that must be appreciated.

Influence of Materials

The majority of stage-by-age development models are based upon graphic representations – on drawing. These models are entrenched in drawing to the point that they lose considerable relevance when different materials are introduced. While almost all children will make marks that depict their worlds, so that drawings are plentiful and easy to generate for the purposes of research, the conclusions about child development are skewed to that particular kind of art. The limitations of the medium are significant if one wishes to more fully understand the ways children create art. Some research involving sculpture has offset the dominance of drawing, however, Claire Golomb (2004) researched developmental stages evident in children's clay sculpture and she concluded that even young children immediately denote specific three-dimensional strategies such as uprightness and balance in their efforts to develop representational concepts. This repudiates previous notions that young children tend to work on a sculpture as a flat two-dimensional "drawing" in clay due to a lack of cognitive development (Golombe, 2004). Materials play a more intensive role in children's art.

Following on this line of research, Victoria Pavlou (2009) found that when child development was considered through the exploration of three-dimensional art activities, teachers' expectations about children's levels of representation were below the levels at which the children actually worked. She concludes that if the number of different materials used to understand child art making were expanded, and the diagnostic assessment criteria align more specifically to the materials in question, this, in turn, can reveal different levels of development in individual children. In other words, a child's interaction with different media can result in specific paths of development, depending upon the qualities inherent in the medium. Using video cameras, for example, favours development of line-of sight and point-of-view that relate to movement and framing, which may not be revealed in other media (Matthews & Seow, 2007). Furthermore, Anna Kindler (1997) comments that the media influences levels of comfort in children's artistic processes. As Sylvia Kind explains, different materials can "evoke different ways of thinking" (2005, p. 12). The nature of a child's affinity to different materials and the different ways she or he approaches the creative process in relation to the media suggests that a variety of materials is necessary within the curriculum to deeply understand each child's developmental and creative state of being within the social context. Thus, investigations about a child's attraction to specific materials are important points of departure for student teachers when approaching children's art making.

The selection of art materials is so significant that processes of art making can seem foreign to children when they use a different, less familiar medium. In his overview of research about artistically gifted autistic children, David Pariser (1997) commented that changing from drawing tools to paint actually caused some children to stop making art. While they typically drew detailed representations of specific subjects at levels that were far above other children their age, when they tried to use paint to make art, they could not create anything but marks and splotches. Such a dramatic difference due to materials highlights a very important aspect of understanding how and why children create art. Selection of materials and/or activities is key to the entire creative process, and in many cases, materials are motivating factors in children's artistic decisions. Therefore, it is important to consider a variety of materials and activities at the very early stages of lesson and unit development. As Kind (2005) notes, "the heavy, damp, dense, texture of the clay, the cold, slippery, gooey feel of wet *papier-mâché*, the warmth and comfort of certain textiles, and the rich, vibrant globs of paint lying waiting on the palate, all are part of the art experience and influence how the art image or art object takes place" (p 13).

Despite this evidence in favour of expanding the kinds of materials for art making, the majority of research on child development in art relies on the assumption that drawing is the main way to define art. This does a great disservice to children and to the field of art education because it limits the definition of art to traditional skills-based drawing techniques. Instead, curriculum that is expansive, including all kinds of materials in art making will result in a corresponding expansion of definitions of art and its possibilities in the eyes of the pupil, the school, and the larger community. This not only reflects the work of contemporary artists, but also allows for more students to feel successful at art even though their drawing skills might not reach the level of realism that is often valued in schools and in the view of the general public in western cultures (Pariser & Zimmerman, 2004). Additionally, materials offer very important opportunities not only to focus on the process of exploring ideas, but also on the validity of the act of exploration in and of itself. In other words, it is through touching, looking, smelling, listening (but perhaps not tasting) a variety of materials that children have opportunities to sensually explore and learn about their worlds.

Socio-cultural Considerations

Understandings about definitions of art, and specifically definitions of child art are tied to social attitude and historical moments (Wilson, 2004). Social and cultural backgrounds hold sway over the kinds of activities of art making that emerge and how art is valued. Stage theories operate under specific Western socio-cultural influences that often go unnoticed. For example, the assumption that children's growth is a linear progression parallels the notion firmly entrenched in western culture that economic progress is desirable and necessary. Brent Wilson (2004) comments that developmental theories are not universal truths that are absolute, and he suggests that notions of child art itself have aligned closely with modernism in the art world. He points out that the fact that child art is actually defined as art, as opposite to play, is a result of culturally specific ideology placed upon childhood (Wilson, 2004). This suggests that student teachers take a closer look at their innate assumptions when it comes to educational systems. The frameworks of instruction and curriculum are always contingent upon the underlying values of the particular culture.

In western cultures, attitudes about how art should be taught typically land somewhere on a continuum that locates technical skill development at one end and self-expression at the other end, but these concepts need not be diametrically opposed (Richards, 2007). Student teachers should be aware that this typical divide is not in the best interests of pupils. Hallam et al. (2008) note three distinct expectations of the learning that are associated with art. Teachers see themselves in the role of expert, valuing technical skills development over other areas of art education; in the role of facilitator, limiting instruction to providing materials and a positive atmosphere in the classroom to foster self-expression; or in the role of one who places art in the service of other curriculum areas, virtually deleting art education as a separate discipline (Hallam et al., 2008). Significantly, none of these three positions in isolation accurately describes the ways that art making can be a generative language that conveys meaning in extraordinary ways when students are taught to consider their embodied relationship to materials and to the world. Regardless of the age of the students, richly layered learning experiences can

Sandbox Art
Age 4

be created with the appropriate combination of both teacher-initiated skills development and student-initiated "ideas" development. As a starting point, therefore, it is crucial that student teachers reflect upon their attitudes and expectations in specific classroom contexts in terms of what they assume the children can accomplish. These assumptions will relate to what student teachers value in art instruction and how they identify as art teachers.

Contemporary Contexts

The world continues to become increasingly image-oriented with technological advances. Many people daily interact through virtual social networks as much as physical ones. Thus, people participate in the creation of their visual culture as well as being influenced by it. In light of this complexity of relations, there has been a call to shift the focus of art education toward a greater awareness of ubiquitous power structures inherent in popular cultural images, and to consider the ways that all of us are active participants in the creation of our visual worlds (Desai & Chalmers, 2007; Duncum, 2010; Gude, 2007).

The visual culture that surrounds us, and that we often take for granted, continues to influence and change art education (Freedman & Stuhr, 2004). Stephen Carpenter and Kevin Tavin describe art education in a state of transition, moving "...toward a profoundly critical, historical, political, and self-reflexive understanding of visual culture and social responsibility, coupled with meaningful and transformative student production in a variety of forms and actions" (2010, p. 245). The significance of this shift from a modern to a postmodern perspective exposes the cognitive developmental theories as narrow descriptions of learning in the visual arts. The influence of visual culture on art education has opened the discipline to a wider exploration of the world, where the search for "correct" answers is replaced by an awareness of the multitude of life's questions that can be shared in a variety of creative ways.

Incorporating social issues such as class, race, and gender into art lessons offers children opportunities to thoughtfully explore their social reality through the visual language of art (Duncum, 2009; Gude, 2007). While every art lesson need not be a political commentary about the world, these social issues are in the forefront of much contemporary artists' work, and should be included in art class in ways that are appropriate, given the levels of student understanding initially gleaned through class discussion. Possible cross-disciplinary connections, for example, between social studies and art, are often evident when topics found in visual culture are introduced into the lesson in tandem with contemporary artists whose work is related to the same theme.

Thus, student teachers who can understand the many connections between contemporary artists' commentary on social issues, the ways an issue is taken up within visual culture, and children's perspectives on the topic will undoubtedly lead their students toward significant learning about their worlds through art making.

Listening and Observing as Teaching Strategy

I observe my six-year old son as he spontaneously begins a drawing inside a homework activity where he has been asked to colour in a photocopied sheet of math problems to discover the hidden image. Inside one section he suddenly starts drawing a narrative about a chipmunk chasing a "bad guy", gives them both parachutes, tumbles one onto the other and finishes with exciting sound effects that represent the climax of the event as his line moves to the edge of the section. He then laughs at his efforts, gives me a knowing smile, and proceeds to cover up his parachuted chipmunk with green pencil crayon in his effort to complete the given assignment. His teacher will see a coloured, completed page, but will have missed much in the meantime. This little narrative gift given to me by my child reminds me that all the adult need do is listen and watch to understand how to situate age appropriate lessons that will excite and encourage children to begin their own inquiries. The meanings that children devise as they create their art can be an evocation of memories, fantasy stories, or other imaginative avenues, where a scribble on the page represents an extraordinary leap into a created world or a portrait of their family members. Lessons generated by listening and observing students in the process of creating art will give new teachers important insights into the contemporary lives of their students, and a high level of interest in the art project will likely emerge.

Christine Marme-Thompson (2009) warns that the developmental theories that have influenced art education over the last century must be carefully located or even left out of the conversation so that they do not unduly shape student teachers' attitudes and expectations. Instead, she calls for direct observation of children making art. Ultimately, this is the best way to learn to be a teacher, although it is not always practical, given the structure of many teacher education programs. Nonetheless, by attending carefully to children when they are in the process of making art, student teachers can find a wealth of information on how students are enacting their meaning making through their art. Critical thinking skills and visual problem solving are evident when children make art, through the thematic exploration with a variety of media (Danko-McGhee & R. Slutsky, 2007).

34

During art class, the room often becomes noisier and conversations flow. There are many reasons for this sense of spontaneity, including the nature of the activity as embodied and social. Making art is an experience where all of the senses are actively engaged. Discussions frequently begin among children due to the urge to share their ideas and questions with their peers while in the process of making art. New teachers sometimes are intimidated by the levels of noise generated, but regardless of personal tolerances to noise levels, all the chatter is indicative of a very important point about the process of making art - that it is a social activity grounded in students' lives (Steele, 1998). By listening, manipulating, seeing, and speaking, as both a personal and public activity, children's perspectives of the world emerge, and student teachers will find that in one grade level there exists rich variety of interpretation of ideas and manipulation of materials.

However, even when student teachers understand and value the embodied nature of art, it is important that they analyze their lessons to consider if and/or how they situate the product in relation to process. Pat Tarr (2008) questions the lack of adequate time and opportunity pupils are given to completely engage with materials without the pressure to have a finished art product. In an educational climate that favours learning outcomes as objectified, identifiable mastering of tasks, I caution student teachers to be aware of the pressure to reward a finished art product at the expense of the vital learning that occurs during the process of experimenting with ideas through the materials. This pressure to have a completed art project that evidences a skill with the materials is partially a result of a culture of early child education craftmaking (Tarr, 2008).

One strategy to focus attention on the creative process is to carefully evaluate the assessment parameters of the assignment so that evidence of process is noted. A second strategy to help parents and the larger community value the creative art process is for teachers to engage in conversations with students during art class, and then to generate a number of student quotations and/or descriptions that are subsequently displayed with the not-so-perfect end result "product" or with photographs of the children in action (provided that appropriate permissions for photography have been granted). In these ways, teachers will have documented the art making with careful listening and observation, and the shift to the child's learning process can be highlighted.

Conclusion

The ways children learn are varied and non-linear in nature. It is counter productive to isolate cognition at the expense of social, cultural, physical, and emotional areas of development. It follows that understanding child development is a correspondingly holistic activity (Richards, 2007; Tarr, 2008). If student teachers begin with the position that knowledge about development in children is contextual and relational (Swann, 2008), and if they have extended contact with children as grounding for learning to teach, student teachers can gain much confidence in their abilities to be successful in the art classroom, regardless of individual skill level with particular materials.

Finally, my advice to student teachers when they ask me questions about specific grades and abilities, is to urge them to understand historical biases from which the developmental stage theories emerged, understand the limitations of these theories, and gather all information that life experience to this point has given them about what actually happens when they make art, and when children make art. Good art teaching is founded upon these reflective habits of mind that are initiated in teacher education programs and nurtured throughout a teacher's career. If student teachers explore with art materials and consider their visual worlds as they listen to children and observe children in learning situations, this will ultimately serve them best as an enduring teaching practice.

References

Carpenter, S. & Tavin, K. (2010). Art education beyond reconceptualization. Enacting curriculum through/with/by/for/of/in/beyond/as visual culture, community, and public pedagogy. In Malewski, E. (Ed.), *Curriculum studies handbook: The Next moment* (pp. 244-258). New York: Routledge.

Danko-McGhee, K. & Slutsky, R. (2007). Floating experiences: Empowering early childhood educators to encourage critical thinking in young children through the visual arts. *Art Education, 60*(2), 13-16.

Davis, J. (1996). *The MUSE book: Museums uniting with schools in education: Building on our knowledge.* Cambridge, MA: Project Zero: Harvard Graduate School of Education.

Davis, J. (1997). The "U" and the wheel of "C": Development and devaluation of graphic symbolization and the cognitive approach at Harvard Project Zero. In Kindler, A. (Ed.), *Child development in art* (pp. 45-58). Reston, VA: National Art Education Association.

Desai, D. & Chalmers, F. G. (2007). Notes for a dialogue on art education in critical times. *Art Education 60*(5), 6-12.

Duncum, P. (1999). A multiple pathways/multiple endpoints model of graphic development. *Visual Arts Research 25*(2), 38-47.

Duncum, P. (2009). Visual culture in art education, Circa 2009. *Visual Arts Research 35*(1), 64-75.

Duncum, (2010). Seven principles for visual culture education. *Art Education 63*(1), 6-10.

Freedman, K. & Stuhr, P. (2004) Curriculum changes for the 21st century: visual culture in art education. In Eisner, E. W. & Day, M. (Eds.), *Handbook of research and policy in art education* (pp. 815–828). Mahwah, NJ: Lawrence Erlbaum.

Gardner, H. (1983). *Frames of mind: The theory of multiple intelligences.* New York: Basic Books.

Gardner, H. (2006). *Multiple intelligences: New horizons in theory and practice.* New York: Basic Books.

Golomb, C. (2004). Sculpture: Representational development in a three-dimensional medium. In Eisner, E. W. & Day, M. (Eds.), *Handbook of research and policy in art education* (pp. 329-358). Mahwah, NJ: Lawrence Erlbaum

Gude, O. (2007). Principles of possibility: Considerations for a 21st-Century art & culture curriculum. *Art Education 60*(1), 6-17.

Hallam, J., Das Gupta, M., & Lee, H. (2008). An exploration of primary school teachers' understanding of art and the place of art in the primary school curriculum. *The Curriculum Journal, 19*(40), 269-281.

Kellogg, R. (1969). *Analyzing children's art.* Palo Alto, CA: Mayfield Publishing.

Kind, S. (2005). Windows to a child's world: Perspectives on children's art making. In Grauer, K. & Irwin, R. L. (Eds.), *StARTing with…* (pp. 9-19) Toronto, ON: Canadian Society for Education through Art.

Kindler, A. (2004). Introduction: Development and learning in art. In Eisner, E. W. & Day, M. (Eds.), *Handbook of research and policy in art education* (pp. 227-232). Mahwah, NJ: Lawrence Erlbaum.

Kindler, A. & Darras, B. (1997). Map of artistic development. In Kindler, A. (Ed.), *Child development in art* (pp. 17-44). Reston, VA: National Art Education Association.

Lowenfeld, V. & Brittain, W. L. (1987). *Creative and mental growth* (8th edition). New York: Macmillan.

Luehrman, M. & Unrath, K. (2006). Making theories of children's artistic development meaningful for student teachers. *Art Education, 59*(3), 6-12.

Marme-Thompson, C. (2005). Under construction: Images of the child in art teacher education. *Art Education, 58*(2), 18-23.

Marme-Thompson, C. (2009). Mira! Looking, listening, and lingering in research with children. *Visual Arts Research, 35*(1), 24-34.

Matthews, J. & Seow, P. (2007). Electronic paint: Understanding children's representation through their interactions with digital paint. *International Journal of Art and Design Education, 26*(3), 251-263.

MUSE Project. (nd). Retrieved on March 25, 2010 at: http://pzweb.harvard.edu/Research/MUSE.htm

Pariser, D. (1997). Graphic development in artistically exceptional children. In Kindler, A. (Ed.), *Child Development in Art* (pp. 115-130). Reston, VA: National Art Education Association.

Pariser, D. & Zimmerman, E. (2004). Learning in the visual arts: Characteristics of gifted and talented individuals. In Eisner, E. W. & Day, M. (Eds.), *Handbook of research and policy in art education* (pp. 379-405). Mahwah, NJ: Lawrence Erlbaum.

Pavlou, V. (2009). Understanding young children's three-dimensional creative potential in art making. *Journal of Art and Design Education, 28*(2), 139-150.

Richards, R. (2007). Outdated relics on hallowed ground: Unearthing attitudes and beliefs about young children's art. *Australian Journal of Early Childhood, 32*(4), 22-30.

Steele, B. (1998). *Draw me a story: An illustrated exploration of drawing-as-language.* Winnipeg, MN: Peguis Publishers.

Swann, A. (2008). Children, objects, and relations: Constructivist foundations in the Reggio Emilia approach. *Studies in Art Education, 50*(1), 36-50.

Tarr, P. (2008). New visions: Art for early childhood. *Art Education, 61*(4), 19-24.

Vygotsky, L. S. (1978). *Mind in society.* Cambridge, MA: Harvard University Press.

Wilson, B. (2004). Child art after modernism: Visual culture and new narratives. In Eisner, E. W. & Day, M. (Eds.), *Handbook of research and policy in art education* (pp. 299-328). Mahwah, NJ: Lawrence Erlbaum.

CHAPTER 4

The Disposition of Creativity in Educational Practice

Introduction

Pink (2005) contends that we have moved into the conceptual age where the exchange and growth of ideas takes precedence over the consumption of information. The implication of this on mainstream educational culture is quite profound as it speaks to the need to go beyond the traditional focus on the acquisition of discipline competency and its accompanying assessment strategies to a culture that values the growth and development of ideas with creativity as the main driving force (Kelly & Leggo, 2008). Leadbeater (2008) contends that contemporary learning culture will be defined by how we share these ideas in a culture of collaborative creativity and social networking pointing to the importance of having educational strategies to enable this.

Creativity is often assumed to be central to artistic practice and art education. However, the complexity of the concept of creativity due to its multi-dimensional nature can lead to diverse views on how creativity is perceived and applied in educational settings. The need for developing creativity competencies in educational practice requires a deeper understanding of the dynamic of creative processes and the concept of creativity and its surrounding vocabulary. In contemporary learning culture developing creativity competencies is as important as developing discipline competencies as there must be meaningful avenues for educators and young learners to apply discipline knowledge to facilitate creative production, invention and innovation. This points to the growth of an impending educational culture that balances discipline competency with the development of the creative disposition.

What is Creativity?

Piirto (2004) describes the origin of the words 'create' and 'creativity' as having roots in the Latin *creatus* and *creare* meaning to *make* or *produce* or literally *to grow*. She goes on to relate that the noun "creativity" is relatively new, appearing in some dictionaries in the 1960s but not in the 1971 Oxford English Dictionary. Piirto further relates that the Dictionary of Developmental and Educational Psychology in 1986 defined creativity as "the capacity to produce new ideas, insights, inventions or artistic objects, which are accepted of being of social, spiritual, aesthetic, scientific or technological value" (p. 6). She goes on to say "To be *creative* is to be *originative*. *Originative* implies making something new. *To be creative then is to make something new or novel*" (italics in original, p. 6). Runco (2007) stresses the importance of applying precision to the use of the term creativity and the need to contextualize its usage because of its inherent ambiguity and complexity. With this in mind it is important to understand the vocabulary related to the concept of creativity and how creativity is applied and can be potentially applied in a variety of educational contexts.

Large "C" and Small "c" Creativity

"Can anyone be creative?" is a question that often arises when discussing the concept of creativity. Czikszentmilhalyi's (1995) "Big C" creativity and "Little c" creativity partially answers this question. "Little c" creativity is the *improvisational creativity* (Kelly & Leggo, 2008) in which every human being engages on a daily basis. This might involve inventing on the spot for a lesson that has gone awry or improvising around the house when cooking or doing repairs. It is human nature to engage in creative acts that are part of every day living. This also speaks to the notion that we all have creative potential. This everyday creativity however does not qualify as "Big C" creativity, which is designated for the very few that have widespread impact on their particular domain. Gardner's *Creating Minds* (1993) profiles the creative lives of "Big C" creativity examples such as Einstein, Gandhi, and T.S. Elliot. The question remains however that if it is human nature to improvise creatively how can creative development be enhanced and nurtured in an educational environment to enable learners to attain deeper, complex and more profound outcomes?

Longitudinal Creativity

From an educational perspective the vertical scaling of 'Big C' and 'Little c' creativity based on the importance of the creative act within a domain or across a particular culture is not as useful as perhaps focusing the nature of idea generation and development and how ideas are brought into forms. Smith (1998) argues that idea generation is the indispensable core of creativity. I would go further and add that idea generation along with idea growth and development and the resultant creation of forms make up the indispensable core of creativity. I use the term *longitudinal creativity* (Kelly & Leggo, 2008) to describe how ideas are generated and developed over time and several iterations into forms in diverse educational contexts. This goes well beyond short-term creative problem solving which typically calls for an acute novel response from a student in relation to a curriculum content issue. These acute problem-solving situations are what many educators come to know as creativity within their educational practice when there are far greater educational potentials for creative development that are possible. Longitudinal creativity speaks to the notion of the creation of original work that is self-instigated by the student and supported through several iterations of development through rigorous research and experimentation. Through the application of this perspective there is greater potential to enable educational environments to evolve into accommodating strategies that are conducive to the attainment of the highest possible creative outcomes through the identification of factors that both limit and enable creative production. *Longitudinal creativity* is inevitably a lens through which one can view educational practice for the purpose of affecting change to maximize the creative potentials of students and educators.

Historical Perspectives and Vocabulary

Historically, there are countless models of creativity. Many of these models can classified as stage theories that consistently deal with the generation of ideas, alternatives, and possibilities, and their evaluation (Lubart, 2000-2001). One of the earliest of these stage theories was developed by Wallas (1926) in his book *The Art of Thought* where he formalized a four-stage model of creative process that heavily influenced creativity theory for over half a century. His four distinct stages of creativity were described as preparation, incubation, illumination, and verification. Incubation was perceived as an active subconscious stage where ideas were reorganized and elaborated. Many stage theory variations followed Wallas's work. Osborn (1953), the developer of brainstorming, describes a seven-stage creativity model that features the following stages: *Orientation* – pointing up the problem; *Preparation* – gathering pertinent data; *Analysis* – breaking down the relevant material; *Ideation* – piling up alternatives; *Incubation* – letting up to invite elaboration and re-organization; *Synthesis* – putting the pieces together; and *Evaluation* – judging the resulting ideas. Osborn's inclusion of an *Ideation* stage is a purposeful stage for the generation of ideas. The underlying belief here is that the creative process can be directed or at the very least influenced. This was a departure from earlier views where the creative process was thought to exist solely in the realm of the subconscious. Koberg and Bagnell (1981), and Isaksen and Treffinger (1985), describe creative problem solving models that feature idea finding and generating options as an important stage. Koberg and Bagnell allude to the development of creative strands that continue perpetually and also concurrently with other creative threads.

Figure 1. An idea

The growth and development of ideas and the realization of these ideas as forms are central to artistic practice. Figure 1 illustrates a representation of an idea. This representation uses a circle with a dot in the middle. An idea can radiate outwards in numerous directions combining and recombining with other ideas or it can close in on itself and not grow at all. Ideally for this idea to grow to its many potentials students and educators would have to be intrinsically motivated to instigate and generate artistic explorations that were personally meaningful accompanied by active research, experimentation and refinement through several iterations of seeking a resolution to an outcome that is unknown. In this ideal world students and educators would create work that is new or novel and display many of the characteristics of creativity described by Guilford (1959) such as: *originality* – new or novel work that is remote or a departure from previous work, *flexibility* - the ability to adapt to new ideas, *elaboration* - the ability to add complexities to existing forms and *fluency* - the ability to easily produce ideas and alternatives though *divergent thinking*. However there are several patterns and forces inherent in mainstream educational culture limiting idea generation and development and inevitably the creative development of students and educators.

Factors Limiting Idea Generation and Creative Development

Figure 2 shows some of the attributes of the predominant learning culture that limit the generation of ideas and creative development (Kelly & Leggo, 2008). The environment of standardization in mainstream educational culture is characterized by short term learning episodes. This is not always the choice of educators involved but is most often due to *time constraints* under the weight of tremendous content volume. This is often accompanied by summative assessment regimens required in this culture to measure student progress against established standards. These factors lead students to develop a disposition of early closure when it comes to the generation and development of ideas, perhaps the single biggest tendency limiting creative development. Focus is often on finding the right answer as quickly as possible without much attention paid to generating alternatives and growing them into different possibilities. The predominant learning culture is also characterized by learning episodes that rely on extrinsic motivation where students spend much of their time restating or retelling outcomes that are already known that leads to a culture focused hyper-consumption as opposed to one of creative production. Eventually, as students ascend grades, this can lead to dissociation where students develop considerable emotional distance from their school environment and the work related to it.

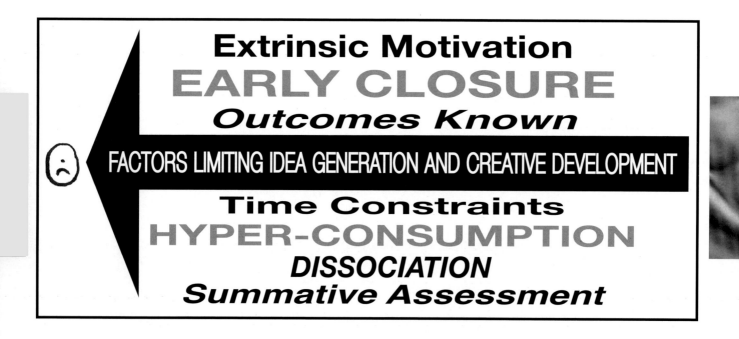

Figure 2. Factors limiting idea generation and creative development

The Importance of Quantity

Figure 3 illustrates the early stages of idea generation and development (Kelly & Leggo, 2008). This depicts the necessary strategy of initially generating idea quantity to overcome some of the factors that limit idea growth. Kelley (2001) of *Ideo Corporation* and Sweeney (2004) of *The Brave New Workshop Theatre Company* both emphasize how important it is to generate as many ideas as possible to come up with a good idea. Sweeney's theatre company generates a minimum of six hundred ideas at the beginning of the development of an original work! Kelley's organization utilizes brainstorming and the generation of hundreds of ideas for innovative product design. A natural tendency of many young artists is to generate few ideas or options and to close early on an idea (Kelly, 2005). Typically, after a teacher has introduced a new creative exploration to a class, there are students who have already closed on an idea as to what they are going to do. The idea might be a good one but there is no way of knowing if this is the best idea and inevitably what the student was potentially capable of. Quantity in the latter scenario enables experimentation, refinement, and the discovery of new, diverse possibilities. It is essential that generating a large quantity of ideas should be built into the beginning of any creative exploration. It is not unreasonable to require students to produce numerous alternatives through thumbnail sketches or models before proceeding with a studio exploration. Developing learning episodes that recognize the value of quantity, risk taking, and idea generation will encourage this practice. Students who are used to early closure patterns will often initially resist this type of strategy. Eventually, with practice, it becomes a way of doing within a creative exploration.

Figure 3. Early stages of idea generation and development

Figure 4. Full inventive momentum

Full Inventive Momentum

Figure 4 illustrates full inventive momentum. In this state, the creative exploration has overcome many of the factors that limit idea generation and development and taken on a life of its own into the realm of *longitudinal creativity* (Kelly & Leggo, 2008). In this stage ideas combine and recombine with others quite readily. Any stimuli generated by research and experimentation by teacher or student is readily absorbed into this process. It is important to note that idea generation is recursive in that new ideas can incorporate older ideas that were previously thought to be irrelevant. Taking this into consideration it is imperative that no idea is rejected and that all ideas are given some sort of form so they can be banked and ready for recall when the moment presents itself. It is not enough for a student to say they have lots of good ideas. These ideas must be given form through the production of thumbnail sketches or building small, three dimensional models or giving thoughts literary form so they can be shared in a collaborative setting or saved for future explorations.

Outcomes Unknown

A learning culture focused on creativity and the creative development of its participants is built around creative explorations where outcomes are largely unknown. The field of exploration or media may be known but the form of the final resolution or outcome is not. Once students learn to trust that engaging in processes and potentials associated with longitudinal creative exploration will yield positive outcomes, the initial anxiety of dealing with outcomes that are unknown will dissipate. Dealing with outcomes unknown implies that parameters for learning experiences allow enough latitude for experimentation, idea generation, and potential diverse resolutions to problems set by the student. If the scope of the learning experience is too narrow because it is overly prescriptive, little room is allowed for idea generation or invention. There is really no impetus to generate ideas in this context or to grow them into new and wondrous forms. On the other hand if there are no parameters for the creative experience, and everything is left totally to the student, it is assumed that the young artist has acquired the necessary strategies and tactics to instigate and sustain a creative exploration. This is where totally open–ended experiences often fall down. On the surface this approach has much appeal from the perspective of giving students complete control and choice over what they do. However, if the student hasn't acquired the mature creative production strategies of intrinsic motivation, research, experimentation, refinement, collaboration and the ability to sustain creative exploration over time then this approach can lead to much frustration and scattered outcomes.

Nurturing Creative Development

With diverse student populations, art educators can construct creative explorations in a balanced, tiered manner to accommodate different levels of artist maturity. Learning experiences can be designed with constraints that will foster creative development on an individual basis to meet student needs that will eventually lead to independent, mature artist practice. Students with specific needs can be engaged in more structured learning episodes to foster creative growth more effectively.

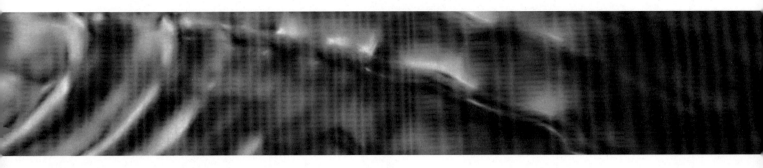

Learning strategies can be differentiated to target specific needs that focus on self-instigation and intrinsic motivation, research, experimentation, inventive sustain, collaboration and refinement of ideas and resultant forms. Students who are working at a more sophisticated level can be coached into further refinement of their ideas and practice at their level, as they are quite likely to have the maturity to create their own constraints.

Intrinsic Motivation

Art educators should constantly strive to employ relevant themes that inevitably enable the student to become intrinsically motivated to develop their own themes of personal relevance. This is built upon a foundation of student self-awareness. As mature artists undertake creative journeys that are relevant to them, developing artists must cultivate and evolve their own personal ideas and themes. Inspiring intrinsic motivation is perhaps one of the most challenging tasks facing educators when nurturing creative development. Valuing student ideas is central to creating an enabling environment for idea generation and having students assume ownership for their creative explorations. Mining personal histories is an important thematic source for creative production in this context. There is always an appropriate place for teacher directed learning episodes and those co-owned by the teacher and student but ultimately the educational dynamic should always be geared towards fostering a learning culture of intrinsic motivation and complete student ownership (Pink, 2009).

Enabling Research and Investigation

Another important aspect of nurturing creative development is to assist in instilling an investigative disposition in the learner. Idea generation requires fuel. Mature artists seek out their own fuel sources (Kelly, 2005). Any form of stimuli that comes across the path of the mature artist is fair game for creative production. This is a form of research. When an art educator sets a creative exploration in motion it is important to continuously provide a variety of stimuli to promote idea generation so as to stoke the creative fires. When students are first confronted with a new art exploration in the classroom it is important that they be given adequate time and stimuli to generate ideas. A teacher in this context can have students visit galleries and artist studios, arrange for guest speakers, or do any number of trigger activities that will enhance the enabling environment. The goal here is not only to fuel student work, but also to model methods of research so that students can research and source information and stimuli for themselves. Previewing the journey ahead and giving students ample time to think about and explore themes enables idea generation. This can be achieved in brief moments before the unit actually begins, while an existing unit is being completed. Mature artists often enjoy the luxury of time while developing their themes. This *leapfrogging* technique (Kelly, 2005), comprised of previewing the learning experience, providing early stimuli, and encouraging early student research is a way of stretching the time window in an environment where time is often at a premium. This will also allow students to gather creative momentum before ever confronting any media.

The Importance of Collaboration

Engaging in collaboration is a critically important avenue to generate ideas by feeding off of the investigations and experiments of others. Collaboration will be most effective in a learning environment where all ideas are accepted and not judged. Early judgment or harsh judgment will inhibit a young artist from developing ideas or volunteering any thoughts in a group forum (Sweeney, 2004). Before students enter a collaborative idea sharing session it is important that they generate some ideas on their own to bring to the group. Having some idea currency in hand before engaging the group can preclude dominance of group discussions by group members who are verbally adept. Sweeney (2004) advocates creating a status-less environment as an optimal forum for collaborative idea generation. If the level of status can be flattened within the collaborative group or class, in other words, if all ideas are valued equally regardless of who generates them or how wild they may seem, the comfort level, openness, and overall productivity of each group member improves.

Figure 5. The idea exchange

Figure 5, *The Idea Exchange*, depicts a strategy that is highly effective for enabling students to collaborate to generate large quantities of ideas in a status-less configuration. Before students engage in *The Idea Exchange* they develop personal lists of ideas and alternatives through investigation and research for whatever creative exploration they are engaged in. The class is then configured into two rows of chairs with students facing each other in pairs. Students then have a few minutes to exchange ideas and to make constructive suggestions on each other's work until the teacher signals them to move one chair to the left or right. The idea is that each student spends one on one time with each other student in the class for a few minutes exchanging ideas. *The Idea Exchange* strategy can be utilized several times at different stages throughout a creative exploration to fuel inventive momentum. Interestingly deployment of this kind of strategy enables independent work in a classroom to become highly collaborative.

Sustaining A Creative Exploration

A creative exploration is not limited to idea generation in its early stages. Idea generation goes through several phases of divergence where alternatives are generated and convergence where alternatives are narrowed down to a potential resolution(s). Several alternatives and possibilities are generated. The artist combines and selects ideas from the available possibilities. These are points of convergence where ideas start to solidify. This pattern repeats itself several times throughout a creative exploration. Composition, form, colour choices, or any design decision are subject to this divergent-convergent pulse. This can be built into the structure of a studio exploration involving creative process. Students can be required to generate alternatives at each stage of the process. The longer this divergent-convergent pulse (Kelly, 2005; Kelly & Leggo, 2008) can be maintained the greater the potential for diverse and interesting outcomes. This enables students to sustain a creative exploration over time through several iterations.

Coaching and Dialogic Assessment

It is prudent to have students explain the thinking behind their generated alternatives literally or verbally. This enables the art educator to take on the role of conceptual coach. The more insight the teacher has into the student's thinking, the easier it will be to help the student generate more alternatives, to converge on ideas, and to fuel the exploration with appropriate sources throughout the creative journey. As the creative exploration unfolds the assessment of the student's work becomes largely dialogic as they are coached and mentored through the development of their forms and ideas. In this context students are not afraid to take a risk or fail as the result of experimentation as opposed to receiving an "F" on a test score in a summative measurement situation.

Emphasizing Process

With prolific idea generation, idea development and the creation of forms comes the development of many creative strands. These strands are the fabric of inventive momentum (Kelly, 2005; Kelly & Leggo, 2008). The works that are produced in a creative exploration are merely convergent points in a very dynamic thought continuum. They are simply moments in time, or snapshots of thought, within a much larger dynamic. It is important for art educators to recognize and capitalize on this body of thought that goes well beyond the production of an actual work. It is easy for one to lose sight of this if the focus is totally on the finished work. This wide body of generated thought is the fertile ground that sustains inventive momentum throughout the creative journey from one learning episode to another.

The Disposition of Creativity

Finally, creative development in an educational setting is not limited to students. Art educators must strive to engage in creative explorations at all levels. This implies growing a creative disposition in personal creative development and professional practice. This ranges from generating ideas for the creation of innovative learning experiences to the development of their own works of personal relevance and value. The development of artistic and creative maturity of the educator can be the single most enabling factor affecting creative development among young learners. Conversely, a lack of creative maturity on the part of the educator can have a profound impact on limiting the creative development of students. The creative disposition of the educator is one that is lived alongside students and although it is most often developed within a domain once creative maturity is attained it is not domain specific (Sternberg, 1999). This disposition transcends every aspect of the educational environment not only in the arts but also across all disciplines and at every level encompassing all participants. Art educators are ideally situated to bring an understanding of the concept of creativity and the dynamic of fostering creative development among learners to the broader educational environment by going well beyond espousing the virtues of the discipline to living the disposition of creativity alongside others.

References

Csikszentmihalyi, M. (1995). *Creativity.* New York: Harper Collins

Gardner, H. (1993). *Creating minds.* New York: Basic Books.

Isaksen, S. G. & Treffinger, D. J. (1985). *Creative problem solving: The basic course.* Buffalo, NY: Beady.

Kelley, T. (2001). *The Art of innovation.* New York: Doubleday.

Kelly, R. (2005). Idea generation: Fueling the creative process. *BCATA Journal For Art Teachers, 47*(2), 4-10.

Kelly, R., & Leggo, C. (Eds.). (2008). *Creative expression, creative education: Creativity as a primary rationale for education.* Calgary: Detselig Enterprises/ Temeron Books.

Koberg, D. & Bagnell, J. (1981). *The All-new universal traveler.* Los Altos, CA: William Kaufmann.

Leadbeater, C. (2008). *We-think: The Power of mass creativity.* London: Profile Books.

Lubart, T. I. (2000-2001). Models of creative process: past, present and future. *Creativity Research Journal, 13*(3-4), 295-308.

Osborn, A. (1953). *Applied imagination.* New York: Charles Schribner.

Piirto, J. (2004). *Understanding creativity.* Scottsdale: Great Potential Press.

Pink, D. H. (2009). *Drive.* New York: Riverhead Books.

Pink, D. H. (2005). *A whole new mind.* New York: Riverhead Books.

Runco, M. A. (2007). *Creativity - theories and themes: Research, development and practice.* London: Elsevier Academic Press.

Smith, G. (1998). Idea-generation techniques: A formulary of active ingredients. *Journal of Creative Behaviour, 32*(2), 107-133.

Sternberg, R. (Ed.). (1999). *Handbook of creativity.* New York: Cambridge University Press.

Sweeney, J. (2004). *Innovation at the speed of laughter.* Minneapolis, MN: Aerialist Press.

Wallas, G. (1926). *The Art of thought.* New York: Harcourt Brace.

CONNECTIONS, REFLECTIONS AND CREATIONS

CHAPTER 5

"So How am I Supposed to Do it?"

The Teacher's Role,
Practices and
Processes
for Teaching Art

Miriam Cooley

By the time you as an aspiring teacher enter a teacher education program you have had at least twelve, perhaps sixteen years of observing what teachers do. Some of those teachers may have inspired your decision to become a teacher and others may have been the teachers who you swear you will never become. Either way, envisioning yourself in the role of a teacher may provoke some anxiety, and considering that not many of those former teachers were art teachers, you might feel that you have very little experience upon which to base your understanding of teaching art.

As a student you may have been exposed to one or both of two very opposite notions of the role of the art teacher. One approach was decidedly teacher directed where the teacher dictated step-by-step directions, often with pre-cut materials so that each child produced an identical pre-designed piece. The result is a class set of decorative pieces in which the students' sole satisfaction is having completed the task as dictated, since they have made no creative contribution to the work. The second approach is quite the opposite. In an extreme approach to child centered learning, some art educators believed that children are innately creative and for adults to give direction at all was detrimental to children's creative development. The teacher was to provide the materials and stand back. While this idea seems to be very affirming of children's abilities, the results are not always so positive. Pre-service education students who took on an assignment[1] where they were asked to provide the art materials but refrained from giving the child any direction, found that not all children happily took up the art materials and spontaneously created vibrant art works. While some children relish the freedom to pursue their own approach to their art making, this was more likely the case for younger children (approximately 2 years to 5 years). The older students, particularly those who had little art making experience, tended to be more hesitant, requested direction, and were greatly frustrated when it was not offered. It might be said that this shows that too much previous adult direction has indeed hindered the children's creativity and self-confidence, however, to persist in the 'hands off' approach will not be very helpful to these students.

Photo By: Antonio Jiménez Alonso

So what then is the role of an art teacher? In this chapter I speak of the *art teacher*, or the *teacher of art* with the understanding that this teacher most likely is an elementary generalist teacher who includes art as part of her or his required program of studies, and in a few instances the *art teacher* may be a visual art specialist. In either situation I suggest that the primary role of a teacher is to provide leadership in the classroom, and in the role of an art teacher your task is to guide as you and your students embark on the adventure of learning in, through, and from the visual arts. In this context leadership involves more than the notion of being 'the Boss' directing the activities and students dutifully following along. Leadership in the art classroom involves the practices and processes that move the whole group through classroom activities to achieve a fulfilling learning experience. As an educational leader you have a vision of the learning that you expect to be accomplished, you take on the responsibility of initiating and assessing learning experiences, and you are flexible and open to the possibility that the route may not be quite as you see it at the outset. As a leader you plan for a variety of learning experiences and prepare the materials and resources for the initiation of the project, but you are prepared for the possibility that your students may also have great ideas that shape the course of the lesson and the eventual outcome.

Creative Experience, Process, and Product

Teaching and learning in the visual arts is commonly understood to be a form of experiential learning. This suggests that students 'learn to do by doing' and that to be engaged in the process of creating art works fosters students' understanding and insight as well as the development of specific art making skills. However, along with the immediate attention to the activity of creating, *the experience* is understood to include the conversations, questions, and reflections that are provoked throughout the process.

The process of art making is honored as a location where learning happens. Some go so far as to make an emphatic valuing of 'process' over 'product,' which may be appropriate if 'product' is judged only by arbitrary standards of attractiveness. However, it is important to remember that what is eventually produced via the 'process' is the trace, the evidence if you will, of the learning experience that has transpired. The finished piece shows where the experience has led, where advances were made, and the meanings that have been constructed via the process in which the young artist has engaged. Moreover, the artwork has value and meaning for the child and it is what will go home to be hung on the fridge.

Strategies, Plans and Approaches

The term 'teaching strategies' is often used when discussing the ways that teachers carry out their responsibilities, although to me, 'strategies' suggests that there is somewhere a list of prescribed plans and courses of action designed to lead to a specific outcome. When teachers are increasingly held accountable to external standards it would seem prudent to be able to lay out such a strategy and assure an approved result. While it is essential to understand the process and plan for how you will conduct your teaching, maintaining a flexible and responsive attitude would relieve some pressure on teachers and students alike, and maybe leave some openings for fun to erupt.

The approach that one undertakes is dependent upon a variety of factors, the most important of which is the children who will be involved in the learning experience. As an elementary teacher you have the day-to-day opportunity to become well acquainted with the personalities, cultural identities, talents, and challenges of the children in your class as well as the knowledge and skills that they have already acquired. You will come to understand the particular interests, needs, and potentials of the children and how they grow and change over the course of the school year. The circumstances of children's lives are varied and each one brings with her or him a complex bundle of experiences, good and bad, that influence responses to what happens in your classroom. Attentive teachers observe their students and initiate conversations through which they learn about children's lives and concerns and devise ways to motivate and promote learning. Such a teacher may be said to be practicing reflection-in-action: "the complex inner dialogue of on-the-spot decisions embedded in the unpredictability of the pedagogical moment, reflection that "not only happens before and after the performed event but informs the very event itself (Taylor 1996, p. 30)" (cited in Cooley & Lugar, 2003, p. 22). The practice of reflection-in-action enables openness to the intuitive and unexpected moments of the art classroom, is grounded in empathetic student/teacher relationships and thus is invaluable to effective art teaching.

The art curriculum as prescribed by your ministry of education is another factor to consider since that document outlines the content that is to be covered. Curriculum documents generally are more explicit about the 'what' that is to be taught than the 'how of doing the teaching. However, careful reading of the introductory chapters covering overview and rationale in your provincial curriculum document can offer insight into the approaches recommended in your particular jurisdiction. As an art teacher your task is to build the bridge between your students and the stated curriculum requirements, to devise the learning experiences through which students' can find relevance in the required material. As a leader you invite your students into activities that build on their abilities and open up new challenges. To use the terminology of the eminent educator Ted Aoki, you become the translator of the 'curriculum-as–plan' into the 'curriculum-as-lived-experience' in your classroom (Aoki, 2005, p. 159-160) – the curriculum that connects with and enriches the lives of children.

Photo by: Valdas Zajanckauskas

With experience, teachers develop a repertoire of teaching approaches that are appropriate to the circumstances in which they work and they learn how to use those approached effectively. One might pursue an inquiry approach through provocative questioning about the subject of an artwork, by inviting children to be curious about the motives of the artist, and by animating the process through which students propose, assess, select, and initiate creative responses to the ideas that arise. A grounding assumption of creative inquiry is that we don't already know the answer. We are actively seeking new possibilities through a process of proposing ideas and then assessing the potential of those ideas for a successful solution. Creative inquiry opens the possibilities for innovation and promotes personal initiative in realizing original solutions.

Art teachers often rely on demonstrations to convey to students an appropriate way to use materials and art making tools. When students see you draw with a paintbrush along the page shifting the amount of pressure you apply, the consequence is evident on the page. As they watch you push your thumb into a ball of clay and begin to press your thumb and fingertips together they understand the movement that is foundational to creating a pinch pot. When you show students how to clean a paintbrush and lay it to dry, the brushes will be ready for the next class. Moreover, when a teacher demonstrates an approach, as when I put my whole hand into the finger paint and sweep the colour across the page, we give permission to our students to step beyond the careful and commonplace and make an energetic, adventurous gesture.

Demonstrations often initiate the mini-lesson for the instruction in an art making technique that will be put into practice in the larger project. If the process involves a number of steps it is wise to introduce the first of them and then call the group back together to demonstrate the ensuing steps. Too much information at once can cause confusion, frustration, and loss of focus. If you are feeling a little insecure about putting your own art making skills on display there are many videos available on line or as DVDs in which an experienced art educator demonstrates the process. Whatever the medium or technique it is well worth your time to try it out yourself ahead of time. First of all you will have the pleasure of doing some creative work that will benefit your own well-being. In addition you will be able to find any aspects of the project that will pose problems for the children. You will be forewarned of such concerns and can modify the project to avoid difficulties

that might overwhelm some students. Remember that the objective is for children, at whatever age, to be able to be successful without having to rely on adults to do more than a little supporting and emergency intervention.

Guided imagining, inviting students to close their eyes while you describe moving into an imagined or remembered situation provides an opportunity for students to form a very strong, personal inner image as the starting point for their art work. It may be the initiation of a personal visual journal or a rich memory of a great family event that come to mind and inspires the clay sculpture or the collage.

The telling of stories, whether by an elder or a talented storyteller, or from storybooks is a very effective way of introducing characters, concepts, situations, and dilemmas that can become the foundation of creative work. What is the story about? What aspects are revealed upon which an art project may begin? For example, in *Anansi the Spider: A Tale from the Ashanti*, (Mc Dermott, 1972) the story unfolds about Anansi, the patriarch of the spider family who has various adventures until he actually gets himself into a difficult situation. His seven sons each possess a special talent that comes into use as they rescue their father. This aspect of each one having a special talent can lead to focusing on your students' special qualities and talents and subsequently into artistic representations of how those abilities can be seen, perhaps through puppetry or a graphic novel.

Looking at art works is of course the greatest way to draw students into the world of art. While the biographical information and formal qualities of the painting are important at some point that is not really what makes anyone take that first look and stop to look again. If you invite a child to take a 'journey' into a painting, to note what draws his attention, what makes her curious or provokes her, then you are inviting that child to recognize and value their own responses. When you then ask the children to tell their classmate what they saw and thought about while they looked at the art, they are able to initiate a conversation about their ideas. If as a group you then stand back and describe the elements of the art work, students can begin to realize how the artist has constructed the work and they can begin to see their subjective response from the beginning of the class along with the more objective view to realize an aspect of how meaning emerges from this 'conversation' with an art work (Horner, 1990; Cooley, 1991).

Becoming the leader in an art education classroom

    is much the same as becoming a leader in any other classroom,

    but if we want children to grow with confidence

    in their own ideas and their ability to express them,

    and if we are committed to the capacity of the arts

    to add value and meaning to children's lives and the culture they create,

    then this requires thoughtful nurturing.

How teachers teach art matters a great deal.

Endnotes

1 This assignment is structured as a participant observation study where the student works with an individual child first as described above, and then develops and conducts art making lessons based on the child's abilities and interests.

References

Aoki, T. T. (2005) Teaching as in-dwelling between two curriculum worlds (1986/1991). In W. F. Pinar & R. L. Irwin (Eds.). (2005). *Curriculum in a new key: The collected works of Ted T. Aoki*, (pp.159-165). Mahwah, NJ: Lawrence Erlbaum.

Cooley, M. (1991). *Changing parts, changing hearts, changing me? An investigation into my response to video art*. Unpublished MA thesis, Concordia University, Montreal, QC.

Cooley, M. & Lugar, C. (2003). (Play)ing > < Living: Researching creative growth. In A. Clarke & G. Erickson (Eds.). *Teacher research: Living the research of everyday practice* (pp. 20-28). New York: RoutledgeFalmar Press.

Horner, S. (1990). Responding to art: 2D and not 3D. That is not a question. *NSCAD Papers in Art Education*, *5*, 31-46.

Mc Dermott, G. (1972). *Anansi the spider: A tale from the Ashanti*. New York: Henry Holt & Company.

stARTing with Art
Relating Children's Visual and Written Expression

Kit Grauer

Alexander is drawing in his visual journal. All around him in this grade two classroom, his classmates are also concentrating on their journals as classical music plays in the background. On this day, Alex is working on a story that he and Ian are writing about Jungle Boy. His drawings are the storyboard for the illustrated book that they will produce later in the week. Some days, his teacher suggests a topic, "what I did last weekend", or suggests an observation drawing of the beans that fill the window sills of the classroom, each in their own paper cup with the carefully recorded children's names printed on the side. Other days, like today, she allows the children to follow their own interests. She wants their work in their visual journals to be intrinsically rewarding and so she provides structure when she thinks the children need it. She also places an equal amount of energy helping them develop their own ideas and interests. In this school, each busy day starts with listening to the music selection developed by the district music coordinator and journal time for the children to draw their ideas onto paper. This teacher has discovered, and many of her colleagues agree, that by starting the day with drawing she has very little difficulty later in the school day when she wants to have the children writing. They always have lots of ideas in their visual journals and lots that they want to put into words and share with their classmates. Visual journals and daily drawing are a school wide focus and the children have little difficulty understanding the close connection between expressing their ideas in images and words. They have lots of time to 'read' back the ideas in the pages of their journals and to use some for their writing class and some as the basis for other larger art projects that they might do later in class. In the primary classroom, integration of subject areas is as common as that separation has become at high school.

At the elementary school level integration of subjects has a long history. Teachers often decide to develop their curriculum units around themes or topics. Dinosaurs and cultural events are common examples of this approach where science, social studies, math, art, language arts and music and movement are all brought in to look at the multiple ways of understanding a particular theme. In this article, I am specifically looking at the similarities in a process approach to teaching the subjects of language arts and art. By concentrating first on these two curricular areas, it is possible to make explicit the powerful associations in student's leaning that occurs when two different ways of representing our knowledge are used in combination. What teachers who use this approach have discovered is that children seem to learn with more engagement when they have a chance to combine their understanding in art and language arts (Steele, 1998). This does not mean that other subject areas are left out of any curricular decisions, it simply means that visual and verbal literacy take precedence when integrating and then the appropriate connections to other disciplines are brought into play. Most teachers at the elementary level are comfortable with their language arts instruction and less sure about the way to teach art. They appreciate that approaching art from a writer's workshop perspective and integrating the two subject areas makes pedagogical sense and also promotes a high level of accomplishment and satisfaction in their children's response to both subject areas.

The idea of linking art and language arts is not new but a recent resurgence in interest (Albers & Sanders, 2010; Cornett & Smitherin, 2001; Fleckenstein, Calendrillo, & Worley, 2002; Piro, 2002) has prompted me to revisit several articles (Grauer, 1984, 1988, 1991, 1999) that explored the relationship between art and whole language. During the last two decades of the twentieth century whole language instruction had started to change the way that many elementary school teachers approached teaching and learning (Fleckenstein, Calendrillo, & Worley, 2002). Teachers were discovering something called the writing process or the writer's workshop approach to teaching language arts (Willis, 1995). Writing was synonymous with thinking and expressing in words, rather than an isolated school activity to teach the skills of spelling, punctuation and grammar. Reading and writing were seen as complementary processes instead of two different areas. Teaching process rather than products became accepted. The two sides of the brain research and early interest in Gardner's theory of multiple intelligence, (Gardner, 1983) provided teachers and administrators access to the ideas of teaching to different styles of learning and encouraging multiple forms of representation.

In art education, an awareness of the importance of including aesthetics, criticism and art history as part of a balanced making and responding art curriculum brought writing and speaking into the art classroom. As well as creators of art, children were expected to become enlightened critics and consumers of art and images. In British Columbia, we were piloting something called 'The Year 2000', built on a constructivist understanding of children's learning. With so many exciting curriculum changes, teachers were given considerable leeway to experiment with changes that made sense to our growing understanding of how children learn. One prominent innovation was the idea that there might be similarities in the way that writing and art were taught (Grauer, 1984). That concept was further expanded to suggest that using both visual and verbal modes of understanding and representing could actually enhance children's expression. By using the unique aspects of knowing represented by visual as well as verbal thinking, children have the opportunity to experience deeper and richer forms of communicating their ideas and to appreciate these capacities in others.

These ideas are continuing to evolve as our strategies for teaching become more refined. Both art and language can be thought of in terms of processes that children and adults engage in to give form to their ideas. If writing is thinking expressed in words, than art is thinking expressed in images. Images are one of our first forms of thought. Long before infants have the words necessary to speak, they have the images necessary to identify, classify and remember important aspects of their world. Image, after all, is the root word of imagination. As children grow and develop, they engage in early scribbling and drawing, developing visual symbol systems to represent their thinking prior to mimicking the symbol system used to represent words. By the time most children come to school, they are often already engaged in talking about their pictures and picturing their thoughts. The relationship between art and language is already established.

If there have been major changes in the way that writing has been taught in the past decades, there are similar changes in our view about art education. Teaching art is not about giving children exposure to a variety of media or about teaching skills in isolation. Skills are necessary, not as the core of the curriculum, but rather in the context of problem solving and thinking within any given medium and within the wider world of images. The current interest in exploring visual culture as way of deconstructing and constructing our identity in a world saturated with media images is an example of how our understanding of the role of art education is changing. A process approach to teaching art that parallels the writing process or writers' workshop approach is a model that both teachers and students have found very useful. Although I will discuss the various 'stages' of the process, it is important to recognize that none of the stages are wholly exclusive and stages often overlap. This model is much more spiral than linear.

Stages in the Art Process

All of the stages in the process can be ongoing, overlapping, and repeated.

Motivating: Getting started. Thinking about the topic or what the artist wants to express. Activities such as brainstorming ideas on a theme, webbing, guided visualization, or looking at slides, films, video or artists' work in other formats, help children generate ideas. Choosing an audience for the work and a medium for the art (clay, paint, ink, etc.).

Drafting: Drawing ideas on paper. Initial attempts at composing ideas in pictures.

In Process Critique: Making it better. Revising the first sketches or drafts by subtracting, adding, rearranging, or substituting material to achieve the results intended. This stage is accomplished in consultation with peers and/or the teacher. Developing the ideas in a suitable medium.

Refining: Checking it. Examining the technical qualities to determine if the result is ready for matting, framing or displaying in some form.

Exhibiting: Sharing it. Sharing the work with others in gallery style as finished art works.

Stages in the Writing Process

All of the stages in the process can be ongoing, overlapping, and repeated.

Pre-writing: What we do before we write. Thinking about the topic or what the writer wants to say. Prewriting activities, such as: making a visual representation; viewing a video or a picture; talking with a friend or in a group; reading an article or a book; listening to a speaker or to music, help pupils generate ideas. Choosing an audience for the finished work and the style or form of writing.

Drafting: Writing the words down on paper. Initial attempts at putting ideas into written words.

Revising or Editing: Making it better. Revising earlier drafts by rewording, altering, adding, eliminating, and rearranging words and ideas.

Proofreading: Checking it. Examining the revised draft for errors in capitalization, punctuation, spelling, usage, and form.

Presenting/Publishing: Sharing it. Sharing the work with others in oral or written form.

Before expressing ideas, artists and writers need to think about the ideas that they want to express. Teachers have learned that it is better to start with the art when combining art and writing experiences. As children think visually first, and as we are becoming more and more an image driven culture, putting the images to ideas prior to the words not only makes biological sense, it also provides a richer verbal experience as children discuss their pictures. At this first stage, visual thinking can be encouraged through any number of techniques: reading to children and having them interpret the pictures in their minds; looking at the work of adult or child artists and illustrators in pictures, photographs, illustrations, videos or children's books; guided visualization or any combination of the above. Motivating children prior to actually making art, allows them to begin to sort through the images in their world and in their minds and develop their own unique thoughts.

'Drafting' is the stage in which ideas move from pictures in the mind to images drawn on paper (or modeled in clay depending on the project). The surprise for many students is that real artists often do many drawings or models of an artwork before choosing one to make into a finished piece. It helps to show artists sketchbooks, or have an artist or illustrator visit the classroom to let children see that all drawings are not perfect the first time. Like practicing artists, their first images are an attempt to make thoughts public and express an idea. The use of visual journals in Alexander's class is one example of drafting ideas first in images.

'In process critique' or 'editing' is a stage that has made a huge difference to building children's confidence and competence in art. At this stage, the artist can examine the rough draft alone or in consultation with peers or the teacher. Here all the elements and principles of art and design can be contemplated for reference: colour, line, texture, shape, balance, harmony, unity, and/or rhythm. It is also a time to look at technical skills and image development strategies. Many teachers find that teaching specific skills at this stage helps children refine their ideas. What changes can the artist

58

make to develop a finished piece so that the work expresses his/her own particular view? Help can come from other children, the teacher, and references to other artists' ideas through looking at books and pictures. Many children appreciate the feedback at the 'in process' stage rather than at the end. For many classrooms, the use of peer critiques are very useful in developing a real audience for the finished work and providing children a chance to share rather than hide, their artistic abilities. This is the stage that many intermediate teachers have found particularly useful. Older children are often particularly reluctant participants in class art critiques. However, by introducing the idea of 'critiques in process', it has taken some of the peer pressure from the critique and turned it into a peer support system. Many teachers now use this technique as an ongoing form of assessment and self-reflection that defines and builds the criteria necessary for more authentic final evaluations.

When the artwork has been completed it is ready to be finished in some type of frame or display format so that it can be properly exhibited for others to see and appreciate.

Art and writing processes are not mutually exclusive. Starting first with an art experience seems to help children discover more about what they want to write. Varying between art and writing, throughout the experience, builds on the strengths of both modes of representation. In many intermediate art classrooms, an artist statement is a requirement of any finished piece.

Later in the day, the teacher in Alexander's classroom is reading the children the story of the Nutcracker. A parent has brought in her Nutcracker collection and the children are taught a simple observation drawing technique and then draw the nutcrackers onto large sheets of paper. They are thrilled with their work and ask to do more than one drawing. These first drafts become finished drawings that the children will be proud to display. Throughout the afternoon, there is plenty of time for the children to talk about their artwork in small groups and pairs. Lots of strong descriptive language is happening as the children describe the various details on the nutcracker figures that they are drawing.

"Let's add one or two sentences of really descriptive writing about your Nutcracker drawing in your draft writing books," the teacher suggests. The process between reading, drawing, talking, writing looks seamless from the outside and the finished products that are displayed at the parent open house later that week are impressive and individual.

This classroom is a good example of what children can accomplish if they are provided with an environment structured around learning. Teaching art and language arts in combination offers these children access to two ways of knowing and helps them celebrate the joy of creation and expression in both.

References

Albers, M. & Sanders, J. (2010). *Literacies, the arts, and multimodality*. Urbana, IL: National Council of Teachers of English

Cornett, C. E., & Smithrim, K. L. (2001). *The arts as meaning makers: Integrating literature and the arts throughout the curriculum* (Canadian Edition). Toronto, ON: Prentice Hall.

Fleckenstein, K. S., Calendrillo, L. T., & Worley, D. A. (2002). *Language and image in the reading-writing classroom: Teaching vision*. Mahwah, NJ: Lawrence Erlbaum Associates.

Gardner, H. (1983). *Frames of mind: The theory of multiple intelligences*. New York: Basic Books.

Grauer, K. (1999). Art and Writing Revisited. *BCATA Journal*. 39(2), pp. 28-32.

Grauer, K. (1991). Artistic knowing and the primary child. *Prime Areas*, 34(1), pp. 67-69.

Grauer, K. (1988). Art and writing: The best of friends. *Prime Areas*, 30(3), pp. 81-84.

Grauer, K. (1984). Art and writing: Enhancing expression in images and words. *Art Education*, 36(5), pp. 32-38.

Piro, J. M. (2002). The picture of reading: Deriving meaning in literacy through image. *The Reading Teacher, 56*(2), 126-134.

Steele, B. (1998). *Draw me a story: An illustrated exploration of drawing-as-language*. Winnipeg, MB: Peguis.

Willis, S. (1995). Whole language: Finding the surest way to literacy. *ASCD Curriculum Update*, Fall, pp.1-9.

CHAPTER 7

Themes, Cross-Curricular Connections and Daily Drawing

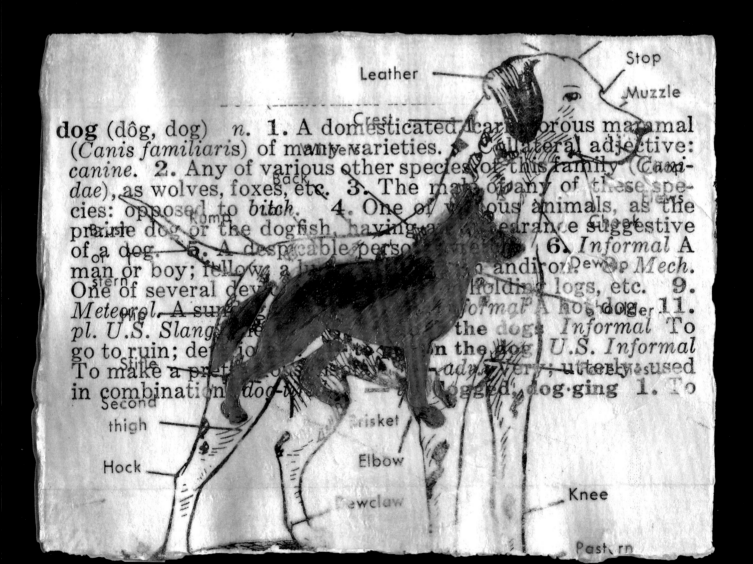

Introduction

If this chapter were to have a subtitle, it would be "Everything I Know about Art and Art Education (well, almost everything) I Learned From my Dog". Why dogs? Well, most people have a dog, want a dog or at least know someone who has a dog. Since interest in dogs and experience with them characterizes many elementary school age students, the subject seems to heighten their motivation to become actively involved in learning. Children tend to learn best when the subject, topic or theme is engaging, relevant and authentic. Artists too, tend to be attracted to certain subjects or topics and to work with themes. They draw their ideas and inspiration from their immediate environment and often in that environment, as part of it, is a dog. Many artists, from Leonardo da Vinci (Roalf, 1993) to David Hockney (1998), have drawn, painted or sculpted their dogs.

The realization of this connection between the way children learn and artists work struck me as over the past decade a dog became part of my family household and my prime subject for daily drawing. I have long advocated an integrated approach to curriculum planning and favoured a theme-based approach to teaching. As I drew, explored and recorded my dog's constantly changing (but somehow constant, like dogs are supposed to be) shape, lines, colours, tonality, body language and attitudes, I became impressed by the richness and depth of "dog" as a theme for meaningful art making.

Using dogs as an *example*, this chapter explores the vital role that a theme-based approach to curriculum planning combined with daily drawing can play in teaching and art making. And since it is grounded in real life experience, it will be both theoretical and practical – ideas and actions. Other examples could have been chosen of course, and the reader is invited to substitute another animal, object or even issue.

Making Connections

First, some terms should be clarified. *Topics* are discrete subjects that relate to students' everyday experiences. *Themes* are broad questions that connect topics to our relationship with the world. The theme should be an overarching, general question or metaphor that ties subjects together in deep and meaningful ways (Koster, 2001). So if my topic were "dogs" my theme could be "dog-human interaction". Themes can be viewed through the lenses of particular subjects or disciplines. When a topic or theme is considered from the perspective of mathematics, language arts, social studies, science or visual art, something essential is revealed about the subject matter as well as about the discipline or art form.

The theoretical basis of art's relationship with other subjects in the elementary school curriculum can be put into historical perspective. A currently fashionable term, "infusion" refers to the injection of the arts into the classroom setting in order to enrich student learning. In the arts infused scenario (a prime example is the visiting artist) the arts enter the scene from the outside in. "Co-relation", a term popularized in the progressive era, is used when art processes or art learning are introduced into (or related to) other school subject disciplines in order to enhance presentation and instruction. A typical example of correlation occurring is when a child is asked to illustrate a story in language arts or to draw an historical event. Illustration, rather than art, is being practiced whenever a child tries to depict an event with which he has had no personal individual relationship (Brittain, 1968, p. 35). There are, no doubt, occasions when illustration and correlation are appropriate and desirable educational objectives. They differ however, from "integration", another term favoured by progressive educators and still a preferred strategy of many elementary school educators.

The Canadian Society for Education through Art (CSEA) defines integration as:

> the making of conceptual or thematic connections between or among the visual arts and other subject areas. Providing additional attention to continuity of curricular concepts, issues, themes, or activities among subject areas, offers an interesting and meaningful exchange of disciplinary knowledge. Often, these integrative practices strengthen understanding across several disciplines. However, great care must be taken to ensure that the integrity of each subject area is maintained in the process of integration. (Irwin, 1997, p.7)

Maintaining a subject's integrity is a difficult undertaking and a large responsibility, since "integration in learning means that the single subjects lose their identity and form a new unit within the student" (Lowenfeld & Brittain, 1975, p. 106). The key point is not so much "what" is being integrated, but "where" or in "whom" the integration is occurring. As W. Lambert Brittain (1968) puts it, "whenever we engage a child in a creative process – a meaningful creative process – the child meaningfully integrates" (p. 34). He adds that this "is the most important contribution which art can make to integrative experiences, because what is integrated is man, not subjects" (34).

When a theme is used, it is not a question of art being integrated with another subject or being in service of that subject. When the theme is "dogs and people" and the student writes a poem about her dog, it is, if a label is required, poetry or language arts. If a dog's age, height and weight is being calculated, the student is "doing math" or science. If she is painting a picture of a dog, paying attention to its shape, texture, colour, the lines and movement it makes and is trying to express its character or her feelings towards it, she is making art. She is also having an integrative experience.

Howard Gardner's theory of Multiple Intelligences provides strong support for an integrative or thematic approach (1983, 1991, 1993) to learning and suggests a central role for art in the school curriculum. Gardner has challenged the pre-eminence of verbal skill as the dominant method of teaching and learning by providing a more complex vision of how people think and learn. He divides intelligence into eight domains representing the biological and psychological potentials within each individual. He calls them: linguistic intelligence; logical-mathematical intelligence; visual-spatial intelligence; musical intelligence: bodily-kinesthetic intelligence; interpersonal intelligence; intrapersonal intelligence; and naturalist intelligence. By identifying distinct but interlocking intellectual capacities or "intelligences", Gardner has reminded us of the breadth of human potential and the many ways that people learn. He has confirmed what many art educators suspected – intelligence is a multidimensional phenomenon that is not fixed and can be enhanced. Intelligence, in the holistic sense, requires integration. It is interesting to note that Gardner does not claim an "artistic intelligence" but believes that all the Intelligences can be used for either artistic or non artistic purposes depending on combinations of individual choice and cultural factors. When an artist is engaged in the art making process, several Intelligences are in play.

Exploring the Human-Canine Relationship

What is common to all of these terms and ideas is the notion that both learning and art making are about making connections. In order to illustrate how a theme based approach to teaching art can generate lessons and activities rich in art learning as well as potential for cross curricular connections, lets look at one topic, "dogs", and related themes in detail. A good way to begin is with a brainstorming session with a group of students to create a concept web. Figure 1 (Student Web) illustrates one student teacher's projection of the kind of responses a group of grade four students might generate as she prepared a unit proposal on the theme of "the Human–Canine relationship".[1] A true brainstorming session can start anywhere and go anywhere. With dogs at the centre and lines radiating, the teacher can name the circles or nodes. "Dogs with jobs", a phrase popularized by a television program, is a good place to start. A list can be made of jobs that some dogs are trained to do, including being guides for the visually impaired; helping the police; searching for bombs, drugs and lost people; guarding homes and businesses; herding sheep or cattle; pulling sleds, racing and acting in movies. Dogs have even gone to outer space!

Most dogs have the job of being friend and companion. Various breeds will be called out starting with a child's own dog. Many children will know names of breeds (Beagle, Poodle, Dachshund, greyhound, cocker spaniel, Rottweiler, etc.). Many breeds are associated with various nationalities or regions, for example German shepherd, Siberian husky, Irish wolfhound, Norwegian elkhound, Australian cattle dog, Old English sheepdog, Labrador retriever and Newfoundland dog. The potential for a geography lesson is obvious. Discussion can move to the training of dogs and terms like "obedience" and "agility". Some students may have knowledge of the world of dog shows and competitions. They may be familiar with various careers involved with dogs: trainer, breeder, groomer, and veterinarian. The history (evolutionary, biological and sociological) of dogs from their prehistoric predecessors to wolves to our present day domestic pets can be elaborated on by the teacher. The types and textures of coats found in various breeds (and cross breeds) of dogs – short, long, wiry, curly, coarse, silky – and the range of colour can lead to discussion of art terms and interpretation in appropriate media.

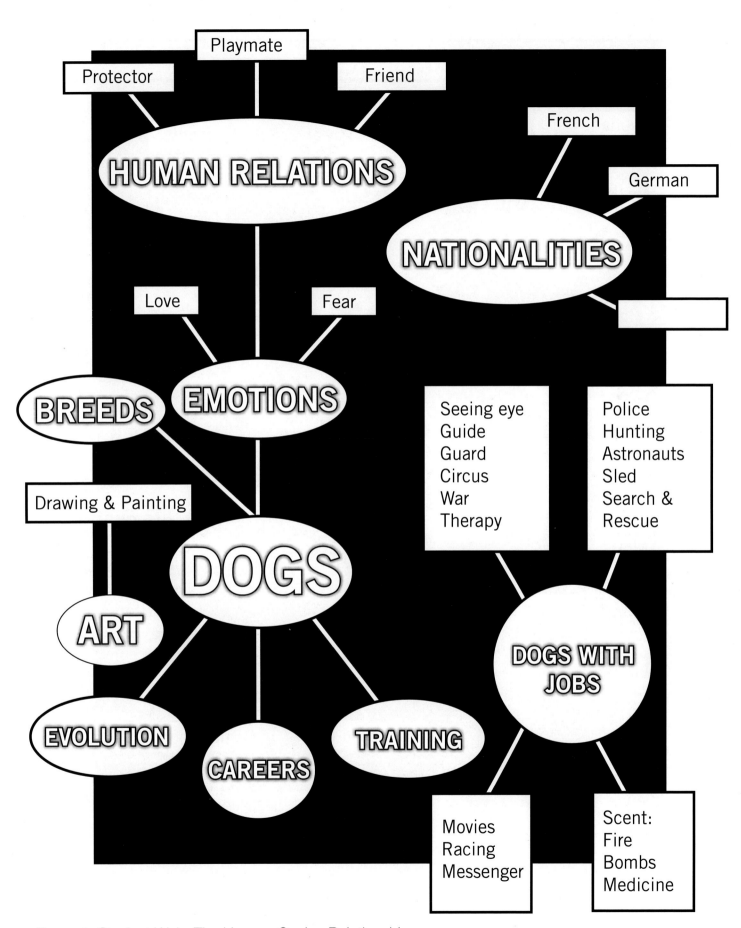

Figure 1: Student Web: The Human-Canine Relationship

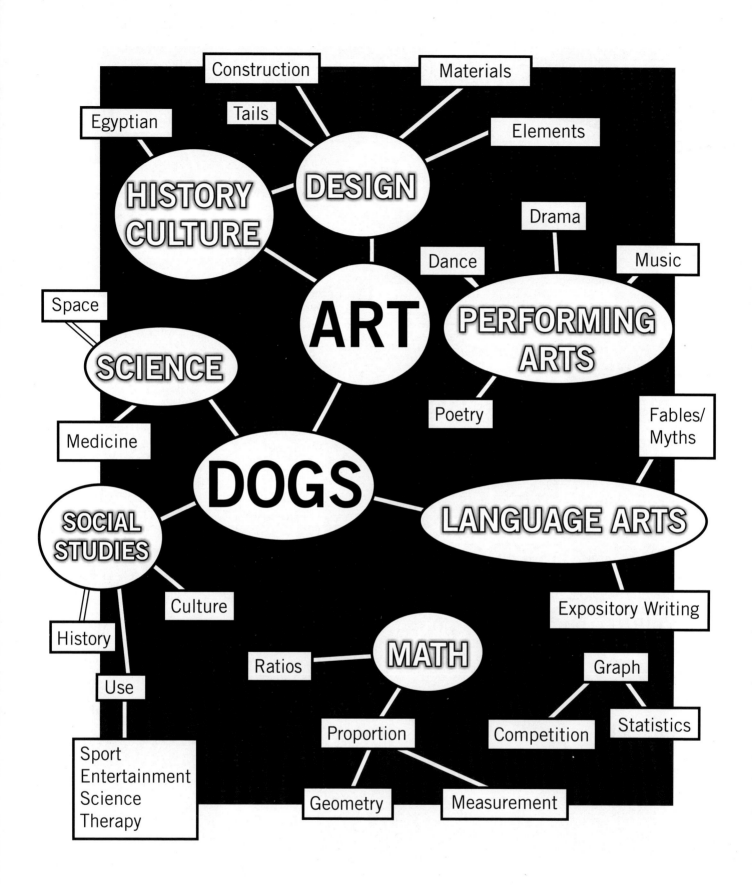

Figure 2: Teacher Web: The Human-Canine Relationship

Figure 2 (Teacher Web) is a concept web of the same theme from the teacher's perspective. It too starts with "dogs" at the centre and leads to various subject areas: social studies (history of the dog; roles of dogs in society); language arts (dog stories, myths and fables; dog novels or expository text); science (breeding, genetics, physiology, etc.); mathematics (proportions, measurements, statistics, graphs) and even physical education (analysis of movement). The dog theme can enlighten and broaden discussions of history and multiculturalism as we uncover humankind's various and often conflicting attitudes towards these ubiquitous beasts. As Stanley Coren outlines, "in some times and places, people have viewed dogs as loyal, faithful, noble, intelligent, courageous and sociable; in other eras and locations humans have thought dogs cowardly, unclean, disease ridden, dangerous and unreliable" (2000, p. 1). The symbolism attached to dogs by different cultures, from being guides for souls or the embodiments of the devil, is ripe and evocative material for art education. It is important to remember the negative side of dogs. Dogs can be fierce and dangerous. A black dog is a symbol of evil and menace. Some people are allergic to dogs.

When developing both the art unit and individual lessons, the "Unit Circle" model provides a useful structure. The four points on the circle: Developing images (the theme and all of its dimensions and possibilities); Elements and principles of design; Responding to art: and Materials and processes constitute the major planning considerations. Each is accommodated nicely in a lesson called "From Picasso Pups to Cajun Canines" in which students learn about the wide ranging styles and other pertinent information of five artists who painted dogs (among other things): Pablo Picasso, Leonardo da Vinci, George Rodrigue (the Cajun), Robert Bateman and Franz Marc. The students respond to these works, learn about personal styles in art, and create a painting in their own personal style using appropriately expressive media and directly or indirectly, particular elements (colour, shape, texture) and principles (emphasis, balance, rhythm, etc.) of art and design. As she points out, this approach incorporates the three facets of art instruction: "Learning *with* art (as a vehicle for studying other subjects), learning *through* art (using art to express ideas and emotions) and learning *about* art (gathering knowledge of media, methods, skills etc.)."[2] Art becomes truly embedded in the curriculum as an integral *learning* language. These examples demonstrate the huge potential of the dog theme and the nature and extent of the relationship between mankind and "dogkind."

Dogs and Art

A short survey of the history of dogs in art is in order. Dogs have had a place in art from what is generally considered to be art's beginnings, the prehistoric paintings on cave walls. The fossil record shows fourteen thousand year old evidence of a domesticated dog, similar to contemporary dogs, as cohabiting with a group of Paleolithic (Old Stone Age) humans who lived in caves in the region that is present day Iraq (Coren, 2000, p. 180). The earliest known graphic depiction of canines is from the late Paleolithic period (15,000 to 10,000 years ago), in caves in the Pyrenean region of Spain (Marley, 2000). These dog-like creatures are crudely drawn and it is not known whether they were companions or competitors in the hunt for game (or the game itself). As domestication occurred, the roles for dogs changed – from hunting, to guarding, to fighting, to herding, to hauling – each task requiring a different type. Egyptian carvings on green slate tablets from at least 4,000 BC portray both Mastiff and Greyhound type dogs, breeds that were also depicted in early Assyrian and Babylonian sculptures. By 800 BC the Egyptians were depicting a small Spitz type toy dog, most likely a pet, in household scenes. Egyptian tomb

paintings from the XIXth Dynasty (c. 1350 –1115 BC) show *Anubis*, the dog or Jackal-headed god of the rites of death whose duty it was to guide the dead on the trip to the underworld. On jugs and urns, the Greeks often portrayed hunting dogs, guard dogs and pets. So too did the Romans. A fine example of a guard dog pulling on its leash in a mosaic excavated at Pompeii is reproduced in Howard's book, *The Illustrated Dog* (1994, p. 24).

While hunting scenes were occasionally the subject of illuminated books depicting the lives of the nobility in the early middle ages in Europe, prior to the Renaissance the major employer of artists was the Christian church and the subjects were religious ones. Consequently, few dogs are found in art from that period - Jesus didn't have a dog. When dogs were depicted it was for symbolic purposes: "A dog with a flaming torch in its mouth is a symbol of St. Dominic" (Marley, 2000, p. 23). The Dominicans, who were called "dogs of the Lord" wore black and white habits. Black and white dogs symbolized this religious order. Dogs were also considered a symbol of faithfulness in marriage. The most famous example is Jan Van Eyck's symbol laden fifteenth century portrait, *Giovanni Arnolfini and his Bride*. The little terrier at their feet symbolizes marital faith. He is probably also just their pet.

The Renaissance, with its advancements in anatomical knowledge and draughtsmanship, along with growing private patronage and the revival of the Greek's keen interest in animals, was a rebirth of sorts for dog imagery in art. Dogs were a favorite subject of tapestry weavers. Leonardo da Vinci and Albrect Durer produced some fine studies of dogs. Venice, which boasted a wealthy merchant class which wanted their portraits painted, preferably with their favorite dogs, supported the painters Titian and Veronese. "Titian", claims Marley, "is well known for his portrayal of small children with large dogs – a device that effectively emphasizes the contrast between vulnerability and security" (p. 22). In Northern Europe, Flemish and German artists included dogs in their commissioned paintings. Certain breeds signified rank and wealth. Eighteenth century British portrait painters such as Sir Joshua Reynolds and Thomas Gainsborough followed this example by introducing dogs into many of their paintings for this purpose, but also as compositional devices. The household pets of common people are found in the Dutch genre painting of Jan Steen, Gerard Ter Borch and others and are often central characters in paintings and illustrations from the Romantic period.

In eighteenth and nineteenth century Britain there was a proliferation of painters who specialized in animals. The best known, George Stubbs, Edward Landseer, and Rosa Bonheur, began their careers as portraitists of human subjects but became famous for their portraits of horses and dogs. Queen Victoria and her family were dog lovers and commissioned Landseer to portray her favorite pets (Howard, 1994, p. 71). The dog portrait as a genre and the dog as a subject for art had arrived. Marley attributes this phenomenon at least in part to "the developing passion for natural history on one hand, and improved printing methods and the invention of lithography on the other" which "provided an enormous incentive for dog artists to meticulously record the breeds" (2000, p. 24). The invention of photography also aided and further popularized this trend. Impressionist painters, notably Renoir and Cassatt, often include dogs in their depictions of fleeting moments of everyday Parisian urban life.

After the Impressionists, dogs as a subject fared less well in modern art, perhaps as a reaction against the Victorian and romantic tendency to sentimentalize and anthropomorphize attributes such as loyalty, obedience and courage. Moreover, photography and the popular media provided ample opportunity for the spread of dog imagery. Still, one of the great landmarks of modern art, George Seurat's *A Sunday Afternoon on the Island of La Grande Jatte* prominently features two dogs and dogs appear, albeit in various degrees of abstraction, in some paintings by Franz Marc and Pablo Picasso. Indeed, Picasso was well known for being a dog lover and had several which are often cited as influences on his art. When the modern sensibility allows for an evocative kind of realism, as in the works of the American Edward Hopper and the Canadian Alex Colville, dogs reappear.

In postmodern and contemporary art with its urge for inclusiveness and embracing of narrative and autobiographical elements, dogs are again a popular, recurring (pun intended) subject. This is probably because dogs, being both a part of (and apart from) human society can serve simultaneously as a metaphor for human beings, a foil for their follies, and as particularized beings. The British-American artist David Hockney unabashedly paints his sleeping Dachshunds in their role as specific pets – both representatives of a breed and as individuals (Hockney, 1998). William Wegman, in drawings, videos, and Polaroid photographs of his Weimaraner, Man Ray and his descendents, treats these dogs less as pets and more as "co-conspirators" as they don outrageous costumes and assume elaborate poses. Similarly the graffiti artist and painter, Keith Haring, often worked with and through an ironically knowing cartoon-like dog. Both artists' work exists comfortably in art galleries and in popular picture books and calendars. It is interesting to note that the postmodern dogs of William Wegman and Keith Haring do not change at all when the art is marketed to children or adults. The format may change but the dogs do not.

As long as dogs have a significant place in human society they will have a place in art. Through art, dogs help us raise questions about that society, be it ancient or post modern, and the nature of social relationships. How we treat our dogs reflects how we value our selves and how we treat other human beings and the environment.

Figures 3 & 3a:
Pages from Harold
Pearse's sketch book.

Dog Based Art Education

In my view, the basis of an art program should be daily drawing. Daily drawing, be it practiced by professional artists, art education students, elementary teachers, or children, is like daily jogging – it keeps the "drawing muscles" (eye, hand, brain) fit. For an adult or adolescent, the routine and discipline of a daily ritual relaxes the mind. With devotion and persistence, increased skill and fluency in drawing (and looking) can develop. For a child, daily drawing can be a kind of game, imbued with the fun that comes with spontaneous expression and the satisfaction that comes with completing a task within or in spite of certain parameters. These drawings (they could be collages or collected or "found" images) need not be large or take long (a few minutes to half an hour). If one is to draw every day in a sketchbook or make entries in a visual journal, the process is expedited if one has an on going topic or theme. I have been drawing daily in a sketchbook since 1988 and a major subject has been my dog - the other subject has been Mounties, but that's another story (see Figure 3: A page from Harold Pearse's sketchbook).

The following ideas could be incorporated into daily drawings or adapted to classroom projects. How about beginning with a page of dog lines: smooth, furry, fuzzy, cuddly, strong, fierce, bumpy, squiggly, wiggly, "as crooked as a dog's hind leg'). A page of dog textures: soft, rough, curly, shaggy, corded. A page of dog shapes: fat, thin, oblong, rounded, long, sausage-like. A page of dog colours: white, black, grey, brown, spotted, striped, banded. Dogs of course can be explored via the essential drawing modes of memory, observation, imagination and description.

Memory: Although not usually described as drawing from memory, young children draw what they remember as a "schema" or routinized graphic representation of a 'dog' - a couple of circles and a few lines that stand for 'dog'. Older children learn to personalize and particularize specific dogs, often drawing things as recalled. Drawing attention to what exactly it is that we are drawing when we draw from memory and where it is coming from (a little TV screen in our heads?) is an important kind of awareness for older children and adults to cultivate.

Observation: First you have to *really* look: at real dogs, photographs, paintings, drawings, x-rays of dogs. Look carefully at these images. How is the dog put together? How does he move? Then put the image away and draw. Draw using a contour line, or what Steele calls the "classical line", the "line of early Greek ceramic decorators or classical artists such as Ingres and Picasso in his classical period" (1998, p. 91). It is the carefully observed and felt line of the contour drawing (the graceful, elegant sweep of a greyhound or whippet); the swift but deliberate and often playful continuous line drawing (the rapid movement of a golden retriever or poodle). The aim is to acheive empathy with the subject.

But as Hubbard cautions, "bringing a dog into the classroom to serve as a model may sound like a good idea and may at first appeal to students, but often can be a frustrating drawing experience because students have not learned enough about the structure of an animal and have not learned about artistic ways of portraying it" (1993, p. 30). In other words, dogs won't keep still for long! But there is always gesture drawing, the perfect way to show a dog in motion. The value of a real dog in the classroom is not so much as a "life drawing" model but the experience of being in the presence of the real creature and the opportunity to analyze its structure and behavior. Hubbard recommends that students take Polaroid or digital photographic images, which in this situation, could be useful references and also give them a sense of ownership.

Imagination: Dogs can be a source for imaginative, fantasy or play inspired drawings. One group of grade six boys I observed with a fascination for collecting beanie baby dogs constructed an imaginary world of a colony of such dogs with their own families and competing armies portrayed in endless drawings, paintings and collages. The design process can be regarded as active imagining. De Bono's classic study, *The Dog-Exercising Machine* (1971), describes the inventive strategies employed by children when asked to "design a machine for exercising dogs." When learning about dog breeds, and collecting images of various breeds, students can imagine and design, draw or collage new combinations (mixed breeds and mixed media). What would a Labracollie, a schnoodle, a Newfy Rotshund look like? In my sketchbook I draw my dog, which I think is a mix of Bichon Frise and Border Collie" – I call him a "broccoli"!

Description: Drawings can be inspired from words, music, plays, films or other symbol systems or art forms. Stories and images are described in some way which can be translated to expressive visual forms. Children's books, from Lassie to Old Yeller to Snoopy contain wonderful dog characters. My current favorite is "Walter the farting dog". The challenge of course is to help children go beyond the stereotypical images often created by adult artists (and the media) to create unique dog characters of their own.

These modes of drawing are combined and extended in a unit I do with my Elementary art students, called *The Dog Collage Project*. We begin by exploring various approaches to drawing including contour drawing, classical line, continuous line, drawing with empathy, drawing from memory, imagination and observation. Even upside down drawing. We consider the notions of topics and theme, using our relationship to dogs as a model. After a variety of dog images are collected and drawn from various sources, a composition (to include at least three dogs or parts of dogs) is created and the outline transferred onto heavy paper. Students are then introduced to a selection of reproductions of paintings with dogs in them: these might include Paul Gauguin, Mary Cassatt, Francisco Goya, Gilbert Sanchez Lujan, Auguste

Figure 6 Elementary Education Student's Dog Collage (Luke Streisel)

"Buddy from photo-sketch"
Jan 18/'10

"Spaniel in Shades"
Jan 18/2010

"Maltise on a Pedastool"
Jan 18/2010

"Snoozer"
Jan 18/2010

Figures 4 & 5 Elementary Education student's dog drawings   (Kristen Nelson)

Figure 7: Elementary Education Student's Dog Collage (Alisha Wamboldt)

Renoir and Alex Colville. These paintings provide the inspiration for the colour palette of their own composition. The colours, shades/tints/values observed in the reproduction, rather than being mixed in paint, are selected from magazines, which become a kind of paint box. The students are encouraged to pay attention also to textures, shapes, lines, mood, contrast, patterns, etc. Using this collage or "paper mosaic" material they give colour, texture, and shape to their own composition drawing. Figures 4 to 10 show Elementary Education students' dog drawings and dog collages inspired by the paintings of a chosen artist – *Magazine Mosaic Muts*!

Figure 8: Elementary Education Student's Dog Collage (Jayde O'Reily)

The above ideas and considerations make for a kind of "dog based art education" (DBAE). But remember, dogs are used here only as one example. Imagine the possibilities using topics and themes like cats, horses, fish, trees, etc. and their place in society, the environment and art. When a theme is explored in depth in one subject, it sets the stage for in depth exploration in others and builds the potential for a truly integrated, renaissance curriculum.

Resources

This resource list of books about dogs only *scratches* the surface. Furthermore, if you *sit* at your computer and *stay* with it you can discover a lot of web sites about dogs (i.e. www.thebark.com; Google Dog Art Today). Who knows what you will *come* up (or *down*) with!

Dog Books for Children

Brett, J. (1988). *The first dog*. Orlando: Harcourt Brace Jovanovich Publishers.

Fanelli, S. (1998). *The doggy book*. Philadelphia: Running Press.

Kotzwinkle, W. & Murray, G. (2001). *Walter the farting dog* (Illustrations by A. Colman). Berkley, CA: Frog.

Roalf, P. (1993). *Looking at paintings: Dogs*. New York: Hyperion Books for Children.

Snow, A. (1993). *How dogs really work?* Boston, Toronto, NY: Little, Brown and Company.

Books on Dogs and Art

Erwitt, E. (1998). *Dogs dogs*. London: Phaidon Press Limited.

Haring, K. (2000). *Dogs*. Boston, New York, London: Little Brown and Company.

Bowron, E. P., Rebbert, C. R., Rosenblum, R. and Secord, W. (2006). *Best in show: The Dog in art from the Renaissance to today*. London: Yale University Press.

Hockney, D. (1998). *David Hockney's dog days*. New York: Little Brown and Company.

Howard, T. (1994). *The illustrated dog*. London: Grange Books.

Merritt, R. & Barth, M. (2000). *A Thousand Hounds: The presence of the dog in the history of photography 1839 to today*. New York: Taschen.

Rodrique, G. & Freundlich, L.S. (1994). *Blue dog*. New York: Penguin Books.

70

Ruben, J. H. (2003). *Impressionist Cats and Dogs: Pets in the painting of modern life*. New Haven: Yale University Press.

Wegman, W. (Photographs and drawings) & Wieder, L. (Introduction) (1999). *Man's best friend*: New York: Harry Abrams.

Books about Dogs

Coren, S. (2000) *The intelligence of dogs: A guide to the thoughts, emotions and inner lives of our canine companions*. New York: Bantam Books.

Coren, S. (2002) *The pawprints of history: Dogs and the course of human events*. New York: Free Press (Simon and Schuster, Inc.).

Cunliffe, J. (2001). *The Encyclopedia of dog breeds*. Bath, UK: Parragon.

McGreevy, P. (ed.) (1999). *The little guide: Dogs*. San Francisco: Fog City Press.

Figure 9: Elementary Education Student's Dog Collage (Kayla Hoffer)

References

Brittain, L. (Ed.). (1968). *Viktor Lowenfeld speaks on art and creativity*. Reston VA: National Art Education Association.

De Bono, E. (1971). *The Dog-exercising machine: A study of children as inventors*. Middlesex, UK: Penguin Books.

Gardner, H. (1983, 1991, 1993). *Frames of mind: The Theory of multiple intelligences*. New York: Basic Books.

Hubbard, G. (1993). Canine connections. *Arts & Activities*, March, pp. 28-31.

Irwin, R. L. (1997*). The CSEA national policy and supporting perspectives for practice guidelines*. Boucherville, PQ: Canadian Society for Education through Art.

Koster, J. B. (2001). *Bringing art into the elementary classroom*. Belmont, CA: Wadsworth/Thompson Learning.

Lowenfeld, V. & Brittain, W. L. (1975). *Creative and mental growth*. New York: Macmillan.

Marley, B. (2000). The illustrated dog. *Dogs in Canada*, 92(1), 22-26.

Steele, B. (1998). *Draw me a story: An illustrated exploration of drawing as language*. Winnipeg: Peguis.

End notes

1. The student and teacher webs described here and the unit concept "Exploring the Human-Canine Relationship through the Visual Arts" were developed in my Curriculum and Instruction in Elementary School Art (EDEL 302, Winter 2002) class at the University of Alberta by Willy Hankinson. Willy also breeds Standard Schnauzers.

2. Quotation by W. Hankinson. See also J. B. Koster, pp. 41-42.

Figure 10: Elementary Education Student's Dog Collage (Taylor Roy)

71

CHAPTER 8

Approaches to Elementary Art Assessment

Fiona M. Blaikie

Assessment of others and ourselves continually takes place. When meeting someone, we interpret their mood. Everything about how others speak, dress, behave, and what they say provides us with information as to how we might respond. Small nuances such as warmth in the tone of voice, or not making eye contact, provide us with clues.

Assessment is one of the most significant educational issues today. Assessment has emerged on the Canadian political stage with some provincial governments demanding teachers be more accountable: that is, teach more content and assess more rigorously. But there is a perception held by the public, parents, teachers and administrators, that art is difficult to assess because it is a 'soft' subject.

Problems associated with assessing art are:

- the *subjective judgement* of the assessor(s)
- the *qualitative* nature of art itself
- the problem of *method*, that is *how* to assess art?

Subjective Judgements and the Qualitative Nature of Art

Assessment is considered difficult to accomplish in art because of the qualitative nature of the subject. How can we grade something as ephemeral as a child's creative expression? This is a valid question. It is unfair when a child produces a piece of creative work -- say a drawing of a cat, and John gets a 'C' while Susie gets an 'A' with no other information from the teacher as to why that grade was assigned. Ash, Schofield, and Starkey (2000) state that "for many Art and Design teachers the idea of examining art work runs counter to a long-held philosophy and imbued ideas about the nature of creativity, self-expression, and the idiosyncratic nature of Art and Design and making. Many will say you cannot assess art, it is to do with subjective opinion, it is creative" (p.145). Not being able to resolve this problem easily, and being expected to assign a grade for art, many teachers have simply relied on their own subjective opinions. However, those arguing against assessment in art would assert that the interpretation of value is so entirely subjectively mediated and defined, that any assessment in art is necessarily flawed. Best (1980) illustrates an extremist's interpretation of this view:

…subjectivists rarely recognize the inherent difficulties in their own position…. A dance professor, who is a convinced subjectivist, commendably recognized that it is a consequence of such a position that anyone's opinion is as good as anyone else's. Hence she was unable to raise any objection when some of her students, as their 'dance performance,' simply sat on the floor of the studio eating crisps. Despite her admirable honesty she lost her job. (p. 36)

If sitting on the floor eating crisps is unacceptable, then there exists a socially and culturally defined conception of what is acceptable: What counts as art or art production is defined socio-culturally. Csikszentmihalyi (1996) explains:

No matter how much we admire the personal insight, the subjective illumination, we cannot tell whether it is a delusion or a creative thought unless we adopt some criterion–of logic, beauty, or usefulness–and the moment we do so, we introduce a social or cultural evaluation. Hence I was led to develop the systemic perspective on creativity, which *relocates the creative process outside the individual mind* (italics added). (p. 403)

Cultures worldwide confer artistic merit based on socio-cultural values, beliefs, and appreciation; as Wolff (1981) asserts, art is produced in a socialized context. The same is true for the subculture of teaching and the school. If art is produced and valued within socio-cultural contexts, we must, as Csikszentmihalyi posits, necessarily adopt socio-culturally defined criteria for determining what is unacceptable, what is better, and what is best.

Learning about art and assessment in the school context is defined by socio-cultural norms and expectations. There is an important difference between valuing art and assessing art in the school setting. This is because *teachers need to be concerned primarily with making educational rather than artistic judgements.*

Assessing Art Qualitatively

As a teacher, you will most likely have to assess students in art. I am not talking about liking or disliking the work produced, I mean considering what educational qualities you believe to be important; thinking clearly about what you aim to teach, what you expect your students to learn, and then turning those expectations into criteria for assessment of a process or product. Thus, assessment involves delineating expectations for what and how your students will engage in learning about art and design, and a range of standards (or levels of achievement) they might attain in relation to your expectations of them. As well, assessment involves deciding what kind of student work will best reveal the learning process. This work may be product, as well as process, or work habit based. In making educational judgments, the multiplicity of variables to be assessed might include "high standards of work; a continuous working process; an independent and responsible attitude; self assessment and evaluation" (Clement, 1986, p. 239). In short, the best qualitative alternative to (indefensible) subjective judgment or simply giving a grade to a piece of artwork based on whether you like it or not is *qualitative assessment by using criterion-referencing*.

Criterion referencing refers to the delineation of criteria for assessment. In order to ensure content validity, you need to assess what was taught. In other words, criteria must reflect lesson expectations. Through defining criteria one can assess specifics such as understanding concepts, the work produced, work habits, skills and techniques, and classroom dialogue. Criterion referencing means that in assessing many variables, the teacher goes much further and beyond a subjective judgment on creative expression alone.

In criterion referencing each child is assessed individually: Susie's work is assessed in terms of the criteria for assessment. Thus, Susie is not compared with John, as in norm referencing where students are compared with one another competitively and in relation to bell curve norms. Rather, in criterion referencing, Susie is assessed in terms of her individual work habits, work produced, and personal potential.

Assessment can be undertaken formally, at the conclusion of a thematic project. This is known as *summative assessment*. Assessment undertaken formally or informally on an ongoing basis is known as *formative assessment*.

Essential to the assessment of art in schools is the need for *dialogue based shared understandings* of expectations and criteria for assessment, which will occur through conversations and art critiques between individual students and the teacher, and discussions with the whole class. This approach will facilitate students' abilities to self and peer assess, and to become reflective learners.

An important aspect of assessment in art is building up individual *student portfolios of visual and written work*. This activity should result in adequate bodies of material to assess, and to discuss with parents and students. Portfolios can and should include written reflective material, sketchbooks, and research materials.

A *portfolio* is a focused collection of visual art, often accompanied by reflective and explanatory written data. The contents of the portfolio and the time frame for production are specified or negotiated between teacher and students.

Krueger and Wallace (1996) hold that a portfolio is:

> constructed according to an explicit purpose. This purpose provides students with a focus for the collection and organization of the evidence, informs them about what they are expected to learn, the types of evidence they can marshal as support for their learning and how they will be assessed…. A major decision relating to the purpose of a portfolio is whether it will contain students' best pieces of work or whether it will be developmental. (p. 26)

There is strong support in the literature on assessment in art education for qualitative assessment of art utilizing portfolios as a significant element of formative or summative assessment, with reference to specific criteria and clearly delineated levels of achievement (Beattie, 1994, 1997; Blaikie, 1997; Boughton, 1994; Eisner, 1985; International Baccalaureate, 2000; Schonau, 1994; Steers, 1994). However, there are many ways to apply criteria.

Comparison of Curricular Approaches to Assessment and Evaluation in Ontario, British Columbia, and Nova Scotia

Barrett (1990) defines assessment as a judgement of a process or product set within a spectrum of explicitly stated criteria. Allison (1986) asserts that assessment and evaluation differ because assessment "is one of the factors upon which evaluations can be made" (p.115). Beattie's (1997) view, as well as definitions in the British Columbia Fine Arts K-7 Curriculum Guide (British Columbia Ministry of Education, 1998), is similar to Allison's. Beattie states that: "assessment is the method or process used for gathering information about people, programs, or objects for the purpose of making an evaluation" (p. 2). In an earlier publication (Blaikie, 1997) I wrote that:

> evaluation tends to be more holistic – one tends to be looking at an overall impression in evaluating; searching out themes, metaphors, patterns and general trends. With reference to criteria for assessment, assessment is specific in its focus on very particular aspects of a student's work and work habits, even though an overall grade or percentage may be the final result. (p. 193)

In assessment the teacher is charged with being specific in regard to individual criteria during the lesson, as well as while providing feedback. Accountability is at issue here, as well as the teacher's ability to explain and defend grading decisions to school administration, students, and parents. If a teacher were being asked to evaluate, s/he might assign a 'C' grade to Jane's drawing of a cat, based on an overall impression of it. But Ministries, Boards of Education, and principals require more data than this. Even when the term used is 'evaluation,' you will be expected to provide detailed information to illustrate how you came to a final grade.

In short, assessment refers to an approach in which greater external control exists, as teachers are expected or required to follow curricular expectations and criteria. In evaluation, control is internal, and rests more with individual teachers. Ideally in both approaches teachers function as respected professionals making informed educational judgements about learning in art.

Ontario

In Ontario, the term assessment is used exclusively in the *Ontario Curriculum Grades 1 to 8: The Arts* (Ontario Ministry of Education & Training, 2009). Teachers are expected to look at specific aspects of learning, rather than making global 'general impression' based judgements. Greater control of teachers and teaching as well as curricular and procedural rigidity are indicated. Specific curriculum content areas and related expectations for learning are organized as follows:

Exploring forms and cultural contexts:	*Creating and presenting:*	*Reflecting, responding and analysing:*
content knowledge	studio work	models for art criticism
(for example, the elements and principles of design, art history, world cultures).	(including drawing, painting, printmaking, three dimensional work).	(including formal analysis and phenomenological approaches).

The four *achievement levels* outlined (p. 34) are to be used along with more traditional indicators like letter grades and percentage marks, and are among a number of tools that teachers use to assess students' learning. The guide outlines four levels of achievement: Level three is the provincial standard, and identifies a high level of achievement where the student's work meets provincial expectations. Level one refers to a student whose work is limited and does not meet the provincial standard, level two refers to a student whose work almost meets the provincial standard, or does meet it some of the time, and level four refers to a student whose work exceeds the provincial standard.

The three curriculum content areas, *exploring forms and cultural contexts, creating and presenting, reflecting, responding and analysing* translate directly into criteria for assessment in the rubric provided, with descriptors in relation to each criterion and the four achievement levels (p. 34). To illustrate how this works, an example of a unit plan for Ontario follows.

The unit plan is for grade one students,[1] and focuses on exploring the art of Roy Thomas, specifically his painting, *Spirit of Anishnabe Art* (Blaikie & Clark, 2000)[2], in which primary colours, shape, and line are examined, along with the meaning of the image. Very brief expectations in relation to each curriculum content area are defined as follows:

Exploring Forms and Cultural Contexts
- Students will learn about and use primary colours, shape, and line.
- Students will learn about the work of Roy Thomas, the cultural contexts for and of his work.

Reflecting, Responding and Analyzing
- Students will engage in Formal Analysis (description, analysis and interpretation) of *Spirit of Anishnabe Art*.

Creating and Presenting
- Students will paint animals, birds, or fish using only primary colours, shape, and line.
- Students will create a stuffed painted sculpture of an animal, bird or fish using shape, line, and primary colours.
- Students will respect art materials.
- Students will cooperate during clean-up time.

The Unit Plan

Lessons 1/2: Formal Analysis of *Spirit of Anishnabe Art* focusing on recognizing the use of primary colours, shape, and the use of line. We will conclude by discussing the meaning of the painting for each of us, as well as its important cultural significance.

Lesson 3/4: Painting of birds or fish using primary colours, shapes, and lines.

Lesson 5/6: Create a stuffed painted sculpture of a bird or fish emphasizing the use of shapes, lines, and primary colours.

Lesson 7: Review and reflection: Students tell one thing they liked best about one of the artworks they produced, and one thing they found difficult. An example of a criterion referenced rubric follows.

Criterion-Referenced Rubric for Exploring Forms and Cultural Contexts

	Level 1	Level 2	Level 3	Level 4
Exploring forms and cultural contexts (Understanding of concepts) Criteria: The student - recognizes and understands the concept of primary colours - identifies and understands the concept of shape - identifies and understands the concept of line - Understands the cultural contexts of the artist and artwork	shows understanding of few of the concepts -rarely gives explanations that show understanding of the concepts	shows understanding of some of the concepts - sometimes gives complete explanations	shows understanding of most of the concepts -usually gives complete or nearly complete explanations	shows understanding of all (or almost all) of the concepts -consistently gives complete explanations

Expectations have become criteria for assessment. Each criterion is assessed in terms of adjectives which describe levels of achievement (levels 1 to 4). These levels of achievement are termed anecdotal or qualitative, because they provide more descriptive information to parents and students.

It should be noted that the approach in Ontario is assessment based and provides less information to parents on work habits; it focuses on art learning, and understanding concepts, an ability to engage in talk about art, and the quality of process and final art products.

British Columbia

In the *British Columbia Curriculum Guide Fine Arts K-7* (British Columbia Ministry of Education, 1998), assessment and evaluation are both used. Four curriculum content areas are defined as:

1. Image-development and design strategies, perceiving and responding as well as creating and communicating are components of all four content areas;
2. Context;
3. Visual elements and principles of art and design; and
4. Materials, technologies and processes.

The curriculum guide provides examples of approaches to assessing student work, based on examples of unit plans. For example, in a grade 7 unit on self portraits, students are expected to do the following:

- view and discuss self portraits by other artists; examining the use of materials, elements and principles of design, and interpreting mood in each image;

- paint self portraits, including symbols, items of personal significance, and "selected use of colour to contribute to the characterization and to develop mood" (p. 6);

- paint using "one colour to convey mood" enhanced by neutrals, complementaries and tonal contrasts;

- experiment with using different painting materials and a variety of "brushstrokes and paint application tools to add texture and details" (p. 6);

- create a "personal web chart of interests, hobbies, friends, concerns, and hopes," in order to convey a sense of 'Who I Am' to the viewer" (p. 6);

- engage in "reflection time" during painting sessions in which students discuss their paintings with a partner, who provides "constructive criticism" (p. 6);

- sign and mat artworks;

- write an artist's statement including reasons for colour choices, style idea, and using particular symbols (p. 6) and

- curate a show of their works and create a catalogue of artists' statements.

Criteria for assessing and evaluating student performance are not defined explicitly in relation to the curriculum content areas: Image Development and Design Strategies, Context, Visual Elements and Principles of Art and Design, and Materials, Technologies and Process. Rather, they are defined in relation to criteria created specifically for this particular project:

- self portrait
- contribution to art show
- artist's statement

A rating of 'C+' in relation to the criterion 'self portrait' is defined similarly to a level of achievement in the Ontario curriculum guide, but more variables are considered here (character, mood, technique, use of elements and principles of design):

May show some inconsistencies. Some features are effective, but there may be problems in another area (e.g., colour may not convey mood; the brushstrokes and paint application may not offer variations in texture). Conveys some sense of character. Tends to reflect 'safe' choices in technique and subject matter. (p. 4)

Overall, in British Columbia, the strategy seems to be closer to evaluation than assessment in that there does not exist a direct connection between curriculum content areas and related expectations and criteria for assessment/evaluation. Teachers are expected to use their "insight, knowledge about learning, and experience with students, along with criteria they establish, to make judgements about student performance in relation to learning outcomes" (p. 1). For the teacher, it seems that one's professional opinion in gaining an overall general impression is important, and seems to count for more than the delineation of specifics, such as how much knowledge a student might have of a very particular aspect of art theory.

Nova Scotia

In the curriculum guide for Nova Scotia Department of Education (2000) *Visual Arts Primary-6* both terms, assessment and evaluation, are used interchangeably. Three curricular areas are outlined:

1. Creative/Productive-Making
2. Cultural/Historical-Looking
3. Critical/Responsive-Reflecting

Several assessment strategies are suggested: collecting portfolios, learning logs and sketch journals; peer feedback through group discussion; performance assessment; student-teacher conversations; questionnaires and surveys, anecdotal records; checklists, observations and questioning (pp. 95-97). Sample assessment questionnaires and rubrics are included. As in British Columbia, they do not relate specifically to the curriculum content areas defined above, but rather, the curriculum content areas are infused within each unit or lesson plan. For example, for a dream catcher's studio exercise (no grade level defined) students are asked to complete a checklist which includes questions such as:

1. I enjoyed (did not enjoy) making the dream catcher because….
2. The part I found most difficult was….
3. I was successful in completing the web design resulting in an exact pattern. (Yes or No).
4. Two things I learned about dream catchers are…. (p. 99)

In peer assessment activities of overlapping line designs (p. 104), the approach leans toward assessment rather than evaluation, as very specific questions are delineated and levels of achievement are defined. Again, there is no evidence of criteria defined in relation to the three curriculum content areas, Creative/Productive, Cultural/Historical, and Critical/Responsive. Rather links to the curriculum content areas are implied.

Overall though, an evaluation based approach is more evident in the Nova Scotia Guide, Visual Arts Primary - 6 (2000): "Evaluation should be based on the range of learning outcomes addressed throughout the year and should focus on general patterns of achievement in learning in and through the arts, rather than on single instances, in order that judgements be balanced" (p. 93).

Photo by: Anissa Barton-Thompson

Conclusion

This chapter began by asserting that assessment goes on all the time, in every aspect of our lives. Three problems were delineated with assessing art in schools: making subjective judgements, the qualitative nature of art, and the problem of method or how to assess art. I defined art as socio-culturally produced. Judgements about art are linked to socio-cultural conceptions and values. I argued that in teaching art we must be concerned primarily with making educational rather than artistic judgements.

I asserted that assessment is specific and looks at particular defined aspects of learning related to specified criteria. Curriculum content areas and related learning expectations are represented in criteria for assessment. Evaluation is related more to a holistic overall impression. Often, evaluation is based on a generalized judgement derived from an initial assessment of learning. In assessment there tends to exist greater external control over teachers, while in evaluation teachers have more internal grassroots control.

In examining three curriculum guides, Ontario, British Columbia, and Nova Scotia, I compared approaches to defined curriculum content areas, assessment and evaluation.

Comparison of Approaches to Curriculum and Assessment in Nova Scotia, Ontario, and British Columbia

Curricular categories and assessment strategies below	Nova Scotia	Ontario	British Columbia
Making Art	Creative/Productive	Creating and presenting	Image Development and Design; Materials, Techniques and Processes; Creating and Communicating; Perceiving and Responding
Theories of/Learning About Art	Cultural/Historical	Exploring forms and cultural contexts	Elements and Principles of Design; Contexts; Creating and Communicating; Perceiving and Responding
Art Criticism	Critical/Responsive	Reflecting, responding and analysing	Creating and Communicating; Perceiving and Responding
Assessment and Evaluation Approaches	Assessment and evaluation; evaluation dominates; criteria for assessment not related explicitly to curriculum content areas defined above	Assessment dominates; criteria related to curriculum content areas defined above	Assessment and evaluation; evaluation dominates; criteria for assessment not related explicitly to curriculum content areas defined above

Similarities between the provinces lie in definitions of curriculum content: Each identifies *studio production*, (creative work or image development) as a specific area of curricular focus. *Theories of art or concepts* are defined as well, although in Nova Scotia the focus is on the historical/cultural, while in British Columbia and Ontario historical and contextual studies are combined with a focus on elements and principles of design. All three include a curricular component focusing on *art criticism or responding to art*. In British Columbia "perceiving and responding" is a sub theme of all four curriculum content areas.

In Ontario, assessment is linked specifically to the three defined curriculum content areas. Overall levels of achievement are outlined with an emphasis on criterion-referenced assessment of finished products. In British Columbia and Nova Scotia, assessment is not linked explicitly to defined curriculum content areas. Rather, links are implied within new criteria defined for each project. Although both terms, assessment and evaluation, are used, the teacher's overall evaluative impression seems to dominate in British Columbia and Nova Scotia.

Finally, effective assessment and evaluation of learning in art is dependent on the following principles: Teachers need to determine what it is they value about teaching art. What aspects of art learning are most important, and how do these relate to provincial curriculum guidelines? Next, goals for art learning based on curriculum guide expectations (as well as one's own) need to be defined for, or with students, along with related criteria for assessment. It is important also to define at least three levels of achievement, for example ranging from 'needs improvement' through to 'good.'

It is imperative that there exists between teachers and students shared dialogue based understanding of expectations and criteria for assessment. Teachers may utilize portfolios, reflective journals, sketchbooks, learning logs, and so on, in order to assess final products as well as ideas and works in process/progress.

Art critiques in which constructive thoughtful responses are encouraged will facilitate self and peer assessment, and reflection. The development of good oral and written skills in responding to art will bring forth enhanced understanding of all aspects of learning in art, providing linkages between theory, studio work, and critical reflection. Reflective self-assessment is the ultimate goal of assessment and evaluation, and is achievable when it is based on socio-culturally and communally defined conceptions of value, creativity, and what counts as good work in learning about art.

Endnote

1. This unit plan idea is taken from Art Kits (Blaikie & Clark, 2000) developed for grades one to eight for schools in the Thunder Bay region. Roy Thomas is one of sixteen artists who participated in this project.

References

Allison, B. (1986). Some aspects of assessment in art and design education. In Ross, M. (Ed.). *Assessment in arts education* (pp. 113-133). Oxford, UK: Pergamon Press.

Ash, A., Schofield, K., & Starkey, A. (2000). Assessment and Examinations in Art and Design. In Addison, N. & Burgess, L. (Eds.), *Learning to teach art and design in the secondary school* (pp. 134-162). London, UK: Routledge Falmer.

Barrett, M. (1990). Guidelines for evaluation and assessment in art and design education 5 - 18 years. *Journal of Art and Design Education, 9*(3), 299-313.

Beattie, D. K. (1997). *Assessment in art education*. Worcester, MA: Davis Publications.

Beattie, D. K. (1994). The mini-portfolio: Locus of a successful performance examination. *Art Education, 47*(2), 14-18.

Best, D. (1980). Accountability: Objective assessment in arts education. In Smith, R. & Best, D. (Eds.), *The function and assessment of art in education* (pp. 27-58). Leeds, UK: Association of Art Advisors: Leeds City Council Department of Education, Printed Resource Unit.

Blaikie, F. M. (1997). Strategies for studio art assessment in Canada: Lana, Brenda, Sharon and Mark. In Irwin, R. L., & Grauer, K. (Eds.), *Readings in Canadian art teacher education* (pp. 193-212). Toronto, ON: Canadian Society for Education through Art.

Blaikie, F. M. & Clark, J. (2000). *Art kits including lesson plans and visual resources for Thunder Bay's elementary schools, grades 1-8*. Thunder Bay, ON: Lakehead University.

Boughton, D. (1994). Evaluation and assessment in visual arts education. Selong, Victoria, Australia: Deakin University Press.

British Columbia Ministry of Education. (1998). *Fine arts K - 7. Victoria, BC*: The Queen's Printer for British Columbia. Retrieved March 23, 2010 at

Clement, R. (1986). *The art teacher's handbook*. Avon, UK: The Bath Press.

Csikszentmihalyi, M. (1996). *Creativity: Flow and the psychology of discovery and invention*. New York: Harper Collins.

Eisner, E. W. (1985). *The art of educational evaluation: A personal view*. Philadelphia, PN: The Falmer Press.

International Baccalaureate Organization. (2000). *Diploma programme visual arts guide*. Geneva, Switzerland: International Baccaluareate Organization.

Krueger, B., & Wallace, J. (1996). Portfolio assessment: Possibilities and pointers for practice. *Australian Science Teachers' Journal, 42*(1), 26-29.

Nova Scotia Department of Education. (2000). *Visual arts primary - 6*. Halifax, NS: Department of Education.

Ontario Ministry of Education and Training. (2009). The Ontario curriculum grades 1 - 8: The arts. Toronto, ON: The Queen's Printer for Ontario. Retrieved March 26, 2010 at

Schonau, D. (1994). Final examinations in the visual arts in the Netherlands. *Art Education, 47*(2), 34-49.

Steers, J. (1994). Art and design: Assessment and public examinations. *Journal of Art and Design Education, 13*(3), 287-298.

Wolff, J. (1981). *The Social production of art*. New York: New York University Press.

CONNECTIONS, REFLECTIONS AND CREATIONS

Greening Our Art Classrooms
Ecologically-aware Health and Safety

Anita Sinner

Beyond lesson plans about environmental issues and student consciousness-raising, we can think about the art classroom as a space where students and teachers embody the qualities and actions of living green, and living green can be the basis for an approach to health and safety. An ecologically-aware art classroom includes informed understandings of a host of key issues: legislation, organization, equipment safety, safe materials, and perhaps most importantly, a philosophy of practice rooted in holistic perspectives. Together these issues and beliefs define how we learn, how we teach and how we make art part of our everyday lives. In this chapter, I share ways to make practice sustainable in relation to the practical requirements of the classroom. I encourage readers to consider their own experiences as students and teachers, and invite readers to develop a philosophy of practice that is authentic to the places they share with learners in schools and in their communities.

The area of health and safety is critical. It is comprehensive, complex, defined by legal language, and often overwhelming in scope and context. There are many excellent resources available to help you get started in your art classroom (see Kalin, 2005; Kalin, 2004). Building on the work of Kalin in previous editions of this book, I suggest weaving into health and safety an ecological approach to manage issues from a preventative perspective rather than a reactionary one, which may be defined by the following dimensions:

Holistic Perspectives

Holistic perspectives in art education focus on engaging the mind, body and spirit of students and teachers in creative expression. The relationships we share with each other and the environment are part of an ongoing dialogue imprinted in our art-making. As London (2003) states, "the quality of one's art flows from the qualities of one's life" and to be in harmony with the world "forms the single most important premise of our holistic pedagogy" (p. 304). For London (2003), recognizing and embracing the whole person begins with: 1) the artful mind, which "cultivates reason ... wonder, memory, awe, intuition, dreaming, fantasy" (p. 307); 2) the artful body, where making art is a physical act of "the multiple intelligences embedded throughout the entire body" (p. 308); and 3) the artful spirit, which involves "any quality we hold to be of ultimate value" (p. 309). In this way, London (2003) suggests, "not only is every portrait a self-portrait, but so is every still life, landscape and abstraction" (p. 229). If we are open to all expressions made by students being a kind of geographies of self, then student decisions on choices of media, elements of design and principles of composition, and materials used is part of a larger embodied encounter with the world around them. From such holistic perspectives, art education brings us to essential questions: Who am I? Why am I here? What is my greater purpose?

To develop an ecologically-aware classroom involves critical thinking on the part of teachers and students to integrate these questions into daily practice. Engaging in the classroom as an open system recognizes that information in relation to health and safety is continually changing, making art and teaching fluid processes that require our ongoing attention. At the heart of holistic practice is a belief that we must model what we teach and be consistent in our methods. In this regard, it is vital that studio courses in university art education programs include the materials that teachers will utilize with students in K-12 classrooms and that adhere to the requirements established under health and safety guidelines for public schools. In some cases, this means shifting from the traditional delivery of art courses and moving to an ecologically-aware mode of delivery. For example, in photography, I only teach techniques like toning with natural food dyes or tea, rather than bought chemicals. Using natural materials wherever possible is a simple step to meet health and safety guidelines, save money on supplies and most importantly, keep chemicals (even when treated) from entering the environment.

Legislation

Schools and teachers have legal responsibilities to ensure the health and safety of students in their care. Such legislation shapes how you will determine your curriculum for your classroom, how you organize and maintain your classroom and how you will manage supplies and organise your activities. Health and safety legislation is complex and the scope of responsibilities for teachers can be daunting. When you enter a classroom for the first time, think about your legal responsibilities, and report any unsafe practices or conditions to your school. Teachers must always demonstrate the same quality of care that a parent would take in similar circumstances. Negligence and failure to do due diligence can make a teacher liable for injury suffered by a student in their care.

At the same time it is important not to restrict learning, but to be within acceptable boundaries of risk. I am reminded of Julie's insights, a senior high school art teacher.
She describes some grade 8 students who come to her classroom and are unsure of protocols and procedures:

Some students are fortunate to have enjoyed a very rich and exciting elementary school experience. They come to my class burgeoning with enthusiasm, timidity be damned! These programs were not 'cookie cutter' at all, and students were exposed to full, vibrant, and visual learning.

But other students arriving into high school tend to come from a VERY protected elementary environment. Some students have had a history of 'Martha Stewart' type art lessons in which everything is cut and ready to go: the papers are pre-cut, the paint is pre-mixed, the glue is pre-poured, and the 'required' supplies are all apportioned. There is little room for student discretion or judgement in this setting. Also, because many elementary classrooms are not

equipped with sinks, students don't always learn about caring for materials and clean-up procedures, such as the used paintbrushes are gathered into a jar at the back of the room. Instead teachers, monitors, or helping parents do the clean up after school.

The net effect is that, when these students arrive into high school, they are almost <u>afraid</u> to have contact and make judgements about art materials, tools, and processes. I've had students ask me if they are <u>allowed</u> to get up out their seats, use scissors, or help themselves to paint. And they cringe at the thought of using the paper cutter. When I teach students how to set out paints on a palette or clean a brush I can tell by the looks on their faces that this is unfamiliar territory.

Within the requirements of legislation, students need opportunities to develop their confidence and take responsibility for health and safety as part of everyday life, and arguably at much earlier ages. Setting a good example is always important, and this can be done in part by creating a classroom of cooperation in which students are involved in decision-making that establishes respectful attitudes for safe practice.

Legislation extends to: 1) ensuring all equipment is in good working order; 2) checking if supplies are flammable or corrosive and storing appropriately in bins or cupboards that are clearly marked and secure; 3) posting sufficient signage of risk and first aid information; 4) reporting injuries or dangerous incidents. For teachers, it is vital to stay informed, in particular on how to take action to facilitate change.

For key technical and educational information, please visit:

Health and Welfare Canada:

see Documents, Reports and Publication:

http://www.hc-sc.gc.ca/ewh-semt/pubs/air/index-eng.php

Environment Canada:

http://www.ec.gc.ca/education

> (Hands-on resources include the "Take Action," "Art Classroom," and "Green School" initiatives, as well as environmentally-friendly lesson plans)

Organization

When organizing your classroom with consideration to issues of health and safety, teachers must consider a host of factors including class size, first aid, protective clothing and gear, options for mobility, cleanup and maintenance of the classroom, as well as off-site visits. A dramatic method of reinforcing the importance of good organization for health and safety is offered by Peter, a secondary art teacher, who with a magician's sleight of hand when demonstrating the use of the paper cutter each year to his new students, purposely cuts off his tie. To the gasping awe of his students he reinforced how easily that could be a finger, and what to do next, using the decapitated tie to demonstrate each step. I'm certain his students never forgot where the first aid kit was and what to do in an emergency.

Layout of classrooms may need to be reconsidered if you are in a school designed for smaller class sizes. The design of your art classroom also involves storage areas, emergency equipment, furnishing and open spaces. We may not be in a position to remodel space, but it is important for teachers to do risk assessments and to bring forward such information to your school. A risk assessment provides an overview of your classroom and an examination of the design. Create your own risk assessment form to reflect the specific situation of your classroom. A risk assessment should include a drawing of room dimensions and locations that map the flow of students (in case of emergency, unimpeded aisles and exits are always challenging with the ever-growing size of backpacks students

now carry), provision for students with mobility challenges as well as accessibility to protective equipment and clothes, where hazards are located, storage areas and in some cases, natural and artificial lighting if lighting is insufficient. Your risk assessment should identify known hazards, prioritise changes that need to be made and offer solutions. Be sure to keep a record of any accidents that have occurred with your risk assessment. Risk assessments should be done annually and include a statement of actions taken to reduce potential harm.

Physical requirements should be at the forefront of inclusive curriculum design and delivery, and this is especially so for planning to work with students who may have mobility and/or dexterity challenges. When teaching pre-service elementary teachers, I stress the importance of providing options and I do so by including multiple tools for our activities. When painting, I encourage them to provide their students with varied brush handle sizes as well as the palette knife, and to look for which tools students select and how

students hold and handle the tools. This is also true when working with clay, when engaging in printmaking, or drawing. And I use myself as an example. I have difficulty with finite motor skills and related art tools, and by sharing this with pre-service teachers I demonstrate that we all have limitations of one kind or another, and it is awareness that matters. Unfortunately, such challenges for teachers and students can be unseen or unknown, and student resistance to an activity is not always behavioural, sometimes it is about accessibility. Making activities flexible and encouraging multiple paths for students to complete a given activity takes into account the potential of mobility, and creates an art classroom that is a more informed site of learning. Advocating for increased awareness of disability services through health and safety, and for attending to personal and professional challenges on a day-to-day basis reinforces the importance of engaging with respect, responsibility and reflection as a holistic teacher and member of the wider community.

Off-site considerations span from daytrips to extended overseas visits with your students, and much of the daily practices relating to health and safety can be applied when away from the school. There are additional considerations, such as the appropriateness of the visit in relation to your students' spiritual, social and cultural experiences and beliefs. Informed consent is always required. An assessment approach to off-site health and safety begins with 1) planning the visit: What are the potential risks to students? Is the site accessible – are there elevators or only stairs? Is there adequate supervision – how many parents or staff do you need?; 2) managing the visit: Are there potential hazards at the site? What if there is an emergency? Do you have student or parent team leaders who know what to do if you become separated?; and 3) evaluating the visit: What can you do to improve the next off-site visit? What unexpected incidents took place? Off-site visit preparation, activities and debriefing should include a discussion of codes of conduct, care of the environment and personal safety and security.

Equipment Safety

The safe use of equipment involves both the equipment and the methods of practice you teach students for ceramics, printing, textiles, painting, photography, computers and related activities. The 'Kit and the Kiln' story is a great example relating to equipment safety. Early in her teaching career, Kit demonstrated to students how to use the kiln, pointing out, "Never touch those wires!" Unbenounced to Kit, the kiln had been turned on, and when she touched those wires, she got an electric shock that threw her back. She's had curly hair ever since. While not suggesting this as a method of instruction, it does highlight how easily as teachers we can assume safety, and we must be cautious to always check and double-check the status of our equipment to ensure it is in good working order.

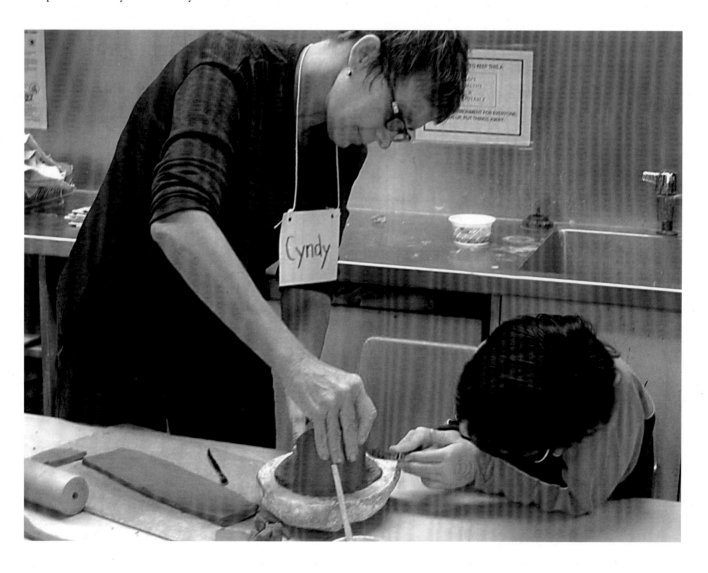

Questions to consider: Is this equipment protected from the source of energy? Is this equipment set up properly and is it stable and secure for student use? Are all hazard indicators working? Is there an emergency power stop accessible to students and teacher? By extension, this is also true for hand-held tools in the art classroom, and for furnishings of tables and chairs. Accidents happen when tools are not used appropriately; get into the habit of using all tools in a motion that moves out from the body, rather than towards the body. Even a pencil can prove dangerous with enough pressure behind it. Some simple tips for teachers and students include:

- tie back long hair

- avoid loose clothes and always wear closed-toe shoes

- use gloves, masks, ear protection and long-sleeved work smocks

- vacuum rather than sweep work areas to reduce dust particulates

- open the windows and doors and/or use ventilation as part of everyday practice

- keep working areas organised

- wash hands after every activity

- if you are pregnant, or a student is pregnant, consult a physician before handling materials, make special arrangements and provide optional assignments

The intent is to ensure everyday practice presents a low risk to students for physical, muscle, eye or mental strain in ways that are consistent with the holistic perspectives of an ecologically-aware classroom.

In a sustainable art classroom, equipment can include considerations often overlooked in general health and safety discussions. The art classroom has different requirements than other kinds of classrooms, and I suggest that aesthetic qualities of the objects in the art classroom become part of the creative experience for students. How students interact visually, emotionally and physically with equipment is a dimension of health and safety that warrants further reflection. For example, display space forms part of the art classroom equipment, and often cabinet doors are the only display available. Making cupboards neutral in colour and within reach of students (yet secure) to post work and discuss it adds an important layer to the aesthetics of your art room. Another example and perhaps

the most taken-for-granted equipment are sinks. Clean-up can be an extension of an art activity when encouraging students to consider the aesthetics of water and the sustainability of water globally. How often do our sinks become clogged? Why do students rush clean-up and create congestion around sinks? If we begin to question these seemingly mundane moments in art practice, we may develop a more holistic understanding of our actions and reactions. Can some water be 'recycled' during clean-up by collecting and using it twice? Demonstrating to students by collecting their waste water that their usage is equivalent (or more) than the average water consumed daily by an individual in drought-plagued regions of our world shows and tells. Ask your students: How can we change our water practices in art? Can we make a difference by not letting water run unnecessarily? What is our contribution to sustainability if we make these daily changes? The challenge is to find ways to integrate all sorts of equipment like display space and sinks into lessons in ways that demonstrate continuity with a holistic practice rooted in an ecologically-aware art classroom.

Safe Materials

Each art activity can involve a wide-range of materials depending on the purpose and design of the activity, and determining which materials are ecologically suitable as well as safe in terms of health and safety is time-intensive and ongoing. By developing lesson plans that are environmentally friendly, reviewing product options prior to purchasing for your class and by selecting non-toxic materials whenever possible, we actively invest in the greening of our art classrooms. Sharing your rationale with students helps develop a stronger understanding of what is good for the community. At the same time, less toxic does not mean there are no toxins, and non-toxic materials also require your attention because products made from organic sources can include wheat, gluten, milk, egg and other common allergens. Share this information with your students and parents and keep communications open.

A starting point for safe materials is to think not only about the eyes, nose and mouth (ingestion and inhalation), but about the skin as a whole organ to be protected from damage. Guarding skin from chemical compounds found in plastics, glazes, pigments, solvents, dyes, recycled materials (handling, reusing, cleaning as well as personal hygiene when using recycled materials), petroleum-based products and more brings a different vision to art education than simply advising 'to reduce irritation, avoid contact with the skin.' Skin contact includes the surface and cuts or breaks in the skin through which chemicals can enter the bloodstream. Reading product labels before the assignment and then using protective gear can prevent exposure that causes skin redness, rash, itching or more severe reactions. This is true too for inhaling fumes and substances that can cause sneezing, coughing, burning sensations, headaches and dizziness. In photography, I prefer liquid rather than powder chemicals to reduce air particulates, even though liquids are more expensive. I always opt for odourless stop, and while that eliminates the intense chemical smell that can cause students to feel sick, the fumes are still in the air and adequate ventilation is a must. Ingestion can happen simply by touching the mouth during an activity, not washing hands before eating or drinking, or by consuming food and liquids while working on an art activity, resulting in nausea, pain or general discomfort. Keep all food and drink away from working areas.

In Canada, materials are categorized based on a national standard governed by the Workplace Hazardous Materials Information System (WHMIS) program. Material information sheets are available, as well as checklists to assess aspects such as: ventilation, ensuring containers are tightly sealed and labelled for long-term storage, and that there is sufficient signage in your classroom to help students become more aware of potential hazards, as well as appropriate clean-up and disposal of chemical spills. The online WHMIS manual is continually updated. The official national site for WHMIS is a key source of health and safety information that regulates all workplaces: http://www.hc-sc.gc.ca/ewh-semt/occup-travail/whmis-simdut

Recycling found materials for art projects and consistently recycling remaining materials from art activities further teaches students the importance of their environmental footprint, and ways to be more involved in making a difference at school, at home and hopefully in their community. This conversation can extend to efficient energy usage by turning off lights when a room is not in use, and converting to compact fluorescent bulbs where possible, showing students you are living your green practice. Instilling an understanding of stewardship for the environment at an early age can contribute to a life-long practice of caring.

Issues concerning health and safety for students and teachers are ever-evolving. Keeping up with the latest information is part of developing a good practice. Some helpful sites concerning safe materials include:

Green Living:

www.greenlivingonline.com/article/safe-and-eco-friendly-art-supplies

Toxic Nation:

www.toxicnation.ca/go-toxic-free/alternatives/artists

(This site includes a Healthy Artist Guide listing toxic and less toxic art materials)

Safe Kids Canada:

http://www.safekidscanada.ca

Healthy School Program:

www.nb.lung.ca/schools/index.htm

Summary

What many ecologically-aware educators are suggesting is that we encourage a paradigm shift and in the art classroom this means encouraging our students to engage with a holistic perspective that extends the instrumentalist views of health and safety as lists of do's and don'ts. The curriculum can become a site where creativity is a conduit for changing behaviours and actions in relation to our changing natural environment.

Awareness of our impact and the costs we are imposing on the world around us demands we take action, and those actions can begin with small steps rooted in sustainability in the art classroom. It is interesting to note that leading manufacturers of art supplies like Crayola are now marketing their products based on how much materials are recycled to make markers. This is a good first step and suggests that shifts are underway in the field, drawing attention to the interrelationships of teachers, students, schools and suppliers as a community of practice within natural and built environments. We can begin to think about art education as a space where we encounter, respond and organise our decision-making and actions in relation to ecosystems. Such holistic perspectives offer an orientation around which to engage in health and safety in ways that are both local and global, demonstrating how an integrative approach of social responsibility, respect for the world around you and ongoing self-reflection makes interconnectedness and accountability the basis for an art practice that is about quality of life.

Collectively we can do and demand so much more, and in the process, we can begin to move the traditional conversation of school art from aesthetically pleasing, to school art that is aesthetically informed by sustainability. Such an approach does not require a major revision of subject matter skills currently taught, but it does require a broadening of perspectives, where the kinds of projects students create stress awareness of sustainability in theme and in the use of art supplies. Perhaps through the ecologically-aware art classroom, art can truly become the voice of a next generation willing to make change part of their everyday practice, fostering curiosity, creativity and consciousness, and in the process, making green the colour of tomorrow.

References

Health and Welfare Canada. (2003). *Indoor air quality – Tools for schools action kit for Canadian schools*. Available at: http://www.hc-sc.gc.ca/ewh-semt/pubs/air/index-eng.php

Environment Canada. (2009). *Art classroom*. Available at : http://www.ec.gc.ca/education/default.asp?lang=En&n=C642D6A5-1

Kalin, N. (2004). Ensuring a safe and secure environment during art activities. In K. Grauer & R. Irwin (Eds.), *StARTing with ...* (pp. 106-112). Kingston, ONT: Canadian Society for Education through Art.

Kalin, N. (2005). Don't run with the scissors. In K. Grauer & R. Irwin (Eds.), *StARTing with ... Second Edition* (pp. 154-160). Kingston, ON: Canadian Society for Education through Art.

London, P. (2003). *Drawing closer to nature: Making art in dialogue with the natural world*. Boston, MA: Shambhala.

CONNECTIONS, REFLECTIONS AND CREATIONS

CHAPTER 10

Sequential Art & Graphic Novels
Creating with the Space in-between Pictures

Michael J. Emme
& Karen Taylor

For the last hundred years, the subject of reading has been connected quite directly to the concept of literacy; … learning to read…has meant learning to read words…but…reading has gradually come under close scrutiny. Recent research has shown that the reading of words is but a subset of a much more general human activity, which includes decoding, information integration, and organization…indeed, reading – in the most general sense – can be thought of as a perceptual activity [that also embraces] the reading of pictures, maps, circuit diagrams, musical notes… (Tom Wolfe, writing in the *Harvard Educational Review* (August 1977) as cited in Eisner, 2008, p.2)

Tom Wolfe, as an author, art critic, and cultural commentator in the 1970s and Will Eisner as a lifelong comic book artist and teacher to the end of the last century were both visionaries in several senses. They each understood before most of us, that stories communicated though layers of image and word combined together reflect the complicated ways that we know the world. Without a particular focus on the internet and digital world, both anticipated the boom in visual resources that demands that the curriculum you must teach now, to be effective now, has to address the full experience of perception. When people comment on the world becoming more visual, they are describing the ways that new technologies have allowed us to create and distribute visual information around the world with a speed and clarity that tended in the past to be limited to the graphically much simpler written word. They often point to how pictures are getting more space and words less space in textbooks (Laspina, 1998). With the advent of the Internet, where the cost of reproducing images is not linked to a printing press or paper at all, this visuality has shifted many people's experience of the world 'out there' away from reading to viewing. The growth of visual communication and the fact that reading images is less bound by a single set of conventions means that students, teachers and schools have an exciting challenge ahead of them.

It is the purpose of this chapter to suggest how art education and creative experiences with sequential art can serve your students in developing the layers of literacy they will need to understand and be understood in their world. All written languages start somewhere on a page. Languages using the Latin alphabet (like English, French and Spanish) start in the upper left, and move right and down, one row at a time. Readers of Arabic and Semitic script start in the upper right, scanning to the left and move down by row. Traditional Japanese is one example where the reader starts in the upper right and reads columns top to bottom. Some pictographic languages can be published in rows or columns from the right or left. As long as the reader recognizes the signs for beginning and ending they can read in whichever direction is used. The point is that every written language has a linear convention, which readers learn. Words, then, are ideas in lines, and the habits of mind associated with reading the printed word involve dedication and discipline in learning the vocabulary, grammar and syntactical conventions. We recognize this as 'linear thinking' and because of the many conveniences of these language systems, we sometimes assume that linear thinking is also 'better' or even, more logical thinking.

If words are ideas in lines, images are ideas in space. The viewer of an image parachutes into the geography of an artwork that has been organized by an artist. Where you land is your first act of perception and it may be influenced by your reactions to the physical properties of the image, by design conventions that you and the artist share, and by moments from your personal or cultural history that resonate with details in the artwork. On landing in the work, your journey through it will continue to be influenced by your physiological, conventional, cultural and personal engagements with the visual terrain created by the artist. As you continue the process of 'reading' or perceiving an image, you have many choices that the conventions for reading words don't allow. Scanning, for example, a written text for every example of the word 'dandelion' is a perceptual feat, but would be of only limited use in understanding the full meaning of, for example a scientific essay. On the other hand, choosing to jump from one instance of the shape and colour recognized as dandelion to others in an image is a very appropriate exploration of motif becoming pattern that might be considered either scientifically or aesthetically. As a viewer, moving our attention through the image supported by the detail of the dandelion is one of many legitimate journeys that make up the meanings of the image. Part of the shift in centuries and millennia past to written language has been to standardize and thus simplify communication, but the cost has been that some of the subtlety, complexity and individual choice of visual experience was lost.

Between a single image and a chapter of a book, there are other expressive forms that work to bridge between the linearity and conveniences of words and the evocative openness of pictures. This chapter is not about movies, but you can see that a movie combines (mostly spoken) words and a series of images presented to us over time. The flow of the story in a movie (and thus, our experience of the time it represents) needs to be carefully controlled by the director and creative team. The only way to dwell in one moment or juxtapose different moments in a movie is through memory. In a way, though movies are pictorial, their narrative flows in a line that we don't control, like a book. Somewhere between the choices when we perceive a single picture and the linear flow of movies is where comics and graphic novels fit as visual story-telling forms.

The notion of telling stories using sequences of images is not new. Cave paintings and ancient Egyptian pictographs are familiar evidence of that. Modern comics are an outgrowth of Mid-19th century 'funnies' that helped bring a broader audience to the growing newspaper industry. As anthologies of newspaper funnies, the first comic books were considered 'low' but popular entertainment. Through most of the 20th century, they have not been considered 'exemplary literature' and have not played a big part in school curriculum. That is changing. Comics and graphic novels, as they have developed into the present, include individual frames that are a collage of words and images. Significantly, each box is also placed in a sequence. Like the pictographic languages mentioned early in this chapter, comic images are read in a language-like line that is usually (but not always), ordered like a sentence. "The reader is thus required to exercise both visual and verbal interpretive skills. The regimens of art (e.g., perspective, symmetry, line) and the regimens of literature (e.g., grammar, syntax, plot) become superimposed on each other" into what (Eisner, 2008, p.2) calls 'Sequential Art'. Like written words and movies, the sequence of images in a comic or graphic novel creates a narrative flow. Many readers might assume that the page must always be read right to left, top to bottom. However, comic books pages, despite being made up of a sequence of images in boxes, are also single visual objects that can be seen as a whole as well. The full page is available to the reader all at once so perceptive readers quickly discover that a single page in a comic can be effectively read in many different ways. There are psychological studies that demonstrate that experienced Manga readers actually scan the page of a comic differently than 'word' readers (Cohn, 2007) by looking first for visual patterns and points of interest before deciding how, or even if, they will focus on the words on the page. Because comics and graphic novels offer such a variety of reading/perceiving strategies they offer a variety of context clues. From body language, through text that gives visual indications about whether words represent dialogue, thought, narrative or sound – if one layer of the story uses an unfamiliar or confusing convention, there is every possibility that another layer will give you a context clue that not only keeps the story moving for you, but expands your viewing vocabulary. This rich, instructive array of clues makes comics particularly suitable to classrooms where students bring many language traditions from home.

After learning from comic artists like Will Eisner and visual literacy specialists that comics and graphic novels represent a powerful, complex form of communication, it is clear how art education, which teaches students to understand the value of visual expression, is a necessary part of each child's development in the classroom. Recent research suggests that schools can and should teach 'studio thinking' (Hetland, et. al., 2007) which encourages students to develop significant 'habits of mind', such as attention to craft, learning to engage and persist, to envision, to express, and to observe.

From Concept to Classroom

Images in sequence can communicate all sorts of things about time, space, and relationships. In *Understanding Comics*, Scott McCloud (1994) developed a detailed, visual history and elements of comic design. In it he gives great visual examples of the ways that the space between images can create narrative. Whether you want viewers to experience 'now-then', 'here-there', 'cause-effect' or any of the complex relationships that we link to prepositions in written language (above, into, among beside, below, etc.) the space between frames and the positioning of those frames are an expressive tool.

Seqential art can be created in a wide variety of ways, including collage, photography and drawing. Young children will be familiar with the collage illustrations of book authors like Eric Carle. While this method is less common in comics, there are a few examples (van Loon, 2005). The process is particularly useful in allowing young students to plan and edit (drawn or photocopied) characters before committing to gluing and completing an image. Photo-based comics (also known as fotonovela[1]) can involve larger groups in the tableaux performance of scenes for a single story (see figure 1).

Figure 1: Excerpt from a fotonovela: 'Lunchtime at Greenview School'

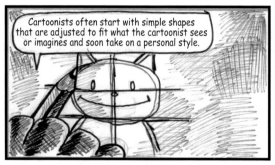

Cartooning with Wolfgang and Pierre.

(sketching, cartoon conventions and character development)

Figure 2

Developing comics using drawing can address several of the big challenges for young artists: being persistent enough in a drawing task to develop skills, while adventurous enough to try different approaches to a subject. Comics and graphic novels can be a compelling answer to both challenges as sequential drawing requires the development of a recognizable character and setting that changes over time to move the narrative (see Figure 2). In many ways, a single comic-style story just a few pages long is a full portfolio of creative effort that includes image development, real commitment to a visual medium, and the critical reflection required to recognize and reinforce visual style as well as imagine the adjustments necessary to ensure that all of the visual parts of the story belong together.

Whichever medium you choose in creating individual frames, the images still need to be organized into a sequence. In the examples included here, we have used the filmic conventions of the '• establishing shot • approach shot • close-up' to show how you can reveal setting, character relationship and mood in three frames (Figure 3).

A second approach (Figure 4) is what is called an 'eyeline match'. In this example, we view a dog from below wearing headphones. He is so deeply and happily into the music that his eyes are closed. The second big frame is actually a mini-sequence of four small frames. The same image, of a second dog, viewed from above, that is pointing and laughing is repeated four times. With each repetition the image transforms from nearly transparent to the same black as the opening image. The final frame, a wide shot gives us a glimpse of a big dog with an arched eyebrow and irritated look peering down at a small dog and we see the headphones from the first frame now discarded on the ground. These last details are also an invitation to revisit the earlier frames and sort out eyelines and points of view. The use of sequencing communicates time passing, eyes opening, and irritatingly persistent behaviour, as well as the space that has been shared by the two dogs and the comic difference in their size.

Figure 3

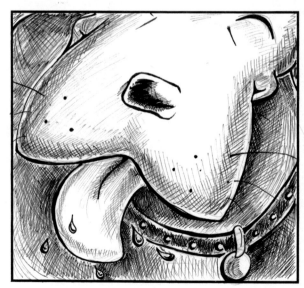

Are you my friend?
(· establishing shot · approach shot · close-up)

97

'Teasing!'
Eyeline and point of view
(Wolfgang's view, Pierre's view, our view, the big picture)

Conclusion

So, sequential art supports multimodal reading habits that are more in line with the way information is communicated in the 21st century. It also introduces an appealing way to support extended commitment to many important visual skills and critical practices that are at the heart of good art education. The last big question could also be a good first question. What kinds of stories could your students tell this way? The history of comic books might seem like it is a history of fantasy and superheroes, which is certainly partially the case. It is also the history of imaginative artists and writers considering science, social issues, and relationships.

In fact, there are worthwhile ways of integrating sequential art approaches across the curriculum. In the form of fotonovela, comics have been used to join with elementary immigrant children to tell stories about their experiences in a new school. They have been used to produce school handbooks for all students. They have been used to work through safety strategies in bullying situations. Sequential art and comic style can be used to do reports about the steps in an experiment in science. They can be a great way to focus a student's attention on a story from history or in their community today. And, of course, they can just be creative, expressive fun.

Comics and graphic novels do assume a classroom where the teacher makes sure students have the time to develop an idea that has many parts. By recognizing how many layers of learning are engaged when students create sequential art, it is possible to see them as projects that integrate a variety of curriculum aims, thus justifying the time that is involved.

Figure 4

Endnotes

1. Fotonovela has a history in popular literature back to the late 1940s. Found in countries like Mexico, Italy, and France, they combined still photographs and text balloons to tell stories that depended less on words and put books into the hands of readers who might find more word-heavy stories inaccessible (Emme & Kirova, 2005).

Resources

http://plasq.com/comiclife

http://plasq.com/comiclife-win
   Comic Life: Software for Mac or Windows. Reasonably priced and great at making comic conventions both accessible and adaptable depending on how adventurous you and your students are feeling.

http://www.jonathondalton.com
   A great example of a website that features the comics created by a single artist who also happens to be an elementary teacher in British Columbia.

Tan, S. (2006). *The arrival: New York*: Arthur A. Levine Books
   A compelling, wordless story about emigrating and adapting with gorgeous illustrations and an amazing invented language that allows each reader to experience being a newcomer.

Grenville, B. (Ed.) (2008). *KRAZY! The Delirious World of Anime + Comics + Video Games + Art* (book cover). Vancouver, BC: Douglas & McIntyre, the University of California Press and the Vancouver Art Gallery.
   An exhibition catalogue and history of trends and innovations in contemporary comics.

Flemming, A. (2007). *The magical life of long Tack Sam*. New York: Riverhead Books
   An illustrated memoir that tells the story of the author's great-grandfather whom she discovers was a world-renowned acrobat. This book is a good story and a great example of combining personalized stick-figure drawing and family photographs to create visually sophisticated sequential art.

Pauli, L. (Ed.). (2006). *Acting the part: Photography as theatre*. London: Merrell Publishers.
   An expensive but very well illustrated collection of historic and contemporary tableau photographs.

https://www.tinlids.ca/Categories.aspx
   And More… Follow the link and select 'Graphic Novels – Children's' for a PDF with over 1,000 titles.

References

Cohn, N. (2007). *Visual language reference bibliography: Development and acquisition*. Retrieved March 1, 2010: http://www.emaki.net/R/refC.html

Eisner, W. (2008). *Comics and sequential art:* New York: Norton.

Emme, M. & Kirova, A. (2005). Fotonovela. *The Canadian Art Teacher, 4* (1), 24-27 (Winter).

Hetland, L., Winner, E., Veenema, S., Sheridan, K. & Perkins, D. (2007). *Studio thinking: The real benefits of visual arts education*. New York: Teacher College Press.

Laspina, J. (1998). *The visual turn and the transformation of the textbook*. New Jersey: Lawrence Erlbaum.

McCloud, S. (1994) *Understanding comics: The invisible art*. New York: Harper.

Van Loon, B. (2005). *The Bart Dickon omnibus*. London: Severed Head Books.

Wolf, T. (1977). Reading reconsidered. *Harvard Educational Review, 48*(3), 411- 429

CHAPTER II

Exhibiting Student Art
for
Understanding and Enrichment

Mary Blatherwick

When student art is exhibited it sets the stage for the final and sometimes most challenging aspect of the creative process. It is at this point that students have the opportunity to respond to each other's artwork and offer interpretations of what they sense and perceive. For students this stage can be exhilarating but also challenging if they lack an understanding of interpretation and its role in exploring personal, social and cultural experiences.

Although there has been a greater emphasis placed on the need to analyze art, and elementary curriculum documents call for the inclusion of interpretive activities, (Barrett, 2000; Eisner, 1972; Freedman, 2003; Gude, 2008; Roland, 1992; Sandell, 2009; Zander, 2003) most elementary teachers continue to focus almost exclusively on art making. When student artwork is finished therefore, it is often displayed without discussion, placed in portfolios, or sent home. As a result, the artwork that students produce seldom becomes a 'catalyst' for class discussions and interpretative activities. Interpretation in this sense refers to responding "in thoughts, feelings and actions to what we see and experience, and to make further sense of our responses by putting them into words" (Barrett, 2000, p.7). When emphasis is placed on interpretation in art programs,

student art takes on a new significance as a rich resource for visual leaning.

Exhibiting student art creates opportunities for students to appreciate their own work and also the artistic achievements of others. Exhibitions of student art take place inside and outside the classroom context. When student art is presented outside of the classroom or school context, it can generate public interest in what young people have to 'say' or communicate visually about their lived experiences.

When student art is accompanied by written texts and response activities it can further engage the viewer (Reese, 2003). If students organize art exhibitions they also have the opportunity to connect with other members of the school or community. In this way student art exhibitions can become important catalysts for discussion and shared interpretative activities.

According to Irwin and Kindler (1999) art learning that takes place outside the classroom is significant. They point out that:

Attention has been drawn in education to learning that occurs beyond the school boundaries. Understanding education in contexts broader than schooling has important implications for art education and calls for an examination of alternative venues, initiatives and strategies that facilitate artistic development, encourage aesthetic growth and

promote reflection about the role and value of art in a society. (p.1)

With a growing focus on visual culture, defined "as the objects and processes, including those created and used by students, that particularly function through visualized forms to affect our lives" (Freedman, 2003, p.39), the value placed on student art exhibitions, both in a school and community context, might increase significantly. Freedman comments that: "from this perspective, artistic production is valued in part, because it has the power to influence, and anyone, including students, can work to initiate social and personal change through the visual culture they produce" (p.39).

For elementary teachers, with little or no background in art education, the idea of organizing art exhibitions, initiating discussions, and encouraging their students to interpret the artwork on display can be daunting. Without exposure to fundamental art education concepts and strategies for analyzing art, it is understandable that many elementary teachers focus their students' attention on making art and not on interpreting it. To prepare their students for interpreting images teachers should first gain an understanding of: 1) how visual images convey meaning, 2) art making techniques, 3) art terminology, and 4) how to increase visual awareness.

This chapter provides a brief overview for teachers of these fundamental understandings that provide a basis for interpretative activities in any context. It also offers effective and innovative strategies for interpreting images in student art exhibitions.

How Images Convey Meaning

Images, as representational entities, are considered to be at the heart of how we form thoughts and therefore, construct meaning. According to Messaris (1994) visual images act as the representations of a person's thoughts and are capable of revealing feelings, attitudes and lived experiences through various media and forms. As a mode of 'communication' mental or visual images share similarities with words because both can convey meaning through an understood code of symbols, which is embodied in what is being said or visually presented. (Curtiss, 1987; Dondis, 1973).

Although Arnheim (1969) connects images with thinking, he suggests that there is a significant difference between images and words. He points out that words reveal meaning, one thought at a time, whereas visual images convey layers of meaning simultaneously. The layers embodied in a visual image however, are not always discernable even though a range of intended meanings might exist.

Visual art images, in particular, are often intentionally ambiguous, and therefore challenge students to think in new and divergent ways. Because art images can also be interpreted in numerous ways, depending on personal experiences and cultural contexts, they present rich forms of expression for reflection. Roland (1992) explains "the purpose of reflection is to make students more aware of what they know; what is going on inside their heads; how one mental activity relates to another; and how their thinking relates to their learning" (p.34). Because student art contains personal and cultural content, it can be a powerful basis for reflection, discussion and interpretation. By encouraging students to interpret each other's artwork, they can learn about each other and gain a deeper understanding of how art conveys meaning.

Art Making

Art making represents the most central activity in the creative process. It is from the experimentation and manipulation of art materials and techniques that students begin to understand and visually articulate their inner thoughts and emotions. Understanding, in this instance, refers to the mental act of perceiving the meaning of something (Chanda & Basinger, 2000). According to Piagetian development theory, in order to choose

appropriate materials and processes, elementary teachers must be aware that children perceive and think differently at certain ages or levels of intellectual development. For instance, he notes that third graders are in the concrete operational stage in which they serialize, extend, sub-divide, differentiate, or combine existing structures into new relationships. Therefore the art making experiences teachers present, should take into account the students' abilities on an intellectual level.

As a child progresses through elementary school, art making provides a vehicle for revealing levels of awareness and understanding about self and others. Researchers in the field of artistic development (Kellogg, 1970; Kindler & Darras, 1997; Lowenfeld, 1957; Wilson & Wilson, 1982) offer different points of view on how and why children's art changes. Becoming familiar with the research on artistic development can provide a basis for determining what art materials and techniques are best to introduce at certain developmental levels.

According to Bolin (1996), once works of art are completed, they become "sources for questions; issues in society and within one's self are seen as places of wonder; art making is perceived as an opportunity to wrestle with the imponderable elements of our lives and an occasion to challenge the mysteries of ourselves and our world" (p.10). Because art presents a particularly rich means for exploring personal thoughts and perceptions, teachers need to encourage students to express themselves through a variety of art materials and techniques. Walker (1996) states:

> Students are not only more engaged when the studio problem is personalized, but they can develop deeper understandings about the artist's creative process.

If students do not have a personal investment in art making, it is difficult for them to realize why art making is about expression and not simply a technical exercise. (p.17)

It is through art making which involves:

bodily manipulations of materials, that much important learning takes place. For as materials bring responses into focus, they simultaneously act as vehicles of reflection provoking new shades of meaning and enriching the immediate significance of the originating thought, memory, or event. (Burton, 2000, p. 334)

Art images, which represent well articulated thoughts through the use of carefully chosen materials, provide especially rich subject matter for discussion and interpretation.

Art Terminology

Being fluent in the terminology of visual art is described by Buchanan (1997) as necessary for eliciting and decoding meanings in art images or extracting information from them. According to Dondis (1973), in order to interpret any image it is important to acquire a vocabulary of terms describing basic components and compositional guidelines that govern how it was formulated. Knowledge of these terms allows for the identification, interpretation and formulation of responses.

Graham (1990), in her research into children's picture books, found that children should be taught the grammar of pictures through investigative experiences which help them to identify, restructure and articulate what they have learned. During the creative process therefore, teachers need to provide opportunities for students to analyze visual qualities such as colour, shape and line in order to fully understand, and utilize them. According to Graham, without exposure to the grammar of art, students find it difficult to articulate what they see in any art image.

Durant (1996) however, argues that before students learn art terminology they should find their own language for making sense of art and not use terms that may seem meaningless to them. She states that art terminology, which describes formal qualities of art such as line, colour, and form, does not need to be mastered before students can personally respond to art. According to Durant, the more comfortable students are with articulating their thoughts using their own art-related terms, the more confident they will be in interpreting art images as they learn more formal terminology.

Visual Awareness

Increasing visual awareness is crucial if students are to capture the details and nuances portrayed in art images. Our eyes can quickly perceive what is identifiable in an image, but to observe or see on a deeper level requires time and concentration. Teachers need to encourage their students to slow down, observe details, and record their discoveries. This in-depth 'way of seeing' instils a sense of wonder and curiosity fundamental to fully appreciating or understanding visual images.

There are simple approaches teachers can take to enhance students' abilities to perceive visual details. For instance, they can create a visually stimulating classroom filled with a wide variety of image and objects to encourage students to contemplate, interpret and respond to their visual surroundings. Taking students outside of school to discover and examine a wide range of visual objects and details can also heighten their visual sensitivity and level of awareness.

Museum and art gallery educators offer many activities to help students observe details. Activities such as asking students to study an object for a short period of time, removing it from sight, and then having the students visually recall what they observed can be very effective. In a gallery context students are often asked to closely examine the content of art images in order to learn how they are composed using various elements such as line, colour and shape. Virtual museums and galleries now offer infinite possibilities for accessing and analyzing art from a wide variety of different social, historical and cultural contexts (Moreno, 2007).

Teaching upper elementary students observational drawing can increase their visual awareness. Contour drawing techniques, in particular, place an emphasis on eye-hand coordination, which enables students to create detailed representational drawings. This skill can be developed, not only as a means of recording visual details, but also to attain a level of artistic achievement which can benefit both self-esteem and confidence at this point in a students' artistic development (Edwards, 1989).

Interpretation Strategies

Interpretation is considered a component of art criticism and it plays a major role in art education literature. Art criticism is defined as the talk, either spoken or written, about art (Geahigan, 1998). The most widely accepted art criticism approach, developed by Feldman (1970), analyzed artwork according to description, analysis, interpretation and judgement. Other art educators have added additional steps, while some use these steps in a random order. Within visual culture however, the notion of following a set of steps or stages can be viewed as restrictive.

Innovative interpretative strategies have been developed that include open-ended questioning, problem-based learning and interactive strategies (Barrett, 1994; Durant, 1996; Freedman, 2003; Geahigan, 1998; Housen, 2007). Before exploring interpretive strategies however, students as well as teachers should be knowledgeable about how images convey meaning, art terminology, art making and visual awareness.

The following strategies have been developed by art and museum educators and could be adapted for student art exhibitions:

1) Barrett (2000) proposes encouraging students to first ask questions to help them understand what they perceive, and then allow them to express their interpretations of what they have learned. He states:

> By carefully telling or writing what we see and feel and think and do when looking at a work of art, we build an understanding by articulating in language what might otherwise remain only incipient, muddled, fragmented, and disconnected to our lives. When writing or telling about what we see and what we experience in the presence of an art work, we build meaning, we do not merely report it. (p.7)

2) Freedman (2003) also suggests that through an inquiry approach to interpretation, where open-ended questions are encouraged, students gain a better understanding of visual art from a personal and social perspective. Like Barrett she encourages the use of questions that allow students to find their own 'voice' and express their inner thoughts and perceptions.

3) According to Zander (2003) classrooms where art is being interpreted should become 'communities of discourse'. For discourse to happen however, she suggests that an open and accepting atmosphere must be established and maintained. Questions that lead to discoveries are considered particularly successful in engaging students in the interpretative process. In her approach students are given a greater opportunity to openly discuss their thoughts and reactions and therefore, teachers play a less dominant role in leading or guiding the interpretative process.

4) Problem-based learning approaches are also used as a means of involving students in interpretation. In problem-based learning the teacher presents a problem to solve and students working in groups begin the process of finding a solution. Beyond information gathering, the students discuss and debate different notions of representation and interpretation, which deepen their understanding of the creative process (Costantino, 2002).

5) Kanatani (1998) describes another approach taken in art galleries and museums that includes open-ended questions, role-playing, improvisational activities and related sensory modes such as sound, movement, and poetry. This approach called *Contemporary Art Smart* or *CAS* encourages teachers to be innovative and spontaneously interactive with students in an exhibition setting. Instead of asking questions that lead to predetermined answers, teachers are encouraged to be receptive to the subjective responses of their students. "For students the message is that the process of observing, thinking and responding is valued over the *quick* or right solution. This acceptance of all considered reflections engenders confidence and encourages maximum participation" (p. 38). According to Kanatani, teachers note changes in their students that include an increase in their use of imagination, development of creative expression, higher self-esteem, self-confidence and keener observation skills.

These approaches for interpretation involve students in the process of looking deeply, visually articulating their thoughts and feelings, and ultimately valuing each other's art. Whether student artwork is exhibited in the classroom, in another part of the school or in the community, these approaches for eliciting responses can be adapted for use in a variety of contexts.

Exhibiting Student Art

Exhibitions of student work can take many forms. Artwork can be exhibited in the classroom, in other areas in the school such as libraries and hallways or in public spaces in the community. When art exhibitions take place outside the classroom labels are attached which have the name and grade level of the artist. In more interactive exhibitions however, personal stories, background information and/or questions might accompany the student art. If the students are also in attendance during the opening of the exhibition, they can share their personal stories and interpretations with other students or members of the community. Student art exhibitions can therefore become rich learning experiences for both the artists and viewers.

Whether the approach for interpreting art is more traditional or innovative, the main objective in exhibiting student art is to celebrate their artistic achievements and provide a place where their work can be seen, reflected on and interpreted. Although student art exhibitions can take many forms, those that include more innovative strategies for interpreting art allow a wider audience to become engaged with the art. Art educators stress that exhibitions of student art are an essential part of the creative process.

Beetlestone (1998) argues that student art exhibitions:

- inform teaching and learning and provide children with further information
- show that children's work is valued and enhance individual self-esteem
- provide an audience for work to be viewed critically, developing the skills needed for appreciation;
- provide examples of aesthetically pleasing arrangements of images and artefacts
- enable interaction so children can learn through enactive as well as iconic and symbolic modes, promoting a feeling of ownership and aesthetic discrimination
- reflect a wide variety of styles and images presenting a culturally diverse society, and promoting positive attitudes towards diversity (p.73-74)

A growing emphasis is being placed on visual culture and new interpretative approaches that encourage students to interact with and respond to the art. Student art exhibitions therefore, can play a dynamic role in the final stage of the creative process. If student art is exhibited, which includes social and cultural content, then their art exhibitions might also appeal to a wider and more diverse audience (Reese, 2003).

Reese suggests expanding the size and content of art exhibitions by asking students to provide texts to accompany each artwork. For instance, students could write autobiographies in which they describe how a piece of art affects them socially, culturally and historically; create stories about where art work 'transports' them; or explain how other disciplines affect the creation and interpretation of the art.

Elementary teachers can do a great deal to enhance the learning that takes place before, during and after art has been made. Each aspect of the creative process should connect whether it is the development of an idea, the creation of the art or the interpretation of the final work. Through the creative process each student also contributes to the experience of learning about oneself and others. Exhibitions of student art, especially those that encourage greater interaction, not only provide rich learning experiences for students but also inform the public about the value and role of student art.

In summary, this chapter provides an overview of how teachers can prepare their students for interpreting art by examining how images convey meaning, exploring art materials, teaching visual language, and increasing visual awareness. It also outlines strategies for interpretation and offers ways to make art exhibitions more interactive. With a greater emphasis on visual culture and innovative approaches for interpreting student art, elementary teachers can enrich this aspect of the creative process and also the lives of their students.

References

Arnheim, R. (1969). *Visual thinking*. Berkeley, CA: University of California Press.

Barrett, T. (1994). *Criticising art: Understanding the contemporary*. Mountain View, CA: Mayfield.

Barrett, T. (2000). Studies invited lecture: About interpretation for art education. *Studies in Art Education, 42*(1), 5-19.

Beetlestone, F. (1998). *Creative children, imagination teaching*. Buckingham, UK: Open University Press.

Burton, J. (2000). The configuration of meaning: Learner-centred art education revisited. Studies in Art Education, 41 (4). 330-345.

Bolin, P. (1996). We are what we ask. *Art Education, 49*(5), 6-10.

Buchanan, M. (1997). *Reading for meaning: critical literacy*. In Mason, R. (Ed.), *Reading visual texts: New directions in art education: conference proceeding* (pp. 20-30). London, UK: Centre for Educational & International Research, Roehampton Institute.

Burton, J. (2000). The configuration of meaning: Learner-centred art education revisited. *Studies in Art Education, 41*(4), 330-345.

Chanda, J. & Basinger, A. (2000). Understanding the cultural meaning of selected African Ndop statues: The use of art history constructivist inquiry methods. *Studies in Art Education, 42*(1), 67-82.

Costantino, T. (2002). Problem-based learning: A concrete approach to teaching aesthetics. *Studies in Art Education, 43*(3), 219-231.

Curtiss, D. (1987). *Introduction to visual literacy: A guide to the visual arts and communication*. Englewood Cliffs, NJ: Prentice-Hall.

Dondis, D. (1973). *A primer for visual literacy*. New York: Harcourt, Brace.

Durant, S. (1996). Reflections on museum education. *Art Education, 49*(1), 15-24.

Edwards, B. (1989). *Drawing on the right side of the brain*. Los Angeles, CA: Tarcher.

Eisner, E. (1972). *Educating artistic vision*. New York: Macmillan.

Feldman, E. B. (1970). *Becoming human through art*. Englewood Cliffs, NJ: Prentice Hall.

Freedman, K. (2003). The importance of student artistic production to teaching visual culture. *Art Education, 56*(2), 38-43.

Gardner, H. (1990). *Art education and human development*. Los Angeles, CA: The Getty Centre for Education in the Arts.

Geahigan, G. (1998). Critical inquiry: Understanding the concept and applying it in the classroom. *Art Education, 51*(5) 10-16.

Graham, J. (1990). *Pictures on the page*. London, UK: National Association for the Teaching of English.

Gude, O. (2008). Aesthetics making meaning. *Studies in Art Education, 50*(1), 98-103.

Housen, A. (2007). Art viewing and aesthetic development: designing for the viewer. In P. Villeneuve (ed.), *From periphery to center: Art museum education in the 21st century* (pp.172-179). Reston, VA: National Art education Association.

Irwin, R. L. & Kindler, A. M. (Eds.) (1999). Art education beyond school boundaries: Identifying resources, exploring possibilities. In Irwin, R. L. & Kindler, A. M. (Eds.), *Beyond the school: Community and institutional partnerships in art education* (pp. 1-4). Reston, VA: National Art Education Association.

Kanatani, K. (1998). Contemporary art start. *Art Education, 51*(2), 33-39.

Kellogg, R. (1970). *Analyzing children's art*. Palo Alto, CA: Mayfield.

Kindler, A. & Darras, B. (1997). Development of pictorial representation: A teleology - based model. *Journal of Art and Design Education, 16*(3), 217-222.

Lowenfeld, V. (1957). *Creative and mental growth* (3rd Ed.). New York: MacMillan.

Messaris, P. (1994). *Visual literacy: Image, mind, and reality*. Boulder, CO: Westview Press.

Moreno, M. (2007). Art museums and the internet: The Emergence of the virtual museum. *Crossings: Journal of Art and Technology, 5(1), 1-11.*

Reese, E. (2003). Art takes me there. *Art Education, 56*(1), 33-39.

Roland, C. (1992). Improving student thinking through elementary art instruction. In Johnson, A. (Ed.), *Art Education: Elementary* (pp. 13-42). Reston, VA: National Art education Association.

Sandell, R. (2009). Using form+theme+content (FTC) for rebalancing 21st Century Art Education. *Studies in Art Education*, 50(3), 287-299.

Walker, S. (1996). Designing studio instruction: Why have students make artwork? *Art Education, 49*(5), 11-17.

Wilson, B. & Wilson, M. (1982). *Teaching children to draw: A guide for teachers and parents*. Englewood Cliffs, NJ: Prentice Hall.

Zander, M. (2003). Talking, thinking, responding and creating: A survey on talk in art education. *Studies in Art Education, 44*(2), 117-13

CONNECTIONS, REFLECTIONS AND CREATIONS

Art Is like a Bowl of Fruit: Aesthetics and Art Criticism in the Elementary School

Steve Elliott

Imagine as an elementary school teacher you have gathered your students together and are sitting in the midst of the group with a painting of large bowl of fruit. You intend to introduce the idea of "still life" as a topic for investigation so you bring attention to the image and ask: "When you look at this bowl of fruit does anything stand out or come to mind that you would like to talk about?" Instantly the students (it is a good day for them) begin to comment on the presentation.

"Look at the yellow of that banana, it jumps right out at me." " The fuzz on that little brown fruit looks like it would scratch if you rubbed it on your arm, What kind of fruit is that?" "It's a kiwi." " Kiwis make me think of my grandma. She always gives me a kiwi for breakfast when I visit her. I love my grandma." "My grandma gives me fruit too." "My mom gives me an apple to bring to school, because she says that apples are school fruit" "What does school fruit mean?" "I don't know but I always see an apple on signs when they talk about schools." "My neighbor has an apple tree, he sprays poison on it to kill the bugs." "I ate a bug in an apple once." "I ate an apple with candy on it when I went to the fair last Saturday. Going to the fair makes me happy."

In school art programs students and teachers engage in talk related to works of art. This talk can take the form of critiques or classroom discussions about art sources, student art projects, or art works of historical or cultural significance. Talk about any of these things can be considered art criticism activity because students explore meanings, understandings, and value associated with art (Feldman, 1994). "Art criticism has become the storytelling aspect of art and aesthetics and transforms visual experiences into verbal expressions that can be shared with others" (Cromer, 1990, p. 9). During these conversations students begin to discover what is interesting about what they see. This chapter introduces a few basic definitions and thinking associated with school aesthetics and art criticism. To facilitate integrating critical talk into classroom practice it concludes by identifying some relevant points of entry for teachers and students to talk about and find value in what they see.

Aesthetic Interest

If you were asked to identify your favorite colour, you would most likely form an immediate answer without much thought. If asked to defend your choice, your argument might include the statement "just because I like it." In this case there is a judgement made about the personal interest or value you hold for the colour you enjoy based on feelings of 'like' or 'dislike'. There are reasons why you like one colour more than another, but you do not have to think about those reasons before you decide which one you like. In the arts we can know things by attending to our feelings. The feelings we have when confronted with a work of art is often considered aesthetic in nature.

Individual feelings are typically subjective rather than rational. This aesthetic subjectivity makes it impossible to decide questions of truth. With a subjective quality at the center of an aesthetic response, artists, philosophers, and teachers look to see if more than one person shares particular feelings or responses when confronted with a work of art. If many people are influenced in a similar way by the same experience, philosophers look for qualities in the work that might have triggered the response. Philosophers with an interest in aesthetics think deeply about, and explore the conditions that cause these feelings. When working with students there may be times when you move from personal interest to general interest

(White, 1999). This validates personal experiences of each student while allowing the group to share a meaningful discussion.

Traditional aesthetics is the branch of Philosophy that concerns itself with theories of art and forms of beauty found in nature and in Art. The thinking involved in aesthetics applies to all of the arts including disciplines such as music, literature, poetry, visual art, theatre, film, dance, etc. Questions that relate to the art objects, the audience, the artists, or the experience of looking, listening, or reading, might be considered aesthetic in nature.

Philosophers typically agree that one necessary quality for something to be considered a work of visual art is that a viewer finds the experience interesting and worthy of attention over a period of time. Although they agree that those experiencing art should find the sights, textures, sounds, concepts etc., interesting, they argue about what does, or should, cause those feelings of interest. Some claim that the feelings must be triggered by what is actually seen or heard in the work while others suggest that the feelings may also be caused by what you think about when you experience the art. Claims about what causes aesthetic feelings, and what we might consider a work of art, have been formed into theories of art.

When you find something interesting to look at (the case with visual art) you may ask questions about what makes it interesting. The answers to such questions are typically concepts associated with aesthetic understanding. One important task of teachers of visual art is to help their students identify and clarify qualities that make art worthy of interest and attention.

What is Art?

We talk about aesthetic questions as a regular part of our daily experience. 'A parent asks how their teenage son or daughter can think that pink hair looks cool.' 'A child wonders how his or her parent can wear checks and plaid together.' 'A citizen thinks a public gallery paid too much money for a painting created by an artist with no apparent skill.' As individuals and cultural groups find different things interesting to look at and question, the set of possible definitions for art increases.

What is art anyway? Is there a definition for art that will accommodate all the variety that can be considered an example of art? Early attempts to define art identified practical objects, like furniture and handicrafts, as art. As time moved on, the categories of things that could be considered examples of art were expanded to include other specific forms of expression like poetry and sculpture.[1] Things like these had no practical use except that people enjoyed them. This kind of thinking represented a refinement, or expansion of the definition of art.

As philosophers thought deeply about the objects that were considered examples of art, they began to realize that some art objects were less interesting than others. This thinking led them to consider the reasons that objects were interesting. Thinking about why art was interesting came to dominate the field of aesthetics. As one set of qualities became popular for definitional purposes, philosophers framed a theory[2] of what makes something art.

Theories of art have traditionally outlined sets of qualities that determine if something should be called a work of art or not. Historically philosophers have used specific theories to define and judge the art that was typical in their culture and time. In current practice, if a teacher limits herself to one theory of

art, she would be unable to analyze and discuss many forms of art that have existed in other times and other cultures. To enable teachers to think deeply about all art they might encounter, they must be able to consider the definitional criteria explained by various known theories and cultures. Individual theories of art represent valid ways of looking at art but if any single theory of art were used as the only explanation of art, it would be too narrow to account for the range of possible art forms. Another problem with using only one theory of art is that the forms of art keep changing. As a result, any single theory of art cannot define all art forms that have been, or will be invented.

Some have suggested that the definition of art was similar to the definition of game (Weitz, 1970). There is no single set of qualities or rules that describe all games. Art, like games, include such a variety of types that no single definition would ever be correct in all cases. As a result, no single set of possibilities will ever be identified (Bryson, Holly & Moxey, 1991). The search for a definition of art has been abandoned and replaced by the identification of art possibilities. This approach requires students and teachers to continually explore the reasons that particular art pieces might be interesting to attend to.

Art Criticism: Process and Attention

Thinking and talking about works of art, in specific terms, is applying philosophy and is called art criticism. Art criticism is the activity of analyzing and talking about specific works of art.

Students often think criticism involves saying bad things about someone's art (Barrett, 1997). The word criticism, when used in philosophy suggests being analytical and insightful about a work. Sometimes the result of art criticism is a judgment or evaluation of a work of art, but any observations, analysis, interpretations, as well as evaluations about art can be considered art criticism. In schools the most instructive talk about art concerns itself with observations, analysis, and interpretations.

To assist teachers in making the perceptions and ideas embedded within works of art explicit, educators in the field have proposed a variety of frameworks or processes to guide classroom art viewing practice. Variations of Feldman's (1994) practical art criticism outline and Broudy's (1987) aesthetic scanning framework probably represent the two most commonly used approaches in North American elementary and secondary schools.

These and other processes for talking about art in classrooms share at least two common elements; looking deeply and making sense of what you see. In all viewing frameworks, slowing down the looking process gives students time to take better note of what they are actually looking at allowing them to thoughtfully consider possible meanings or value associated with each work. An important part of putting aesthetic thinking into practice is learning to look, listen, and think carefully. This process tends to heighten student sensitivity toward things visual. Through this heightened sensibility, they begin to look at ordinary things in extra-ordinary ways.

The process of looking deeply, creating meaning, and assigning value requires teachers and students to consider specific things in each art work to make sense of. By considering sets of worthwhile things to attend to, teachers can more productively guide students through criticism sessions.

As mentioned earlier, individual theories of art claim that art should be or do something in particular to engage the audience, capture attention and sustain interest. If we analyze the definitional criteria suggested by various theories of art, we can construct a list of specific things about individual examples of art that make them work as expressive, or at least attention worthy, presentations. These things could be called qualities of the works and, in the case of art forms would be called aesthetic and artistic qualities.

Artists use aesthetic and artistic qualities to create their work, individuals respond to them with interest while looking, and teachers and students consider them while thinking and talking about works of art. To account for past theories, current production, and some future possibilities in art, it might be productive to consider artistic qualities under three categories, perceptual, conceptual, and cultural.

Perceptual Qualities

"Look at the yellow of that banana, it jumps right out at me." " The fuzz on that little brown fruit looks like it would scratch if you rubbed it on your arm."

Individuals can experience an aesthetic response to art forms through qualities that are interesting simply because they are seen, felt, or heard. These are called perceptual qualities because simply perceiving them creates interest.[3] Some distinctions of perceptual interest might include sensory, formal, expressive, and physical qualities of a work.

Sensory qualities are those attributes in works of art that directly stimulate the senses. They include all qualities that can be seen, felt, or heard. Humans find intrinsic interest in stimulation of their senses. Things to look at and discuss under the sensory category of interest might include qualities like colours (i.e. red, blue, orange), tones (i.e. light, dark, bright, dull), textures (i.e. rough, smooth), lines (i.e. thick, thin), lights (i.e. bright, dull), movements (i.e. twirling, leaping), sounds (i.e. tapping, rustling), etc.

Formal qualities are those attributes in works of art that expose how the parts of a presentation or work are put together or relate to each other. This putting together is often called the composition or design of the work. The interest and value in these qualities resides in the structures inherent in the works. Things to look at and discuss under the formal category of interest might include qualities like form or shape, (i.e. round, triangular, flat), balance (i.e. symmetrical, asymmetrical, radial), rhythm (i.e. repetition, pattern, disruption, connections), emphasis (i.e. focus, attention, contrast), unity (i.e. chaotic, integrated, harmonious), etc.

Expressive qualities are those attributes that make us feel a mood or emotion by the way they look. This expressiveness can be created by the personal associations we make with facial expressions or other life experiences. Colours, lines, sounds, words, movements, performances, can each look or sound expressive. They can imitate or suggest many emotions like sad or happy, anxious or calm, warm or cool. Things to look at and discuss under the expressive category of interest might include qualities like moods (i.e. somber, menacing, frivolous,), emotions (i.e. happy sad, angry,), or states (i.e. warm or cool, tense, relaxed, conflicted), etc.

Physical qualities are those attributes in works of art that are physical or technical in nature. There is a different expressive quality to steel in a sculpture than that created by stone or glass. There is a different feel to acrylic paint than watercolour or oil. The audience responds in a particular way when viewing a work of installation art made up of rocks on a hillside. The physical qualities of a work of art can shape the felt experience of the work. Physical qualities of art works might include considerations like material aspects (i.e. paint on canvas or steel, Helvetica or Times text), technical aspects (i.e. watercolour wash technique or impasto,), or environmental aspects (i.e. seashore or countryside), etc.

Conceptual Qualities

" My mom gives me an apple to bring to school, because she says that apples are school fruit" "What does school fruit mean?" "I don't know but I always see an apple on signs when they talk about schools."

Aesthetic and artistic responses can also be created by qualities that are interesting because of what one thinks about when they see, hear, or read a work of art. These are called conceptual qualities because interest is created and shaped by thinking about what is perceived.[4] The conceptual experience of art can be meaningful to the audience if their thoughts about the work either denote or exemplify something that is connected with their lives.

A work of art denotes something when it reveals, stands for, or identifies it plainly. For example, the name BatMan denotes a mysterious masked man with a cape and a winged car who helps people in distress. An image with two red stripes, on either side of a white stripe with a red maple leaf in the middle, denotes Canada. As works of art denote understandable symbols, they bring to our minds and our feelings, all that those things stand for and represent to us.

A work of art exemplifies when it serves as an example, illustrates or suggests something that we understand. Exemplification can illustrate, suggest, or represent ideas or concepts. A red circle can illustrate the features of an apple. A trapped animal can suggest an animal rights issue. A hymn can represent a religious experience.

Works of art can, denote, and /or exemplify ideas that make us feel. Some qualities in the conceptual category might include social, symbolic, contextual, and narrative aspects of art works.

Social qualities are those attributes in works of art make us feel by presenting social issues that are current, interesting, and important for us to think about. These qualities are usually connected with issues that are part of a pressing concern to a community of people. All those who experience the art might not share the same attitude about the issue, but they will understand that it is a concern that many feel requires debate and attention. Social qualities may include thoughts about issues (i.e. animal rights, democracy, bioengineering), events (i.e. man walking on the moon, bombing of the world trade towers), beliefs (i.e. democracy, religion), etc.

Symbolic qualities are those attributes that make us feel by presenting objects or images that have come to stand for some general notion or concept. When a group of people think of the same thing when confronted with an image, idea, sound, or word, that thing acts as a symbol. Symbolic qualities are usually connected to objects or ideas that have been associated with a particular thing over a long enough period of time that the meaning is generally understood. . Symbolic qualities may be connected with representations of: archetypes (i.e. hearts, democracy, bioengineering), icons (i.e. movie star, politician), emblems (i.e. national flags, crosses), etc.

Contextual qualities are those attributes that shape our thinking and feeling when works of art are presented as part of a meaningful context or environment. Works of art can be presented in endless different contexts, each having the potential of shaping the way you feel about the work. When you attend to objects, sounds, or words in a gallery they are affected by the fact that you interpret them as a work of art. When you look at an ancient water pot you see it as an object of interest that also carries water. If we see a painting in a church we bring to our view of the painting, feelings and interpretations with religious considerations. Contextual qualities may be noticed in presentations associated with environments (i.e. galleries, churches, schools), objects (i.e. books, house-wares), settings (i.e. at night, in private), etc.

Narrative qualities are those images, sounds, words, and movements that tell a story. People intrinsically enjoy stories and find them interesting because they organize related parts of general experiences that help us create mesning. When things have meaning for us we relate to them with increased feeling and interest. Stories or narrative qualities in art offer accounts of real or fictional events, situations, or circumstances. Although literature is most often associated with narrative qualities because it tells stories with words, Artists can also tell stories with pictures, marks, sounds, and movements. Narrative qualities can be found in story and storyboard-like presentations that are personal (i.e. my family, I am a woman), public (i.e. the buffalo hunt, 911), invented (i.e. life as an ant, 2025), etc.

Cultural qualities

"I ate an apple with candy on it when I went to the fair last Saturday. Going to the fair makes me happy."

In addition to perceptual and conceptual qualities that create inherent interest in things associated with visual presentations, we are integrally connected to a current culture that shapes our attention and interests. Concepts in this category of interest have come to be known as visual culture which consists of venues in our environment that occupy our attention to such a degree that we look to them to satisfy and shape our interest and need for visual stimulation. For most young people this consists primarily of the visual aspects of their popular culture as expressed through life experience, media, and worldview.[5] Because aspects of this category are so pervasive and compelling they tend to reshape in a powerful way, even the aesthetic interests and judgements that we at one time considered universally human. Some considerations in the cultural category might include qualities in events, media, and popular culture.

Qualities in events are those parts of events or community experiences that hold a high degree of interest for your students. The idea of "event" itself might suggest that students either attend significant happenings or make an event of some experience (like going to the mall). In these instances the event carries greater impact than one might typically think the situation warrants. Here students seem to assign larger than life value to everyday life experience. Within our culture we, at times, look for qualities to help us define our visual importance. Qualities in events can be associated with happenings (i.e. fashion shows, concerts), places (i.e. the mall, amusement parks), etc.

Qualities in media can be observed in many forms of public communication. Due to the pervasive place it occupies within our life experience and the sophistication of the presentations, media has a powerful impact on the way we process information.

Qualities in media can be distilled from print material (i.e. fashion magazines, motorcycle zines), television (i.e. situation comedies, music stations, reality shows), the internet (i.e. web sites, chat rooms), etc.

Qualities in popular culture are those aspects of the dominant culture for any group that holds their attention and causes individual members to adopt, copy, emulate, and at times idolize observable features of the group. Discussion items in this category might help students clarify embedded messages, values, and impacts of cultural decisions. Qualities in Popular Culture can be found in fads (i.e. tattoos, piercings, border clothes), film (i.e. music videos, movies), games (i.e. nintendo, web games), activities (i.e. skateboarding, parties), etc.

To the Classroom, a Few Closing Thoughts

In schools, teachers might be considered leaders, facilitators and participants in classroom activities. The main goal of art talk activities in elementary classrooms is to have the students look more carefully, think more deeply, and talk more often about the things they see (Barrett 1997). Through art criticism, teachers and students clarify experience and find meaning and value in their art encounters. Teachers who are able to direct both the looking and the talking associated with student attention can enrich student search for visual value.

As a leader in the classroom teachers review student and historical works that will be discussed in their class. With careful attention they decide which categories of artistic and aesthetic value might represent the most productive point of entry for their students. With these qualities in mind they create leading questions that will both direct student attention and focus thinking and talking about the works they view.[6]

As a facilitator in the classroom teachers allow time for careful looking and strategically pose questions to stimulate conversation. At Harvard students were asked to find the thing about each work they viewed, that carried the punch, or generated the strongest response as their entry into critical dialogue (Perkins, 1994). By keeping the discussion moving all students will have an opportunity to look, think, and participate in worthwhile critical activity.

As a participant in the classroom teachers talk about their own observations and give both time and consideration to all student responses as they explore the visual field together. Art is a living part of our human experience. Learn to look carefully, think deeply, feel freely, and share openly through effective critical talk in the classroom.

Notes

1. As an example, Plato stated that art was considered good if it imitated nature well (mimesis). Using this theory of art he stated that the purpose of poetry was to accurately copy or portray the activities of the gods.

2. Some historical theories of art include: Imitationalism, Expressionism, Formalism, and Institutional definitions of art.

3. Harry S. Broudy (1972, 1987), a professor of philosophy at the University of Illinois developed a list of perceptual aesthetic qualities to guide the looking, listening, and thinking about art. For him, interpretation is based on identifying the perceptual qualities within works of art that create feeling in the audience. His set included sensory, formal, expressive, and technical (physical) aspects of art works.

4. Nelson Goodman (1968), an American philosopher, was instrumental in explaining the conceptual side of art expression. He was a professor of philosophy at Harvard University and, as a young man, ran an art gallery. He argued that understanding a work of art is not matter of appreciating it or finding beauty in it, but it is a matter of interpreting it correctly. Interpretation is based on how and what the work of art symbolizes, and how that meaning relates to the individual looking, listening, or reading the work.

5. For discussion about the place of visual culture within our schools see Studies in Art Education v (40)-(44), Duncum (1999, 2000); Freedman, K. (2000); Giroux (1989).

6. For suggestions about creating sets of discussion topics with your students see Elliott (2001).

References

Barrett, T. (1997). *Talking about student art.* Worcester, MA: Davis Publications.

Bryson, N. Holly, M. & Moxey, K. (1991). *Visual theory, painting and interpretation.* Cambridge, UK: Polity Press.

Broudy, H. S. (1972). *Enlightened cherishing: An essay on aesthetic education.* Urbana, IL: University of Illinois Press.

Broudy, H. (1987). *The role of imagery in learning.* Los Angeles, CA: The Getty Center for Education in the Arts.

Cromer, J. (1990). *Criticism, history, theory and practice of art criticism in art education.* Reston, VI: The National Art Education Association.

Duncum, P. (2000). Visual culture: Developments, definitions, and directions for art education. *Studies in Art Education, 42*(2), 101-112.

Duncum, P. (1999). A case for an art education of everyday aesthetic experiences. *Studies in Art Education, 40*(2), 259-311.

Elliott, S. (2001). Some Thoughts about Viewing Art in Schools: "Building Viewing Art Categories with Students". *British Columbia Art Teachers Association Journal. 41*(2),17-21

Feldman, E. (1994). *Practical art criticism.* Englewood Cliffs, NJ. Prentice Hall.

Freedman, K. (2000). Social perspectives of art education in the U.S.: Teaching visual culture in a democracy. *Studies in Art Education, 41*(4), 312-329.

Giroux, H. & Simon, R. (1989). Popular culture as a pedagogy of pleasure and meaning. In H. Giroux, R. Simon, & Contributors. *Popular culture: Schooling and everyday life* (pp.1-29). New York: Bergin & Garvey.

Goodman, N. (1968). *Languages of art.* New York: Bobbs-Merrill.

Perkins, D. (1994). *The intelligent eye.* Santa Monica, CA: The Getty Center for Education in the Arts.

Weitz, M. (1970). The role of theory in aesthetics. In Weitz, M. (Ed.). *Problems in aesthetics* (pp.169-180). NY: The Macmillan Company.

White, B. (1999). A fish tale metaphor. *CSEA Journal, 30*(2), 19-25.

CHAPTER 13

The Magic and Mystery of Image Development

Sharon McCoubrey

Defining Image

The magic and the mystery of art reside in the image. Without an image, there would be no art. Whatever materials or processes were used to make the artwork, it is the image of the artwork that makes it distinctive and unique from any other artwork. And so, as the image carries the mystery and the magic of art, image development is a vital part of making and looking at art.

An understanding of image development is best started with an understanding of image. The term "image" is used in many different contexts but is somewhat difficult to define. The image of an artwork is its appearance, what it looks like. When trying to describe the appearance of a painting, a photograph, a sculpture or a video, one might refer to the colours, or perhaps the subject, the style, the art process, or the materials. In fact, none of these factors is the image, but they are all used to make the image.

Certain factors can be used to describe an artwork, including materials, process, style, subject, colour scheme, composition, use of elements and principles, emotions, or special effects. A specific image is what it is because of how these factors have been combined.

Generally, the Postmodern inclusive lens for looking at art will include many forms of art, including installation art, earth works, photography, performance art, conceptual art, media arts, or folk art. The diversity of art also includes the images found within magazine adverting, interior decorating, fashion design, videos, landscaping, product design, cars, flower arranging, jewelry, fabric, wallpaper, wrapping paper, theatre set designs, puppets, greeting cards, book illustrations, tattoos, and many other visual features of our world.

Images are in all these forms of art. Images take the many forms that artworks take. In a similar way, images are created for the many purposes for which artworks are created, such as to illustrate, celebrate, advertise, give a message, provoke, adorn, challenge thinking, or to express ideas. Images are within two-dimensional and three-dimensional artworks.

The word *image* is found within the word *imagination*. An artist uses imagination to create unique images by selecting, combining, or applying the factors available to create art. Even though we seem to deal with image and with image development predominantly in the creation of art, it is also significant to deal with image and image development when viewing artworks, and when considering art in terms of art history, aesthetics, or critical analysis. As we provide opportunities for students to look at art, we need to make reference to the image, and the artists' image development decisions and processes. "The meanings of artworks can be made clearer and art appreciation can be enriched when viewers consider the strategies employed by the artist in creating or transforming images in innovative ways" (Zuk et al, 1997, p. 115-116).

With this understanding of images, it is now possible to explore image development, the processes of creating the images that become the art.

Defining Image Development

Image is fundamental to all art. Whether looking at a First Nations carved mask, an Expressionist abstract painting, or an embroidered shawl from the Ukraine, all the artworks consist of an image created by an artist using an image development strategy.

Even though artists have always used image development to create art, it is still somewhat elusive. Learning about and working with new materials, such as the latest fabric paint, or learning about and applying new processes, such as non-toxic printmaking, is what generally fills art workshops and courses. Learning about image development is less common.

Of course, image development processes change as materials, technologies and processes change. Monoprinting resulted in a different approach to image development than did the traditional printmaking methods of etching or woodcuts. The myriad of tools available in computer graphics software lead to different image development processes than those used with charcoal pencil on cartridge paper. The key to image development lies in the ways in which the artist uses the available tools, materials, and processes to visually problem solve, to use the components of an image in such a way as to express an idea, represent a subject, portray an emotion, or present a concept. "It is the way in which ideas are translated into visual statements that is the essence of image development" (Ministry of Education, 1985).

Under the Bow Branch   by: Sean Duteil

Although art curricula vary somewhat from jurisdiction to jurisdiction, each with slightly different organizational structures and use of terms, it is the case that image development is part of each curriculum in some way. Image development might be referred to within the various sections or approaches of a curriculum, or, it may form a distinct section of a curriculum, with information provided under that heading. Recognizing the key role that image development plays in the creation of art, and when responding to art, image development is an essential part of art curriculum.

Young children in grade one use image development strategies to paint their story telling pictures, and although the complexity would vary, senior students will also use the same image development strategies to create their artworks. The process of creating an image is perhaps best explored through an examination of specific image development sources and strategies.

Image Development Sources

As artists use materials, select processes, apply elements and principles of art, and deal with many other factors in order to create images, their ideas for images can come from a number of different sources. Typically, the following six sources of images are used.

1. **Observation**: looking at the subject, be it a landscape, person, object or still life, then creating an image that is about that observed subject in some way.

2. **Memory**: recalling past experiences, situations, locations and then creating images from information contained in those memories.

3. **Imagination**: imagining something entirely new, making it up and putting it down as an image.

4. **Concepts/Ideas**: using a specific concept, such as a social issue, growth, loyalty, reflections, contrasts, or any number of other concepts from which to create an image.

5. **Sensory Experiences**: creating images as suggested by experiences involving one or more of the senses.

6. **Feelings/Emotions**: creating an image that emerges as the artist endeavours to express an emotion or as stimulated by a feeling.

It is not possible to totally isolate these sources from each other, as there is often some overlap. For example, an artist may be painting an abstract image from imagination, but will be partially influenced by memories of landscape forms. However, there is usually one dominant source.

As teachers plan art activities for students, the source of the image should be identified. For example, if the students will be creating watercolour paintings about spring, or about the concept of "belonging", will they use their memories to create the image; will they create original images from their imaginations; or will they observe a specific subject in order to create the image? Identifying the source of the image at the lesson planning stage is essential so that the teacher is able to determine the preparation for the creating stage of the activity, and perhaps for the evaluation.

118

Image Development Strategies

Creating an image is often a process of editing, adjusting, reviewing, and changing before the final image is reached. As with writing, editing and refinement are important processes of image development. Artists can use a number of strategies during the creating process. The following is not necessarily a definitive list , as many resources and curricula will have slightly varying lists of strategies. Typically, many strategies involve manipulating a starting image, which was previously created by the artist, or some other subject or visual reference point.

Abstraction: to depict an idea or subject by reducing it to its basic visual properties, to depict an idea or subject with less than accurate representation.

Elaboration: to embellish, add pattern, detail and adornment to an image, attach, append.

Magnification: to increase a portion of a subject or an image to larger than natural size.

Multiplication: to multiply parts of an image to produce a pattern or sequence in the image, to repeat.

Reproduction: to reproduce a component, and perhaps to alter it in some way such as size or tone, and use the reproductions in some way within the image.

Point of view: to depict a subject from unusual points of view, for example, a bird's eye view, an ant's point of view, eye level, aerial, profile, angled, x-ray, or through a telescope.

Juxtaposition: to combine two unlikely or very different elements or subjects together in an image, to create an unusual relationship or a new synthesis by placing unlike subjects together.

Metamorphosis: to depict objects or forms in progressive stages of growth or change to create new images.

Distortion: to bend, twist, stretch, compress, warp, melt, or deform an object or subject.

Exaggeration: to represent some component of a subject in an exaggerated way, making that component unrealistically prominent.

Fragmentation: to split, fragment, insert, invert, rotate, shatter, superimpose or divide an image and then reconstruct it to create a new image.

Minification: opposite of magnification, to reduce a portion of an image to a smaller size, to diminish, contract.

Serialization: to create a set within an image, to group, link, show progression.

Reversal: to reverse the laws of nature, such as the time of day, the seasons, gravity, size, age, function, and other such factors of the components of an image, rotate, reflect, reorient, such as back to front or mirror image.

Simplification: to reduce the details of an image until it is represented in a simplified way, to eliminate, subtract, delete, remove, and erase details.

Superimpose: to cover, overlap, or merge some part of an image, to place one component over another component in the image.

Polarize: to place opposites together in an image, such as beauty/beast, good/evil, life/death, involves duality.

Substitute: to substitute a component in an image for another, to replace, exchange, switch, or swap.

Disguise: to place almost hidden images within the image, to hide, conceal, camouflage, screen or shroud some component of the image.

Isolate: to separate within an image, to segregate, seclude, exclude.

Stylize: to simplify the subject of an image to achieve a stylized representation.

Animation: serializing images in various stages of action to depict movement and progression.

Valuing Original Images

A fundamental aspect of art is the uniqueness and originality of the images. In the same way that an author does not copy word for word the contents of a book and then publish it as a new book, visual artists do not copy another artist's image and present it as a new work of art. Wouldn't we get tired of going to art shows if we looked at only repeats of previously seen images? Art would quickly limit itself and expire if that were the case. "Imagination and individuality are critical to successful production in art…Individuality of outcome, not conformity to a predetermined common standard, was what I was after" (Eisner, 1998, p. 118).

The Postmodern idea that art carries a social responsibility (Albers, 1999) leads to many artists and art students investigating social issues, such as poverty or racism, through their imagery. This further confirms the requirement for original artwork, as the use of art to provoke reactions or to make a statement about a social issue would not be possible except through personal expression. Much of the artwork we look at from any culture, from any time, is a reflection of a life situation or a significant event. Our means of feeling the emotion of another person is communicated through art images. Art images must be original in order to allow relevant and meaningful communication. "Artists are concerned with exposing aspects of reality through symbols, they are not imitators, but interpreters of reality reacting with feelings as well as thoughts" (Schinneller, 1968, p. 198).

Counter to the misconception that art is only relaxing handiwork, creating an original image is an extremely complex, cognitive process involving many decisions and much thinking, often divergent rather than linear thinking. Creative thinking is intellectual. "There is no competent work of the hand that does not depend on the competent use of the mind" (Eisner, 1998, p. 23).

Creating original art results in intellectual development, "different forms of representation develop different cognitive skills" (Eisner, 1998, p. 47). Therefore, thinking skills, the essence of an educated person, are developed when creating original images. Original thinking, creative thinking, critical thinking, and problem solving are all desired and essential cognitive skills for successful learning, successful work, successful relationships, or a successful life. Every opportunity to develop and value creative thinking skills should be embraced by the school system.

Current practices in many schools and classrooms do not embrace such creative work by children. Unfortunately "we are far more concerned with the correct replication of what already exists than with cultivating the powers of innovation or the celebration of thinking. Perhaps a little parity among these educational goals would be appropriate" (Eisner, 1998, p. 26). Copying, tracing, and colouring stenciled pictures have nothing to do with art or education. This 'busy work' may keep their hands busy, but their thinking and feelings take time off (Gaitskell, Hurwitz & Day, 1982). School is not about busy work. School is about learning, developing, and about thinking.

It is not uncommon to see elementary art, in particular primary art, that merely consists of following given instructions to complete a pre-planned project. In these cases, the students are not creating their own images, and as a result, are not going through the thought processes required to create and problem solve. Unfortunately, the tremendous benefits that come from creating their own images is lost to these students. Fortunately, those non-creative projects can easily be converted to creative art activities. This conversion can happen by simply changing that part of the pre-planned project that dictates what the final product is to look like, and instead, letting the students decide that part for themselves. For example, the students can use brown paper and coloured stickers to create gingerbread characters (a project that a primary teacher might want to coincide with the reading of that story) but rather than having a gingerbread man tracer to draw around, let the students draw their own men, and all features of the gingerbread men.

Students of all ages must be allowed to create their own images. This is essential for long-term development of their skills and confidence in art. Not only is this creative approach essential for meeting the learning outcomes of the curriculum, it is also essential for gaining the benefits inherent in art experiences.

Sometimes, pre-planned art projects are given to primary aged children because it is thought that there is no choice, that young children cannot yet draw pictures and therefore, the tracers and outline drawings are used until they are able to. That would be a little like saying young children should not make sounds until they are able to speak. In the same way that those beginning babbles lead to speaking, those beginning scribbles lead to drawing and original art images. Young children's drawings and art creations are delightful, and would be missed if students are not allowed to create their own images.

Art education is all about development and creativity, not about completing pre-planned projects. As Zuk and Dalton (1997) clearly state "…learning how to create and transform images for expressive purposes, should be emphasized at every opportunity in art education" (p. 119).

Developing Image Development Skills

A common misconception is that images in artworks are somehow 'inspired' and magically come to the artist who then creates them on canvas or from stone. Although inspiration may be part of the process for some artists, art making is in fact about skills. Image development is clearly a skill that can be developed. The use of various strategies, reference to or manipulations of existing images, critical analysis of beginning efforts and exploration of various compositions are all part of the image development skills that can be developed.

Those students who approach an art activity with reluctance, or those who stare at a blank page with anxiety, or those who say 'I can't draw' will be helped tremendously with specific image development skills. They will be able to move beyond these hurdles by having a place to start, by having specific strategies to use, and by having a means to assess their efforts.

Many decisions are necessary as images are created. A first step for art students is to clarify the idea that will be represented in their image. The idea may be a straightforward record of some object, person, or place, or it may be a social message or a feeling. The creator works to make the idea known in the image. Students can be encouraged to create well-designed and meaningful images by stressing the need to plan ahead, to think about how to put their ideas together, to use the elements and principles of art to create effective images, and how to make their images intriguing and extraordinary (Changar, 1992).

Making working sketches of the idea is often an important part of image development. The sketches help the creator work through the decisions that are part of the final image. It helps make obvious and therefore allow elimination of the representations that 'don't work'.

Teachers have an opportunity to support and facilitate students' image development skills by providing the following:

1. **Opportunities** – teachers must provide many and varied occasions in which students are required to create their own images. Working with pre-drawn images, tracers, or copying images all take away such opportunities.

2. **Encouragement** – some students need prompting and a great deal of encouragement to create their own images until they have gained confidence in their image development skills.

3. **Acceptance** - teachers must accept the imagery that matches the age and development stage of the students. That might mean accepting scribbles from very young children. The development in drawing skills and image development skills will progress only if the early efforts are accepted. "If a thing's worth doing, it's okay to do it poorly. Otherwise, you'll never give yourself permission to be a beginner at a new activity" (von Oech, 1990, p. 146).

4. **Positive Feedback** – appropriately respond to students' early efforts so that they will be encouraged to continue and their confidence can be built.

5. **Enthusiasm** – students learn through modeling and will become enthusiastic about creating their own images when the teacher values that skill and is enthusiastic about art, and about the students' potential, and the resulting artworks.

6. **Guidance** – as students progress, particularly when they reach the Realism Artistic Development Stage, suggestions and specific instruction may be needed to help the students progress with their image development skills.

7. **Variety** – providing students with a great deal of variety of art processes, subjects and challenges will address their varying interests and preferences, and thereby provide essential motivation.

8. **Motivation/Preparation** – the challenge and anxiety of facing a blank page, of thinking of what to create, will be minimized when the teacher provides some image development preparation, such as key questions to trigger memories, or visual references for observed subjects, or intriguing scenarios for creating through imagination.

Some Activities Working with Images

The following suggested activities can be helpful explorations with image development for pre-service teachers or for their students. During these exercises, attention is given to the potential image, the essence of any artwork.

- Each person is given an assortment of coloured shapes of paper, varying shapes, sizes and colours, but the same set for each individual. Working on a blank piece of paper, arrange the paper pieces to create a picture, a composition, a design. Compare each other's images. Discuss variations possible with same starting pieces. Refer to the elements and principles of art and design, then create new compositions by changing the paper pieces to create specific effects, such as a center of interest, formal balance, or movement.

- Use a viewfinder to select an image while looking at a portion of the room, at a landscape, at a still life arrangement. Move the viewfinder to change the image, move the viewfinder in all ways possible including its distance from the eye. Consider all the possible images from one setting. Determine which is the most effective image and why.

- Search magazines for pictures of jewelry, examining the range of images. Choose a particular type of jewelry, such as a ring, watch, lapel pin, necklace, pendant, earrings, bracelet, hair barrette, etc. Design a new piece of the chosen type of jewelry to match a particular generation, era, or style. Other items could be used rather than jewelry, such as cars or furniture.

- Each person will work with one of the many possible image development strategies, selected by drawing names from a hat. Everyone will work with a selected image that is displayed, but will create a new image by manipulating the starting image using the selected image development strategy.

- Include dialogue in the image development process. A small group of classmates can discuss or critique each other's artworks at an early stage of creation to consider if other options or refinements might be useful.

Image Development Activities for Students

Art education involves students creating images that are meaningful to them. Art education is not about completing pre-planned projects that involve someone else's image. It is not possible for those images to be personally meaningful to students when they did not create the images themselves. In order to provide art activities that result in personally meaningful images, students need to be given topics or challenges that require thinking as they develop their unique images. The following list provides some examples of image development starters. These suggested activities are only brief descriptions here, and will need to be fully developed into lesson plans. Variations of these ideas are possible, and may allow for the customization needed to suit the age of students or the class situation.

- Have the students do a drawing or painting of this topic: "The police are coming! What is happening?" Students will choose to do different things with this topic based on their varying experiences with this topic, or based on their imagination about the kinds of events police have to attend.

- Ask students to recall their own experiences related to a variety of topics, then to create images from those experiences, such as: - the most frightening thing to me would be…, my favourite movie is…, if I could invite a famous person for dinner, it would be…, my hero is… because.

- Provide opportunities for students to discuss, research, and then create images related to social issues, such as poverty, the environment, loneliness, or racism.

- Students can give their personal interpretations of topics such as my best adventure, my ideal house, my favourite alien friend, or my innovative vehicle.

- In a similar way, have the students think about and create images from the following topics:
  - Someone who is sad, and why
  - A group of people each with something different in their hands
  - People in a circle
  - People gathered but each arrived by different means
  - A memory of cats
  - What I saw when I reached the top of the mountain
  - The strangest person I have ever seen

Motivating for Image Development

For many students, having to create a work of art from a blank piece of paper or a pile of raw materials is an intimidating and daunting task, enough so that many are reluctant to start, and many are unhappy with what they do put down. Teachers need to stimulate the imagination and get the students to the point where they can't wait to get their hands on the materials. Teachers can help students over the "blank page" hurdle by providing experiences, inspirations, and challenges to trigger thinking and imagining. Some of the ways in which teachers can provide the pre-image development preparation that will 'fire their imaginations' include:

- Tell a story without showing the book illustrations so that pictures can form in their minds, from which they then illustrate some aspect of the story, or create an entirely new image. The same could be done with poems, plays, and other literary works.

- The lyrics of some songs may provide a starting point for creating an image. An instrumental piece of music could stimulate image development.

- Experiences provide great material for image development. Sometimes teachers are able to provide such experiences, such as field trips, special quests in the classroom, or special activities.

- Movies, pictures, films and a host of other pictoral resources may provide the basis of an image.

- Characters, whether actual people, pets, wild animals, alien creatures or any host of imaginary characters could be represented in images.

- Collaborative image development can be an effective alternative to individual art making.

- Challenges of all sorts can trigger the students' imagination for image development, and result in a unique image. One such challenge might be to create an image that shows what the characters in a chosen painting are looking at.

- Some of the preparation for image development might include a brainstorming and discussion session related to a specific topic.

- The materials or the art process itself might trigger ideas for creating images. Simply make a random start with the chosen materials and techniques, respond to the start, add to and alter until a final image is achieved.

- The use of visual reference may be helpful to the students' image development. The visual reference might include photographs taken of the subject, looking directly at the subject, or more subtle influence from other artworks. Rather than directly copying the other artwork or the photograph, the student may refer to them in order to get the required visual information needed to complete a new image.

- Visualization can be prompted by providing descriptive scenarios and action.

- Students' image development will be greatly facilitated and will result in richer final images when teachers provide pre-image development preparation.

Conclusion

Teachers have the opportunity to take the mystery out of image development for their students, but maintain the magic. The value of creative image development directly leads to creative thinking, a major goal for education. "The function of art education is to provide opportunities for creative experience" (Hausman, 2010). Fortunately, there is currently a renewed interest in creativity in art education (Marshall, 2010). Working directly with learning outcomes related to image development; planning for the image development stage of the art activities; providing opportunities for students to create their own images; facilitating image development skills; and providing pre-image development preparation are all ways in which teachers can nurture their students' creativity.

References

Albers, P. (1999). Art education and the possibility of social change. *Art Education, 52*(4), 6 – 11.

Changar, J. (1992). *"Time…. pieces" curriculum resource packet*. St. Louis, MO: Craft Alliance.

Eisner, E. (1998). *The kind of schools we need*. Portsmouth, NH: Heinemann Press.

Gaitskell, C., Hurwitz, A., & Day, M. (1982). *Children and their art: Methods for the elementary school.* New York: Harcourt Brace Jovanovich.

Hausman, J. (2010). An almost forgotten 1953 conference on creativity. *Art Education, 63*(2), 6-7.

Marshall, J. (2010). Thinking outside and on the box: Creativity and inquiry in art practice. *Art Education, 63*(2), 16-23.

Ministry of Education. (1985). *Elementary fine arts curriculum guide/resource book*. Victoria, BC: Ministry of Education Curriculum Branch.

Schinneller, J. (1968). *Art search and self-discovery*. Scranton, PN: International Textbook Company.

Von Oech, R. (1990). *A whack on the side of the head*. Menlo Park, CA, Warner Books.

Zuk, B. & Dalton, B. (1997). Expanding our vision of image development. In Irwin, R. L., & Grauer, K. (Eds.) *Readings in Canadian art teacher education* (pp. 115-124). Boucherville, QU: Canadian Society for Education Through Art.

CHAPTER 14

Exploring the Elements of Art

Heather A. Pastro
*with visual resources
by : Laura Mann*

Learning about the elements of art is critical to the understanding of art and the language of vision. The elements of art are Line, Shape, Colour, Texture, Form, Value and Space. It is essential for students and teachers to have a good working knowledge of these elements and be able to apply that knowledge when viewing, creating, and discussing works of art. Furthermore, students need to be able to see these elements in their own work and the work of others, and be competent in visual and oral expression of the elements of art. What follows is a description of lesson planning ideas that may be used to teach elementary students about the elements of art.

Creating a Visual Resource Collection

A particularly successful project is the creation of a set of images or posters that describe the elements of art. This activity allows the student to create a collection of seven visual aids – one for each of the elements of art. This collection can be presented as a series of seven posters or PowerPoint slides. Both are illustrated here and should be referred to as one reads the remainder of this article. The student should go through a process of collecting images from a variety of different sources – magazines, calendars, books, the internet, etc; and incorporate these images onto the posters. This collecting process is critical as it encourages the student to make meaningful decisions about the choices of images. One of the requirements is to include at least one artwork created by the students themselves. It is recommended that at least three to five images are used on each poster. There may be text that is presented on the front and the back of the posters. The text component of the posters is for use by the teacher, but also will be viewed by the learner. For example, it is suggested that the definition of each element be formed in a manner that will allow the learner to understand the element, especially in combination with the images presented on the posters. The lesson ideas are for the benefit of the teacher – they are the activities that would be taught in the classroom to accompany the posters and further the student's understanding of each element. It is suggested that a lesson idea be written for primary and for intermediate levels.

These posters/images are a rich and rewarding resource in the classroom, both for teachers and for learners. They can be displayed permanently and referred to at any time, or in other situations, they can be brought out as needed for a specific lesson. The possibilities are endless, but the benefits are definitely invaluable, especially in terms of increasing the visual literacy of the teacher and the student. The more often that the posters are utilized in reference to discussion about the specific elements of art, then the learners' knowledge and understanding of that element increases. It is a very rich and rewarding experience as an art teacher to witness students engaged in conversations about the elements of art when they are viewing, creating, or discussing art. This level of knowledge and understanding is so important for their own growth as an artist and also for their appreciation for the work of others.

Preparation for a Lesson in the Elements of Art

Materials

- Sources of images: magazines, calendars, books, the internet etc.
- An assortment of art supplies such as crayons, felt pens, paint, etc.
- Bristol board or similar card stock
- Scissors
- Glue

Processes

The student works through a process of collecting images from a variety of different sources – magazines, calendars, books, the internet, etc. Throughout this exercise, students are creating, communicating, perceiving, and responding. Students are also making decisions and thinking critically.

The Assignment

Create a visual aid for each of the following Elements of Art:

- Colour
- Shape
- Texture
- Value
- Line
- Form
- Space

Images/Illustrations

- You may use real examples that you have made, or examples made by children, or images generated by computer, or pictures from books, magazines, or calendars, or other sources.

- Be creative in the use of images, but make sure that they are good examples and clearly define the element.

- Consider choosing images that will be of interest to children.

- Use many different images to define the element as this will help in clarity and understanding (at least three to five images for each element).

- Consider choosing images relating to a theme or topic (i.e. Canadian Art, Children's Literature, Animals), etc.

Text

- All text should be typed and/or computer generated.

- Be very neat and professional with all text and written work.

- Use bold headings. Keep text simple and accurate.

- Include at least one lesson idea/activity for primary students and one lesson idea/activity for intermediate students to accompany each element. This can be written in point form.

- Include the definition of each element on one side of the poster.

Layout/Design

- Present visuals and text in an organized format.

- Create these posters as a collection, so you may consider a theme approach or some sort of unifying device.

- Use borders to define edges.

- Cut out all examples neatly to create a professional appearance.

- Present your artworks in a finished format: i.e., mounted and free of ragged edges/pencil marks, unplanned borders.

Evaluation Criteria

Visuals: Examples of Colour, Shape, Texture, Value, Line, Form, Space.

Text: Headings - Bold, clear, easy to read.

Lesson idea/activity: specific and clear.

Definition: clear language that is accurate, yet concise.

Generally, your work should demonstrate the following:

1. Evidence of imaginative and creative thinking through the choice of images.

2. Sensitive appreciation of the medium at hand and its expressive potential, through original artworks.

3. An awareness of, and a feeling for, the language of vision and the elements and principles of design, as demonstrated in the layout and presentation.

4. An understanding of and ability to articulate the language of vision in artworks.

Images/Illustrations: relevant, interesting, appropriate, good variety

Presentation/Organization: professional, applicable as a teaching tool, creative, neat layout and design, interesting.

Resources

K-7 Visual Art I.R.P., British Columbia Ministry of Education

LINE

The path of a point moving in any direction

Thick or thin, bent or straight, broken or solid,
Angular or curvy

Creates an infinite number of configurations

Defines the edges or boundaries of shapes and
forms

SHape

A two-dimensional image created with lines

Composes two images:
The positive (inside) and negative (outside)

Regular or geometric examples are
rectangles, ovals, trapezoids

Irregular or organic examples are
a paint spill, the outline of a lake on a map,
an unusual puddle

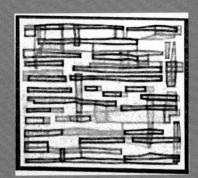

An actual or simulated appearance

Evokes the sense of touch

Suggests rough, smooth, bumpy, grainy, prickly, fluffy, hard

space

The illusion of depth and/or form on a two-dimensional surface

Techniques used to suggest depth are perspective, overlapping, and variation of size

Extension Activities

Line

Using tempera paint, make lines of different colours covering a piece of paper. Consider thin, thick, straight, curved, short, overlapping lines to create a non-objective painting.

Shape

Create a dramatic abstract collage with shapes. Cut out many different organic shapes including flower shapes and leaves. Cut out a large geometric shape which will be the vase in this collage. Arrange the shapes on white paper, then glue the pieces down, overlapping the shapes. When it is dry, cut around all the shapes and glue the collage on black paper.

Form

Cut from magazines, pictures illustrating different forms from nature and architecture. Arrange the pieces on a piece of cardboard and glue down in an interesting and creative way.

Colour

Using tempera paint, make a colour wheel. Draw a large circle on a piece of paper, then draw twelve circles or squares evenly spaced around it for the three primary colours, red, yellow, and blue, the three secondary colours, green, orange, and violet, and the six intermediate colours, red-violet, blue-violet, blue-green, yellow-green, yellow-orange, and red-orange. (For variation and interest, draw the outlines of animals or flowers instead of circles or squares.)

Value

Using only black and white tempera paint, paint five or six 4 x 6 inch pieces of paper in different values of grey. Make a collage by arranging and gluing the shapes on a larger piece of paper (ground.)

Texture

Using a rough object as the subject for a rubbing or frottage, use crayon to pick up the texture, then paint the paper with tempera paint. The crayon resists the paint, creating an interesting textural painting. Cut out or tear pieces of paper, from your rubbing, in different sizes and make a parrot from the shapes. Glue the pieces down to make a textural collage on black paper.

Space

Cut out people shapes, dog shapes, flower, or fruit shapes from different coloured paper in different sizes. Cluster them together in groups on a white piece of paper placing the larger ones below or on top of the smaller ones or both. You have developed a sense of space. Glue down after you have achieved a pleasing arrangement.

The lightness or darkness of any colour

Bright, dark, light, and muted
are some terms used
to describe the
value of a colour

Three-dimensional:
forms occupy space or give the illusion of
occupying space

Created with sculpture, photography,
papier-mâché, glass, etc.

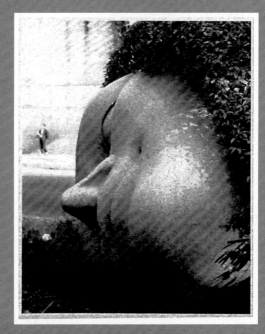

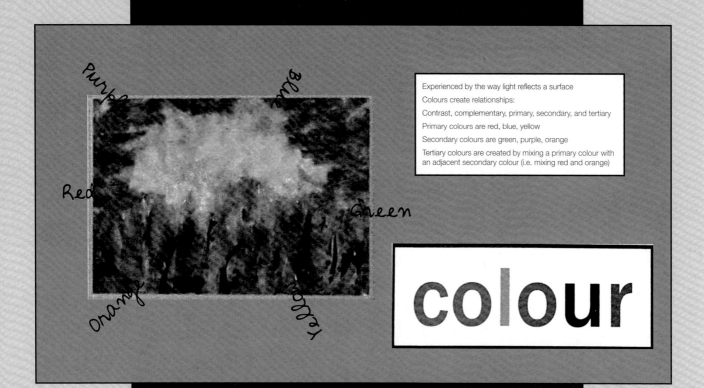

Purple

Blue

Red

Green

Orange

Yellow

Experienced by the way light reflects a surface

Colours create relationships:

Contrast, complementary, primary, secondary, and tertiary

Primary colours are red, blue, yellow

Secondary colours are green, purple, orange

Tertiary colours are created by mixing a primary colour with an adjacent secondary colour (i.e. mixing red and orange)

colour

CONNECTIONS, REFLECTIONS AND CREATIONS

CHAPTER 15

Making Meaning
with Holiday Crafts

Aileen Pugliese Castro
Juan Carlos Castro

Photo by Hilde Vanstraelen

Recently we received an email from a former teacher candidate who was completing her long practicum. In her email she asked a common question often raised by teacher candidates working in elementary schools.

Teacher Candidate: Hi Aileen, My practicum is going well but it is pretty exhausting. I just learned that I have to do a lesson on picture framing for mother's day and my budget is pretty low and I am not sure how to go about it. I thought about popsicle sticks, but my kids are in grade 4 and 5 and I want it to look presentable. How can I make this a success?

There is a lingering problem with contemporary elementary art education, in the context of generalist classrooms, where art is equated with a certain conception of craft, product, and decoration (Smith, 1995). It is a conception of art education that is about highly contrived and predetermined "make-and-take" projects that are supposed to represent complex ideas about family, religion, culture and personal experience in a few simple steps. Many of the art activities that happen in classrooms usually center around using "crafty" or step-by-step "cookie cutter" approaches. They also are centered thematically around holidays that often end up stereotyping religion, culture, gender, and race. Rather than just replace craft and holiday art with an approach that is focused solely on fine art, aesthetics, and design (Greer, 1993), we propose that elementary contemporary art and craft practice such as DIY culture, craftivism, and sustainability offer a way to rethink, repurpose, remix and recycle materials and ideas in the elementary art classroom. It is not just about making pretty things, but rethinking our relationship to meaning and objects (Gude, 2004).

In the email, this teacher candidate was struggling with not only financial limitations but the complexity and diversity of her students. How many students do single parents raise? How many students have two mothers? And when it comes to holidays, how many students celebrate Christmas or Easter? We live in complex times where the diversity of cultures, beliefs, and personal experiences of students are not the same. In this chapter we explore ways to rethink relationships, meaning, and materials that honor the diversity of our classrooms.

From Holiday Crafts to Asking Meaningful Questions

The holidays are coming and what are we going to make this year? This was a common question asked of us by our colleagues early on in our careers. There are expectations that art in the elementary art classroom is about making holiday crafts to celebrate holidays (Stankiewicz, 2004; Stokrocki, 1986a, 1986b). And in our culture crafts have been commonly associated with holidays. A visit to any craft store during the more traditional western holidays will confirm this phenomenon. There are many issues regarding holiday crafts, such as creating gifts for family members, costumes to represent ethnic holidays, or decorations to show a festive spirit. Teachers have been faced with these issues for years. To what extent can we celebrate Halloween, Christmas, Valentine's Day or Mother's Day? The major issue arises from the fact that our classrooms are made up of diverse cultures, religions, race, gender, and family structures. In our experience some parents will protest the celebration of Halloween because of the costumes, or Christmas because of the family's religious beliefs. Again, even on Mother's Day some families don't have a mother in the home.

How can the holidays be opportunities to both celebrate diversity and build meaningful connections between our students? Instead of asking students to construct a predetermined solution to a teacher-centric assumption about religion, culture, or personal experience this can be an opportunity for students to share, explore, and understand their own local context and experiences. It is also an opportunity for students to research the history, differences, and evolutions of their cultural heritages (Stokrocki, 1997).

Returning to the example of Mother's Day frames we start by asking ourselves: what is a picture frame? What does it mean to frame something? What does framing signify? What will be framed? Who are my students? Where do they come from? Do they have a mother in their lives? What does it mean to be a mother? Who cares for them? How can this be more than just about someone's mother expanded to include the role of women in our lives? From this kind of questioning we can begin to move our teaching towards big ideas (Walker, 2003), and meaningful inquiry (Gude, 2007). It is about expanding our interpretive frames to reconsider our relationships to meaning and objects (Castro, 2007). The kinds of questions we need to ask should reference the personal history and experiences of our students while prompting opportunities to meaningfully connect those histories to present conditions and contexts. We should also make clear that the kinds of questions and meaning making in the classroom should be about cultural and ethnic stereotypes. We can avoid this stereotyping by constructing questions and inquiry that asks students about their specific experiences.

In the example of Mother's Day perhaps we could ask: Who are the women in our lives who have cared for us and how can we recognize their specific contributions to our lives? How can we create a visual representation of a special artifact from this person? Instead of assuming that we all have a mother caring for us, we ask: who are the women in our lives and how have they cared for us? This expands the lesson to create a space for our students to respond without feeling that their differences exclude them from being what the curriculum describes as being "normal."

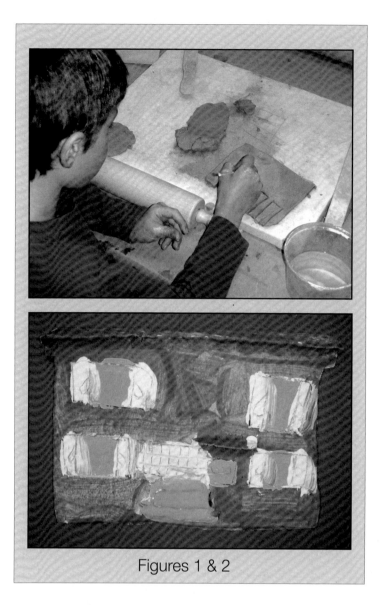

Figures 1 & 2

Figures 3

Making Meaning From Our Materials

The other dimension of holiday crafts in elementary art education is how we understand and define craft. The mention of crafts in the context of elementary art and what comes to mind are popsicle sticks, cotton balls, felt, and paper plates used to make hand turkeys, Santa Clauses, and Easter bunnies. The Oxford English Dictionary (Craft, n.d.) definition states *craft* as "an activity involving skill in making things by hand" (¶ 2). Its origins come from the German *kraft* meaning strength and skill. Although glueing cotton balls to pre-cut bunny rabbits is technically making something by hand it trivializes the potential for everyday materials to be assembled in meaningful ways. Considering the metaphorical value of materials and assembling them in ways that consider relational meaning our students can understand that all materials and objects can be assembled to

136

create meaning (Marshall, 2008). We think with and through metaphors every day (Lakoff & Johnson, 1980) and it is possible to teach deliberate metaphorical thinking in elementary art classrooms. One important characteristic for teaching metaphoric thinking through art making is allowing students to research and self-select materials (Castro, 2004). This includes materials that are found outside the classroom. Having the ability for students to select their own materials to assemble gives students ownership and autonomy over their decisions as they inquire into their experiences and ideas.

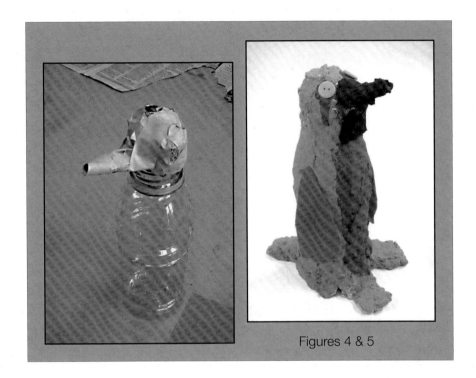

Figures 4 & 5

Understandings of craft are changing from the well-made and holiday art to forms of public and social activism. The rise of D.I.Y. cultures and movements such as craftivism signal a shift in how we use, repurpose, and engage with material culture. D.I.Y. or Do It Yourself is making and repurposing things that are personally relevant, meaningful and address a need in one's life (Lupton, 2006). Craftivism engages the public in rethinking social or political issues (Greer, 2007). Graffiti knitting, where craftivists interact with public spaces through knitting things such as parking meter cozies and signpost sweaters are examples of rethinking what is considered craft, art, and activism. What both the D.I.Y. and craftivism movement do in the context of this chapter is present opportunities for elementary art teachers to rethink what materials we use and how we use them. Using recyclable materials like bottle caps, cardboard, bottles, jars, cans, and paper prompts our students to see how everyday materials can be transformed. Given the current state of our environmental crisis and the ever-growing rise of disposable products, we need to provide opportunities to think about what we use differently.

Figures 6 & 7

Again, we return to the example of Mother's Day picture frames and ask: Do picture frames need to be made from wood? Does the closest approximation to a wood picture frame need to be popsicle sticks? What are the materials that are meaningful in the lives of our students? How can they be used to create works that rethink the relationship of materials and meaning? We have suggested to our teacher candidates that instead of spending money on popsicle sticks, foam, and other materials from the craft store, to look for recyclables in the school that could be used instead. Could the students choose materials from home that are significant to the woman in their life? Are there old cards, fabric scraps, or other everyday disposable artifacts that are either metaphoric or artifacts from their significant woman or mother? Then we asked again what is the purpose of framing and what materials support, highlight, and portray what is special to this person? This is a process of dialogic conversation between students, teachers, materials and meaning. By expanding our frame of reference, perspectives, and the experiences of our students, we hope to create a space that values the visual expression of our students.

Figures 8

Summary

We are not advocating for a removal of all celebrations throughout the school year. Rather, what we suggest is a rethinking of what it is we celebrate, how we celebrate it, and who it is that is celebrating with us. Our classrooms today are rich with a diversity of experiences and cultural backgrounds. By asking ourselves: What are the big ideas behind why we celebrate? How can the many diverse experiences in our classrooms be represented? By asking these questions we hope to move away from monocultural activities and viewpoints, consider how everyday materials in our lives can be repurposed experiences for celebrations, events and holidays, remixed, and assembled into meaningful metaphors.

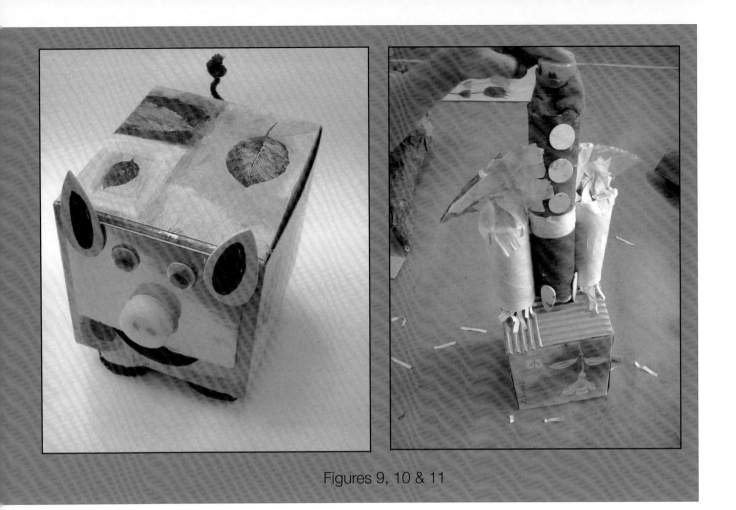

Figures 9, 10 & 11

Figures

Figures 1 & 2. Using air drying clay and tempera paints, young artists (6-8 years old) create portraits of where they live.

Figure 3. Instead of a Christmas holiday scene young artists (4-6 years old) were asked to consider their favorite winter memories. It was up to the child to select and incorporate their own materials to bring this winter wonderland to life.

Figure 4 & 5. Young artists (6-8 years old) recycled plastic bottles to make penguins. Sculptamold was added on like icing and they created Pop Penguins inspired by Andy Warhol and the children's book *And Tango Makes Three* by Parnell and Richardson.

Figure 6 & 7. How Am I Feeling Puppets inspired by *Where the Wild Things Are* by Maurice Sendak (1988). Young artists (4-6 years old) were asked to make expressions of how they were feeling today on the front of a flat paper bag. Inspired by the textures on the characters from the book, the young artists created their own textures using a variety of paper techniques such as crumpling, tearing, folding, curling, etc. They also used additional found materials to embellish their puppets with hair and arms.

Figure 8. It just snowed in our city! What would a snow person look like if it was made by Pablo Picasso? Starting with squares of white foam core, young artists (4-6 years old) selected from a variety of materials to create their interpretation of the question.

Figure 9, 10, & 11. Recycling disinfected square tissue boxes, young artists (6-8 years old) were asked to re-imagine what a box could be. The children's book *Not a Box* by Antoinette Portis was used to stimulate an inquiry to look at everyday objects differently. The book begins with the main character, a rabbit, sitting in a box. On the next page the rabbit used its imagination to turn that box into something new like a race car, or a hot air balloon. The story is used to encourage young artists to turn their boxes into something new. They used found objects that would normally be thrown away or may not be recyclable to build their "not a box."

Figure 12 & 13. Limited budgets can be an issue for many teachers. Young artists (6-8 years old) were asked to bring in objects from home that they may recycle or throw in the trash. In this example, young artists were asked to bring in a cereal box from home. It was used to create cereal box weavings.

139

Resources

Books

Augatis, D. (2010). *Brian Jungen*. Vancouver, BC: Douglas & McIntyre. A catalog of artist Brian Jungen works. He is known for his innovative remixes of aboriginal and contemporary culture using everyday materials like sneakers, golf bags, and plastic chairs.

Berger, S., & Hawthorne, G. (2005). *Ready made: How to make (almost) everything: A do-it-yourself primer*. New York: Clarkson Potter. A Do It Yourself resource for rethinking the uses of everyday materials.

Edgar, D., & Edgar, R. (2009). *Fantastic recycled plastic: 30 clever creations to spark your imagination*. New York: Lark Books. A how-to book on using recyclable materials to make animals, masks, planes, and more.

Lupton, E. (Ed.). (2006). *D.I.Y.: Design it yourself*. New York: Princeton Architectural Press. A Do It Yourself resource of how to create, customize, and design everything from t-shirts to websites.

Lupton, E., & Lupton, J. (2007). *D.I.Y.: Kids*. New York: Princeton Architectural Press. A Do it Yourself resource for children.

Montano, M. (2008). *The big ass book of crafts*. New York: Simon Spotlight Entertainment. A book for rethinking everyday materials through innovative combinations.

Parnell, P., Richardson, J., & Cole, H. (2005). *And Tango makes three*. New York: Simon & Schuster Children's Publishing. A children's book based on a true story of two male penguins who raise their own child.

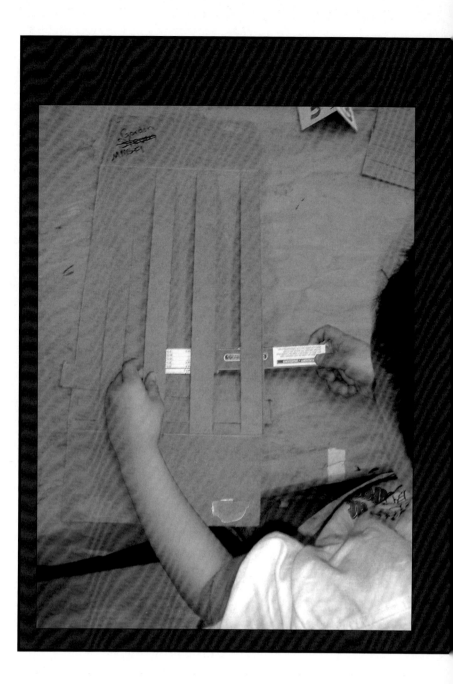

Websites

Craftzine http://craftzine.com/ From the magazine *Craft*: transforming traditional crafts, a blog full of innovative craft how-to articles.

D.I.Y. Kids by Ellen & Julia Lupton: http://www.diykids.org/ Great ideas to get you started on doing D.I.Y. activities with children.

Inhabitat: Green design will save the world http://inhabitat.com/ A blog devoted to highlighting sustainable design.

Instructables http://www.instructables.com/ A D.I.Y. social network site committed to users sharing how-to guides on just about anything. Complete with image and video tutorials.

Makezine http://www.makezine.com/ From the magazine *Make: technology on your time*, a blog on how to make just about anything with a focus on D.I.Y. mechanics, digital technology, and electronics.

Figures 12, & 13

References

Castro, A. P. (2004). *Introducing metaphorical thinking to children*. Baltimore, MA: Maryland Institute College of Art.

Castro, J. C. (2007). Enabling artistic inquiry. *Canadian Art Teacher, 6*(1), 6-16.

Craft (n.d.). In *Oxford English Dictionary*. Retrieved May 16, 2010, from http://dictionary.oed.com

Greer, B. (2007). art+ craft = craftivism Retrieved May 11, 2010, from http://craftivism.com/definition.html

Greer, W. (1993). Developments in discipline-based art education (DBAE): From art education toward arts education. *Studies in Art Education, 34*(2), 91-101.

Gude, O. (2004). Postmodern principles: In search of a 21st Century Art Education. *Art Education, 57*(1), 6-14.

Gude, O. (2007). Principles of possibility: Considerations for a 21st-century art & culture curriculum. *Art Education, 60*(1), 6-17.

Lakoff, G., & Johnson, M. (1980). *Metaphors we live by*. Chicago: University of Chicago Press.

Lupton, E. (Ed.). (2006). *D.I.Y.: Design it yourself*. New York, NY: Princeton Architectural Press.

Marshall, J. (2008). Visible thinking: Using contemporary art to teach conceptual skills. *Art Education, 61*(2), 38.

Sendak, M., (1988) *Where the wild things are*. New York: Harper Collins.

Smith, P. (1995). Art and irrelevance. *Studies in Art Education, 36*(2), 123-125.

Stankiewicz, M. (2004). A dangerous business: Visual culture theory and education policy. *Arts Education Policy Review, 105*(6), 5-14.

Stokrocki, M. (1986a). A portrait of an effective art teacher. *Studies in Art Education, 27*(2), 82-93.

Stokrocki, M. (1986b). Expanding the artworld of young, elementary students. *Art Education, 39*(4), 13-16.

Stokrocki, M. (1997). Rites of passage for middle school students. *Art Education*, 48-55.

Walker, S. R. (2003). What more can you ask? Artmaking and inquiry. *Art Education, 56*(5), 6-12.

CONNECTIONS, REFLECTIONS AND CREATIONS

CHAPTER 16

Visual Journals in the Elementary Classroom

Kit Grauer

One of the ways that elementary teachers have found to help children record and reflect on their thinking is through the use of visual journals. Visual journals expand children's understanding using both images and words and are a daily feature in many classrooms. The visual journal moves beyond the writer's concept of a diary or writing journal by including thought expressed through images and moves beyond the artist's concept of a sketchbook by integrating images with words. This integration of image and text is complementary and interdependent, building on the thought processes familiar to children. As one child suggested 'I think my think and then draw it on paper.' Starting each day or each subject unit with drafting ideas in the visual journal allows children to capture their thinking and reflect upon it. This article will provide a brief introduction to the idea of a visual journal and possibilities for incorporating its use into the elementary classroom. A wealth of resources in the form of books or online websites and images can encourage even the most reluctant teacher to give daily visual journaling a try.

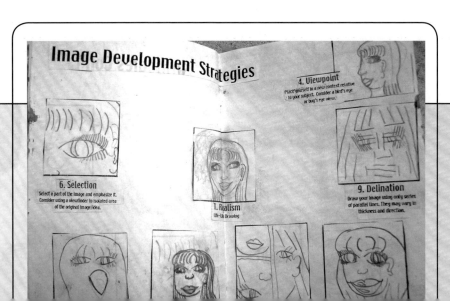

The idea of a visual journal is not new. Great thinkers across time have used some form of visual journals to observe, record, document and reflect on their ideas across a wide range of disciplines from science to art. Leonardo da Vinci is perhaps the most famous example of an artist/scientist who used what could be called a visual journal. Leonardo developed his habit of recording his studies in meticulously illustrated journals. These studies and sketches were collected into various codices and manuscripts, which are now collected by museums and individuals. A quick Google image search will provide hundreds of sources to see and discuss these amazing drawings. Many other famous inventors and artists used journals and sketchbooks that are available in print and online and can be used as inspiration for children. The list available later in the reference section of this article is by no means extensive. Teachers can search for local artists or artists' journals on line that call to the particular themes or communities that would inspire their students. Looking at artists' journals, children can see evidence of artists' thinking and in developing their own journals they see a record of their own ideas over time. Visual journals may also be known as: image journals, visual diaries, drawing and writing files, notated sketchbooks, visual thinking journals or workbooks. The name doesn't matter; it is the process of collecting ideas and images over time that does matter. The journal that that emphasizes creation values process over product and allows students to gain confidence in their own ideas (Pearse, 2007).

Why are visual journals valuable in the elementary classroom? For the individual child, they are records of process, evidence of their engagement with some aspect of their world. As teachers, we can see how each child's thinking changes and develops over the course of a school year (Fahey, 1996). Especially for young children, they can readily see how their ability to draw or write improves from their first entries to the end of their journal and how they can 'read' their journals through the use of their own growing symbol system. Visual journals allow the interplay between image and language, forms of expression that capture thought differently. Often a child's drawing or painting will trigger oral language that is far more eloquent than their written ability. Images are strong springboards for oral and written expression and act as a visual/linguistic record of thinking. The visual can also provide an immediacy that may not be as accessible as the linguistic. A child starts to scribble and draw long before they learn to write. Using the visual journal with an art activity first, can often lead to greater fluency in the written activity (see the article on Art and Writing in this book). Children learn to trust this way of processing information. Individual ways of working through visual problems and concepts in the visual journal should be respected (Grauer & Naths, 2001). Exploration and creation are individual processes and should be encouraged through regular activity (New, 2005).

Of all the information available to the teacher, visual journals provide us with the more personal evidence of a child's thinking. The form of the journal, its intimate scale and insistence on interactivity, connects the viewer to the 'artist' in a very personal way (Hall, 2000). When children express their ideas through drawings and other image making techniques, they often express emotive as well as conceptual understandings. Drawings are ways of noticing specific details, setting up compositions, and combining information from our eyes with images from memory and our imaginations. Some images come from the child's world, and some are based entirely in memory or creative imagination. Journal drawing differs from finished drawings in that sketches are intentionally vague or exploratory, encouraging reinterpretation upon revisitation (Szekely, 1982). They can be annotated, with color, collage or explanations, "to translate categorical information into depictive information" (Fish, Scrivener, 1990, p.121). Many of the drawings in a visual journal might be considered 'voluntary drawings' (Thompson, 1995), drawings that are made in response to a prompt, but with the topics freely chosen by the students. In this way, students use drawings to integrate their personal experiences with studies of their environment, or connect their understandings from various subject areas. Here the journal serves as a place to store these explorations and observations (Szekely, 1982). Visual Journals give us a glimpse of the ongoing life of a child, connected to the past and the future while working in the present. Moreover, they capture as Julia Cameron (2007) suggests, "an instantaneous form of meditation focusing on the worth of every moment. So often the great adventure of life lies between the lines, in how we felt at a certain time and in a certain place. This tool will help you remember and savour the passing parade" (pp. 299-300.) This combination of visual and text is very appropriate as evidence of learning , a picture is worth a thousand words and students can effectively encapsulate a number of things that they have learned within the immediacy of a visual journal.

Visual Journaling with your Students
Setting up an ongoing practice

Start with a blank book.   The books you use in your classroom should reflect the students who use them. Many teachers use the making of a journal the first activity thereby encouraging students to personalize their books. While it is always special for students to make their own journals, it is not necessary. Many dollar stores sell blank books that are inexpensive and have blank covers for embellishing. For those students or programs that can afford it, hard cover sketchbooks are an option that is sure to make the journaling experience feel like the creative process of a real artist. Visual journals can even be created from discarded atlases, colouring books or discarded books. Pages can be revisited, collaged, or blank paper can be partly glued on or into what is already there. We have found that finishing the cover art in a journal is best done after the journal has been in use for some time and the children are more experienced with possible art techniques and images they might want to express.

Include lots of materials and techniques to stimulate idea generation.   Encourage children to collect images from magazines or the internet , articles and images from newspapers, a variety of papers from tissue to construction and photo copied pictures, found objects, poems, quotes, text that can be collaged or used as the basis for adding drawing, painting, or printmaking. An envelope for these collections of each child can be stored in the classroom to be accessed at journaling time. Felt pens, inks, paint washes, fabric, crayon resist, or any artistic technique can be demonstrated and encouraged for the unique qualities that will inspire an image. Try text as pattern, repeat images through stencils, make a print from material, expand on an inkblot… Sometimes serendipity or lucky mistakes can help make connections and generate ideas that were not previously conceived. This is a place for process over product, allow children to take risks and experiment.

Use the journal regularly.   Encourage students to draft their ideas for writing, science or social studies projects or any school related work in the journal. You as the teacher can suggest prompts such as: combine any two animals together to create a new creature; what really surprises me is…; draw yourself the way others see you and another portrait the way you see yourself; look at the work of children's book illustrators and storyboard your own story. At some schools, a daily journaling time begins the day or follows recess or lunch. At this time it settles everyone into a more contemplative and focused activity. Demonstrate a technique, use a prompt or give students free time to explore their own themes. Asking students to date each entry allows them to see that a journey is a series of daily journal encounters and our life is a gift of accumulated moments captured to recall.

Set up opportunities for children to learn from each other and other artists. Too often we deny children the excitement of sharing their work with others under the guise of 'copying.' Setting up an environment where great ideas, images, techniques and surprises are encouraged, valued and shared is a natural and inspiring way to learn and encourages rather than discourages creativity. Children should learn by sharing their success and viewing their classmates' work on regular informal and celebratory basis, free of criticism and supportive of risks. It is also inspiring to see how adults have learned through process journals and sketchbooks not always viewing the finished art works. If you as the teacher share in journaling and sharing, so much the better but there are fabulous journals available on line and in book form.

Suggested Books and Websites to Get Started

Books

Cezanne, P. (1951). *A Cezanne sketchbook: figures, portraits, landscapes and still lifes.* New York: Dover.

Eldon, D. & Eldon, K. (1997). *The Journey is the destination: The journals of Dan Eldon.* San Francisco, CA: Chronicle Books.

Gregory, D. (2008). *An illustrated Life: Drawing inspiration from the private sketchbooks of artists, illustrators and designers.* Cincinnati, OH: HOW Books.

Kahlo, F. (1995). *Diary of Frida Kahlo.* (Carlos Fuentes, Trans.) City of Mexico: Banco de Mexico.

Robinson, G. (1995). *Sketch-books, explore and store.* Portsmouth, NH: Heinemann.

Shu. H. A. (Ed.). da Vinci, L. (author). (2005). *Leonardo's notebooks.* New York: Black Dog & Leventhal.

Sokol, D. D. (2008). *1000 journal pages: Personal pages and inspiration.* Beverly, MA: Query.

Someguy. (2007). *The 1000 journals project.* San Francisco, CA: Chronicle Books.

Thiebaud, W. (1987). *Wayne Thiebaud: Private drawings, the artist's sketchbook.* New York: Abrams.

Wolk, J. (1986). *The seven sketchbooks of Vincent van Gogh.* New York: Abrams.

Websites

http://www.1000journals.com   This is a collaborative web site that shows a wealth of images from literally thousands of people around the world. '1000 journals are traveling from hand to hand around the world. Those who find them add their stories, drawings, and pictures, and then pass them along in an ongoing collaboration.'

http://www.daneldon.org/journals   This site is especially inspiring for older children as it chronicles Dan's journals from age 15 to 22.

http://www.accessart.org.uk/sketchbook   One of many UK resources where sketchbook journals are encouraged-many great teacher ideas from making books to idea starters.

http://sketchbooks.org   This website gives artists a platform from which to display their work – by using it they can explore their own creative process while building links with others.

References

Cameron, J. (2007). *The Complete artist's way: Creativity as spiritual practice.* London: Penguin Books.

Fahey, P. (1996). Magic eyes: Transforming teaching through first grade sketchbooks, *Visual Arts Research*, 22(1) 34-43.

Fish, J. & Scrivener, S. (1990). Amplifying the mind's eye: Sketching and visual cognition. *Leonardo*, 23(1), 117-126.

Grauer, K. & Naths, A. (2001). The visual journal in context. *ARTicle: The Journal of Art Education Victoria*, 3(2), 29-33. Reprinted from Grauer, K. & Naths, A. (1998). The visual journal in context. *CSEA Journal*, 29(1), 14-19.

Hall, J. (2000). Sketchbooks and artists' books. In Addison, N., & Burgess, L. (Eds.). *Learning to teach art and design in the secondary school* (pp. 207-219). London: Routledge/Falmer.

New, J. (2005) *Drawing from life: The journal as art.* New York: Princeton Architectural Press.

Pearse, H. (2007). Sketchbooks, workbooks, visual journals: all in a days work. In Irwin, Rita L., Grauer, K. & Emme, M. (Eds.). (2007). *Re-visions: Readings in Canadian art teacher education (3rd ed)*. (pp. 224-231). Toronto, ONT: Canadian Society for Education through Art.

Sanders-Bustle, S. (2008). Visual artifact journals as creative and critical springboards for meaning-making. *Art Education*, 61(3), 8-14.

Szekely, G. (1984). A case for student sketchbooks. *Arts and Activities*, 96(3), 36-37.

Szekely, G. (1982). Creative learning and teaching of the gifted through sketchbooks. *Roeper Review*, 4(3), 15-17.

Thompson, C. M. (1995) "What should I draw today?" Sketchbooks in early childhood. *Art Education*, 48(5) 6-11.

Chapter 17

Learning in the Art Gallery
Essential Not Enrichment!

Often we think that it would be nice to enrich our art programs through field trips to our local art galleries or museums. I would like to suggest that such experiences are not an extra activity, any more than trips to the library are enrichment to our language arts programs or that reading is an enrichment to literacy. If regular visits to the library and a regular reading program are necessary to our language literacy, then visiting an art gallery or museum and viewing original works of art are equally necessary for our visual and cultural literacy. In this chapter, I will explain how visual literacy is developed and how educators can use visits to art galleries as an integral part of an art program. Further, I will discuss alternatives to traditional art galleries that provide students a broader exposure to the arts of other cultures within our communities. Finally, I will discuss how a school can set up its own art museum, similar to the school's library, in order that original works of art be available to teachers and students on a daily basis.

Visual Literacy: Learning to 'Read' through Art

'Literacy' is one of those nebulous terms which have powerful significance yet are not well defined. Often definitions of literacy conflict and there exists much misunderstanding about how literacy functions in our everyday lives. I propose the following definition for use in this discussion: The ability to understand all the symbol systems through which our society exchanges ideas and sends information, enabling the individual to communicate effectively, think critically, and participate fully in their culture. There are several assumptions about literacy embedded in this statement. The first assumption is that definitions of literacy limited to decoding are not adequate. Statistics Canada uses this decoding definition: "the skill to use everyday printed material at home, at work, and in the community." Literacy researchers like Tuman (1987) have identified that the individual not only decodes information, but creates meaning which is contextually dependent. Our definition of literacy assumes that literacy education requires learning to decode signs and to build meaning within the given context.

This leads to the second assumption that our definition makes: the 'signs' decoded in the literacy process are not restricted to printed texts. We assume, with Gardner (1985) that "there exist many kinds of symbol systems, many of which are not closely related and which can be conveyed through a multiplicity of media (p.39)." Eisner (1991) elaborates on this idea by identifying the object of the decoding process as the content of forms that are intentionally patterned, serve a purpose, have a history and a set of conventions.

By introducing notions of history and convention to the definition of literacy I propose, cultural context becomes an issue. Our definition assumes that literacy has a cultural component. Broudy (1990) defines cultural literacy as "the ability to construe the characteristics of a culture..." (p.10). This is important, for as the work of sociologist Bourdieu (1993) reveals to us, without access to the symbol systems of a culture, when one is unable to decode cultural 'forms' or 'construe the characteristics of a culture,' one is disenfranchised. Disenfranchisement means that one is unable to be proactive in determining the conditions of one's personal life or in the goals and values of one's community. Research by Johnson (1989) elaborates on the method of participation. She stresses that the learner needs to approach the cultural construction activity critically. She explains that cultural literacy requires "an active examination of the meanings, values and behaviours in a culture" (p.45). Johnson's concerns outline the final assumption on which our definition of literacy has been built: that literacy enables critical thinking and full participation in the culture.

Visual literacy focuses on the visual symbol systems of art and their role in literacy education. With Gardner and Eisner, I believe that visual art forms have an important role to play in the literacy process. With Bourdieu, I assert that the ability to participate in the symbol system is necessary for full participation in a cultural community. When Gardner (1983) describes the way in which the different intelligences function, he stresses that 'art' is not a separate intelligence, but a way of exercising an intelligence. This is significant to the issue of whether one simply constructs and decodes signs or whether one is involved in critically exploring meaning. The aesthetic manipulation of a symbol-system means that one is literate, that one is aware of the history and conventions (the culture) of that system (Eisner, 1985). This goes beyond simply the way in which symbols can be intentionally patterned. The notion of *reading* an image thus involves an aesthetic orientation to the symbol system that constructs meaning.

Cooper, in his book *Literacy: Helping Children Construct Meaning* (2000), identifies four principles of meaning:

1. Reading, writing, speaking, listening and thinking develop simultaneously as learners grow in literacy.

2. Individuals learn to read and write by reading, writing and responding to their reading and writing.

3. Prior knowledge and background are major elements in one's ability to construct meaning.

4. Comprehension is the process of constructing meaning by relating ideas from a text to one's prior knowledge and background.

The museum visit is vital to supporting visual literacy. Cooper stresses that students need to interact with 'real' texts. By 'real' Cooper means texts as they are found in the real, lived world of the students. He believes 'real' texts support literacy in three ways:

1. They motivate, captivate and engage the students;

2. They provide a natural base to develop and expand upon; and

3. It is easier to read and understand real texts than those contrived to 'fit' the learners level of literacy.

The art museum provides 'real' experiences of both visual and language-based symbol systems to the students. Art is seen within its real, lived context. An art exhibition is the 'real' text of the western visual arts community and works of art are found primarily in art museums in our culture. Festivals, celebrations, faith acts, architecture and the home provide real contexts for the art of other cultures. Thus, in order for students to engage with 'real' visual art symbols, field trips to sites where real art is found are not just nice, but are a necessity to a child's ability to learn through art.

Visiting Your Local Art Museum

Now that I have established the necessity for children to see art in the many real contexts in which it exists, I will explore how to incorporate the museum visit into the learning activities of the classroom. The first task is to review the curriculum objectives for the year, then to survey the educational programming offered by local art galleries and museums. Museums typically have three different kinds of programmes available: guided tours; self-guided tours; self-guided, self-directed tours.

Guided Tours

The first kind of programme, the guided educational tour, is developed by the museum and taught by a museum educator. Guided tours are usually between one and one and one-half hours in length. They usually combine looking with discussion, participatory and hands-on activities. Students will not only listen, but will talk, write, and draw. They might even engage in dramatic play, dance or music activities. Some museums are able to provide a studio component to the students' experience making the media and techniques of the artwork come alive.

Guided tours are usually developed in one of two ways. First, a museum may have standard programs that they offer regardless of the exhibitions on display. These programmes usually deal with basic formal, conceptual or historical concepts in art. For example, a museum programme may deal with colour, abstraction or Early Colonial art. They are excellent opportunities to explore universal issues within the art of a given culture. These programmes are often developed with a sensitivity to the provincial curricula and address learning objectives for grades one through six. Review the stated learning objectives for these programs to determine if any of the set programmes offered by an institution will meet the needs of your art programme.

Art museums also organize educational programmes specific to a temporary exhibition (an exhibition that remains at the museum for only a limited period of time). These programmes are often much more specific in their scope. The programme may introduce students to a particular artist, a particular artform or genre of work. These specific programmes are a wonderful way to explore particular concepts with which you may be less familiar or not able to explore at school. For example, an exhibition of work by Québécois sculptor and poet Gilles Mihalcean would allow students an opportunity to explore how artists use found objects to create poetic interpretations of the landscape. This understanding could be taken back to the school in a unit that develops the assemblage technique and the landscape genre in visual art. Interdisciplinary links could also be made to poetry in language arts. Although more specific to a given grade level, these programmes are also usually designed with provincial curricular requirements in mind. Teachers need to discuss this with the educator at the time of booking.

When planning a visit to an art museum, remember that the teacher and the educator are teaching partners. Teachers know their students' strengths and their limitations. They know the context into which the tour will be place within the art programme. Teachers need to discuss their expectations, teaching objectives, the concepts and skills that need to be addressed with the museum educator. Most museum education programmes will accommodate students' special needs as well. Teachers should visit the exhibition to be toured prior to the class's museum visit to ensure that the content supports the values represented by your school and community.

Self-Guided Tours

Some art museums offer tours that the teacher can lead. They can be of either standard tours or tours of temporary exhibitions. They will not, however, be taught by a museum educator. Instead, materials will be made available to teachers to enable them to teach the programme outlined. This might include written and audio/visual materials. The self-guided tour provides more flexibility for the teacher, enabling her to tailor the visit to her art programme and students' needs more closely than perhaps the guided tour would. It requires quite a bit of preparation on the teacher's part. Teachers planning a self-guided tour should plan to visit the museum before hand to familiarize themselves with the tour and to customize it as they find it necessary.

Self-Guided, Self-Directed Tour

A teacher may choose to visit a museum without the aid of a museum educator. This is appropriate when the teacher has sufficient knowledge of the work and when the art museum does not offer a pre-prepared programme that meets the needs of her art programme or the learning needs of her students. In order to develop a meaningful self-directed programme, the teacher must identify very clear learning objectives for the visit. Open-ended wandering of the museum will accomplish very little toward evolving the students' visual literacy. First, the teacher should visit the museum herself in order to be completely familiar with the work involved. The teacher may choose to focus on a particular exhibition or on particular works in several exhibitions, depending on the concepts she wishes to teach. Next, the teacher will develop learning activities that call on different learning styles, engaging the students in research, discussion, writing, drawing and performance activities. This will provide the students with a variety of entry points to the work, it will teach them a variety of strategies for 'reading' art. Below I outline some strategies teachers can use to plan tours for their classes. The advantage of a self-directed tour is that it will fit seamlessly into your own art programme. The disadvantage is that it requires a good deal of time and commitment to develop a successful experience for your students.

Incorporating The Museum Visit Into Your Classroom Teaching

Ideally, the museum visit is a development of learning that first occurs in the classroom. Students should engage in studio, research, or other related activities that build upon the concepts explored in the museum either prior to or after the visit. Such activities will link the museum tour to the art programme at school, creating a meaningful context for the field trip. These 'pre-tour' and 'post-tour' activities weave the learning engaged in at the museum into the work in the classroom. This is why it is so important for teachers to work with the museum educator or to evolve a self-guided or self-directed tour that responds to the classroom context.

In order to make this integration effective, teachers need to be familiar with some strategies for teaching in the museum, whether you are working with an educator or developing your own tour. I will review three models that I have found useful in developing programming in the art museum. The first is a model of aesthetic development proposed by Micheal Parsons (1987). Parsons' model allows us to understand that an individual's response to a work of art is subject to their level of development. The second is based on the research of Andrea Weltzl-Fairchild (1991) that examines the different states of aesthetic experience engaged in by viewers. It provides the understanding that viewers engage in different kinds of cognitive activities while experiencing an artwork. Finally, I will review the model of aesthetic interaction developed by Henry Birk Feldman (1981). Feldman's model is used widely by museum educators as a framework for touring. In understanding the developmental, cognitive and practical issues involved in interacting with works of art, teachers can confidently develop meaningful visits to art museums for their students.

Parson's Model

Parson's model of aesthetic development recognizes that different levels of sophistication exist in a viewer's response to a work of art. He identified five stages to aesthetic development, based within Piaget's model of cognitive development and Kohlberg's theory of moral development.

Stage one response is characterized by an egocentric approach to the work. The viewer is consumed by her own response and is unaware of the experience of others. That the experience of another might be different than her own is completely out of the question. The response is spontaneous and idiosyncratic; the viewer will happen upon the separate components of the work one at a time without understanding that each contributes to the creation of a whole.

Stage two responses seem to focus on the subject matter of the work. The work is about what is pictured, and that which is good is usually beautiful. Stage two viewers are aware that others are experiencing the work, but assume that everyone experiences the work as they do. The stage two viewer believes his perception to be the norm.

At stage three viewers understand that the subject matter points to the meaning of the work. They expect to find meaning in a work of art. They believe that meaning is derived from her subjective experience of the work. The stage three viewer is conscious that the work is affecting her; she is able to reflect on that affect. Further, a third stage viewer is beginning to be aware that a work may affect others differently than it affects herself.

The stage four viewer becomes aware that the medium of the work plays an important role in its significance. Stage four viewers understand that the medium is "an active partner…a collaborator with the artist, having its own potential, bigger than [the artist], a sea in which she fishes" (Parson, 1987, p. 49). This viewer is aware that the success of the work depends on the artist's ability to balance virtuosity of technique with exploration of content.

At stage four the viewer becomes aware that the meaning of a work of art is also affected by the art world. The norms and expectations of the arts community become meaningful to the viewer. He can now understand that a work of art exists as part of a larger dialogue about concepts of art.

The stage five viewer is aware that art is an abstract concept; that its nature is subject to philosophical debate. This is the stage wherein the different philosophical definitions of art evolve: art as expression; art as communication; art as social arbitrator; etc. The stage five viewer will explore a given work within this philosophical context. She will explore how a work represents a given definition or functions within a certain philosophical context. The stage five viewer may affect particular philosophical

attitudes to examine the work. She may view the work through a formalist, feminist, or Marxist lens. She may examine the work through each of these and compare the meanings achieved through this exercise.

What this model suggests is that an educator cannot expect a coherent theory of art from a viewer who is responding within the third stage. As with all developmental theories, Parson's model suggests teachers need to be aware of the kinds of experiences possible within a given developmental stage. Further, the teacher needs to lay the foundations for the learner to move from that stage to the next. For example, it might be expected that grade three students will be situated in the second stage of Parson's model. Therefore, the teacher can expect that the students will engage with the subject matter of the artworks. They will believe the meaning of the work is the subject matter pictured and that everyone experiences the work in a similar fashion. Grade three students will have a more successful experience with art if it is representational, with clearly articulated subject matter that points unambiguously to its content. For example, Ken Danby's work, *At The Crease* (1972), is a carefully rendered portrait of a goalie waiting expectantly to intercept a goal. The goalie, as subject matter, is also the content. *At The Crease* is a painting about the role of the goalie in hockey. In the next developmental stage, students will be able to understand that individuals may have different responses to the work, depending on their own experience. Teachers can lay the foundation for this development by exposing students to works with the same subject matters that point to obviously different meanings. For example, David Thauberger's *Niagra Falls at Night* (c.1985) and Thomas Davies's *Niagra Falls From Above* (c.1762). Although both works take the famous falls as their subject matter, the content of each work differs significantly. The former explores the notion of tourist attractions, the latter examines the sublimity of Nature. If a grade three class is visiting an exhibition the teacher might want to plan to engage in some of the following activities:

- Draw/write about what happened just before the pictured event or what will happen in just a few moments;
- Copy the picture, but change one of the pictured elements. Describe how this changes the meaning of the picture;
- Compare the depiction of similar subject matters in different works of art and describe how the meanings of each work differ.

152

Weltzl-Fairchild's Model

Andrea Weltzl-Fairchild (1991) discovered that viewers engage in different kinds of cognitive activities when viewing works of art. She found that viewers will engage in activities she characterized as *dreaming, play, metaphor and concept*.

When viewers dream they engage in an identification with the artwork. They associate aspects of the artwork with memories or experiences they have had. They will make statements like, "This reminds me of…" or "This makes me feel sad." While in the dream state, viewers will also make initial judgments; they will either 'like' or 'dislike' works. In order to support *dreaming* activities, teachers can provide students with activities that encourage free association. Some of these kinds of activities might include: spontaneous interpretative dance, matching a sound to the work or element of the work, creating titles for the works. Teachers can validate students' initial attraction or indifference to certain works by asking them to explore why they like or dislike the work. Students can choose a work they like very much and one they dislike. By comparing and contrasting the two works, students can explore their values, realizing that these are subjective and personal.

Viewers will also *play* with the work of art. In their imaginations, viewers will wonder how the work might look if it were different colours, if objects within the work were placed differently. They will muse about the subject matter. Viewers will compare works of art within the exhibition to one another. Teachers can encourage playfulness by asking students to re-create the works through drawing or collage activities that change the colours, shapes or position of elements. Students can engage in dramatic play or can compare works in a guided discussion.

When viewers begin to evolve meanings from their experiences, they are engaged in the *metaphor* state. Viewers will talk about what the piece means to them, not just what it reminds them of. Perhaps the piece reveals something new to the viewer about a feeling or a person or an object. Perhaps the viewer understands a social situation or an historical event in a new way. The viewer has discovered the metaphorical function of the work for herself. Teachers can support the evolution of metaphorical significance through activities in which students examine prior understandings and decide whether the work they are examining has led them to any new insights. Creative writing and dramatic play are often excellent ways of supporting this metaphorical activity.

During this state viewers are also re-examining what they believe art is and what museums are. Young children who entered the exhibition believing art is painting, may leave realizing that art can also be sculpture. Sophisticated viewers may leave coming to a new appreciation of the role of art in society. An important aspect of developing visual literacy is the evolution of these aesthetic concepts. Guided discussion and reflective writing can help students engage in these dreaming activities.

When viewers end their visit they will evaluate their experience. In the *concept* state, viewers will decide how and why the entire experience has been valuable to them. This is a deeper, fuller experience than the initial impressions of like or dislike elicited in the *dream* state. Teachers can lead students through an assessment of their visit by asking them to describe how the museum visit met their expectations, what they saw that they did not expect, what new things they learned during their visit. Concept activities will provide the teacher with an opportunity to assess the student's learning and to plan for future experiences.

Feldman's Model

In the 1980s, Feldman purposed a systematic approach to examining works of art that helps viewers focus attention and engage in meaningful looking. Feldman's model is comprised of five or six major activities: *First Impressions, Description, Analysis, Interpretation and Judgment.* Some viewers might also engage in *Research* between the analysis and interpretation activities. These six activities are characterized by different questioning strategies that a teacher can use to guide the students' interaction with the work of art.

First Impressions

- What does the work sound like?
- What is the temperature of the work?
- What adjective describes the work?
- What does the work feel like?
- How does the work make you feel?

Description

- What colours has the artist used?
- What shapes are used? Are they organic? Geometric? Representational? Abstract? Non-objective?
- What kinds of lines do you see in the work?
- What are the real textures of the work (the ones you can feel with your hand)?
- What are the implied textures of the work (the ones the artist wants to remind you of)?
- What is the range of values present in the work?
- What is the work made of?
- Is the work two or three dimensional?
- Is the work an object or a performance?
- Does the work stay the same or does it change?

Analysis

- What are the colour relationships in the work?
- What is the heaviest part of the image? What makes it that way?
- What is the lightest part of the image? What makes it that way?
- How has the artist balanced the composition?
- How has the artist arranged the parts of the image to lead our eye from one to the next?
- What parts of the image hold our attention the longest? Why?
- Does your eye move smoothly from place to place or does it jump from one place to the next? Why?
- How has the artist handled the materials?
- Are elements repeated in the work? What patterns or rhythms are created? How?

Research

- Who is the artist? When did s/he live? What other biographical details can you discover?
- Why did the artist make this work? Was it a commission? Was it a personal choice? Was it part of a body of work?
- What ideas about art was the artist interested in when s/he made the work?
- What inspired the artist to make this work?
- Was this work a new direction for the artist?
- Who curated this exhibition? Why was this exhibition organized? Is this a temporary or permanent exhibition? If temporary, will it go to other museums? Where has this exhibition been?
- What do the artist, curator or critics say about this work or exhibition?

Interpretation

- What is the main content of this work?
- What are the themes explored by this work?
- What stories does this work tell?
- What does this work reveal to you about its subject matter? Its content?
- What does this work reveal to you about the medium? The technique?
- What does this work reveal to you about this kind of art?
- What does this exhibition teach you about the artist? This kind of art?
- What does this exhibition teach you about artists? Art? Museums?

Judgment

- What are the successful aspects of this work? Why?
- What are the unsuccessful aspects of this work? Why?
- Do you want to see more work by this artist? Why or Why not?
- Do you want to visit this museum again? Why or Why not?

Putting It All Together

The three models I described address different aspects of a students experience with a work of art. How does a teacher synthesize these three different approaches into a coherent museum visit? Below is an outline that teachers can use to plan a museum visit that responds to the developmental, cognitive and practical issues involved in responding to works of art.

Developmental Issues:	Dream State Activities: (First Impressions And Description)	Play State Activities: (Analysis)	Research Activities:	Metaphor State Activities: (Interpretation)	Concept State Activities: (Judgment)
Stage(s) of Aesthetic Development present in my class:	Activities to address present stage(s):	Activities to address present stage(s):	Activities to address present stage(s):	Activities to address present stage(s):	Activities to address present stage(s):
Foundational Activities for next stage(s):	Activities for next stage(s):	Activities for next stage(s):	Activities for next stage(s):	Activities for next stage(s):	Activities for next stage(s):

Using Other Community Resources to Develop Your Own Program

I suggest that the teacher collect information about all the art galleries and museums, cultural centres and cultural activities within her community. Often, we are unaware of what is available for our students because we depend upon those institutions that provide educational programming to inform us of their activities. However, there are valuable resources in both the public and private sectors that can provide our students with meaningful, real 'texts' to support visual literacy.

For instance, shops that feature the work of indigenous artists and the arts of other cultures can provide the raw materials for a field trip. These sites do not usually have formal educational programs, however, the owners of these establishments are usually very knowledgeable about the work they sell. By visiting the shop beforehand and discussing the work with the owner, the teacher can learn the background information needed to develop an educational program.

Cultural centres and associations often have collections of art representative of the cultures they promote. Again, although no formal educational programming may be provided a meeting with the administrator of the collection can provide the teacher with context appropriate to her program.

Small museums and commercial art galleries often do not have educational programming either. Again, the teacher should not be put off if the site has works of art integral to students' learning. The directors and owners will be knowledgeable about the work and can provide the teacher with background that can be developed into an appropriate program.

Developing a School Art Museum

The school library is an invaluable source of materials to support learning in all the curricular areas and to promote reading. A school art museum can be equally valuable. Real works of art can provide students with source materials for visual literacy development, but also for work in all the curricular areas. A painting can be a source of information about social history, a geography lesson or even a math class. A sculpture may provide information useful within a physical education context or a science lesson. All works of art can support the language arts curricula when students talk and write about their experiences of them.

A school that wishes to establish a 'museum' will need a dark, dry space in which to store the works. Light can fade sensitive pigments and too much moisture can wreck havoc on any work of art. A storage closet fitted with shelves for three-dimensional work, racks for paintings and framed drawings and drawers for works on paper, jewelry and textile works will work well.

The school can collect original works through donations from parents, staff, or others associated with the school. Particularly fine examples of student work can be collected as well. The school does not want valuable works as students need to be able to handle them, study them, use them to learn. This is called a 'Study Collection.'

The collection should be catalogued through a simple filing system. I suggest a number be assigned to the work when it is acquired. This accession number is written in pencil or white marker on the object and is recorded on a card with a description of the work. When a teacher wants to use a work, she signs it out just as she would a library book, referring to the accession number.

155

A school art collection also offers students an opportunity to learn to how to organize exhibitions of art themselves, how to display the works effectively, how to create useful labels and didactic support materials. Works from the school collection could be combined with student work in an exhibition.

Concluding Remarks

Just as there is no substitute for books and other printed materials when students are learning to read, there is no substitute for the experience of real works of art when students are learning to make and view art. Each community in this country has some form of original work of art available for students to see. It may be held by a museum, a cultural centre, a private gallery or 'craft' shop. There are 'artmakers' in every community. They may be professional artists, commercial photographers, amateur artists and artisans. Parents and grandparents of students may have original works of art they are willing to share, including not only paintings and sculptures, but also textiles, jewelry, carvings, embellished home accessories. I urge teachers to find real works of art for students to work with. The benefits of the experience are worth the time it takes.

References

Bourdieu, P. (1993). *The field of cultural production: Essays on art and literature*. R. Johnson [Editor and Introduction]. New York: Columbia University Press.

Broudy, H. (1990). Cultural literacy and general education. *Journal of Aesthetic Education, 24* (1), 7-16.

Cooper, J. D. (2000). Literacy: Helping children construct meaning [Fourth Edition]. Wilmington, MA: Houghton Mifflin Co

Eisner, E. (1991). *The enlightened eye: Qualitative inquiry and the enhancement of educational practice*. New York: Macmillan.

Feldman, H. (1981). *Varieties of visual experience* [Second Edition]. Englewood Cliffs, NJ: Prentice-Hall.

Gardner, H. (1985). *Frames of mind: The theory of multiple intelligences*. New York: Basic Books.

Johnson, D. & Roen, D. (Eds.). (1989). Richness in writing: Empowering ESL students. New York: Longman, 1989.

Parsons, M. (1987). *How we understand art: A cognitive developmental account of aesthetic.* Cambridge, GB: Cambridge University Press.

Tuman, M. (1987). *A Preface to literacy: An inquiry into pedagogy, practice, and progress.* Tuscaloosa, AL: University of Alabama Press.

CHAPTER 18

Art Education for our Time
Promoting Education over Conservatism

Dónal O'Donoghue

Marina Abramovic: The Artist is Present
March 14, 2010 through May 31, 2010
The Museum of Modern Art, New York.

What does it mean to teach art in our time, in a time of great uncertainty?

Recently, at the Museum of Modern Art (MoMA) in New York, I encountered Marina Abramović's live art performance titled "The Artist is Present". As I write this chapter, several days after encountering the work, the performance continues to take place at the Museum, and can be watched online during Museum opening hours through a live stream from MoMA. "The Artist is Present" is the longest durational work ever mounted in a museum to date, and Abramović's longest performance: Beginning on March 14, 2010, the performance, which is staged in the Donald B. and Catherine C. Marron Atrium of MoMA, is a new work that runs until to May 31, 2010 – a total of seventy-seven days. It is one of several performances being staged on the occasion of the first retrospective exhibition of Abramović's work in the United States[1]. As I observed Abramović sit upright and motionless on a wooden chair at a wooden table[2], wearing a long dress that pools at her feet[3] and staring into the eyes of the audience member who sat opposite her about six feet away – a practice that she engages in for the duration of the seventy-seven day performance[4] – I once again found myself asking questions about Art and Education that have engaged me for some time: What does it mean to teach art in our time, in a time of great uncertainty? What does it mean to teach art in a society that is increasingly diverse, fluid, complex, unstable, depersonalized, globalized, and media-saturated, where 'everything is always constantly changing' and constantly being updated and reformatted? In what ways might contemporary artists and their practices help us, as art educators, to educate students for a constantly changing and unpredictable world; for a world where new horizons are always coming into view while old ones are disappearing without trace; for a world where new possibilities of living differently are offered? What should art education programs focus on, develop, trouble, and extend? What should an art education that is committed to educating students about and through art of their time look like? My questions come from a larger question: What does it mean to educate a public for a global world?

As an artist and educator, Abramović's performance invited me to consider how art education in schools might be considered otherwise and practiced differently. Because her work makes visible several issues that artists are grappling with in the opening decade of the twenty-first century, I believe it warrants our attention as educators. First of all, her performance, "The Artist is Present' challenges our traditional notions of what art is and what it does. Second, it challenges how we look at, experience, and interpret artworks. Third, her performance questions the codes of participation in art museums by altering the nature of spectator participation. For example, Abramović introduces the living, breathing artist back into the museum space as the object and subject of the artwork; museum-goers rarely get to encounter the artist in the flesh at the exhibition site, and almost never as an artwork in the show; viewers rarely get the opportunity to engage with the artist in the production of his/her artworks, especially in such a public way. While at the museum audience members encounter work that artists produced, artist are absent. As Jennifer Gross (2000) observed, "[In exhibition spaces] the viewer is more likely to be invited to look, read, and listen his or her way into art on display through the digestion of didactic information presented through a concise wall label, audio tour, or docent" (p. 1). Furthermore, Abramović's performance gives form to Nicolas Bourriaud's claim that "the exhibition is no longer the end result of a process, its 'happy ending' (Parreno) but a place of production" (Bourriaud 2005, p. 69). Abramović's performance insists that we ask different questions of art of our time – different from those that we have asked of works from the past. Jeffrey T. Schnapp and Michael Shanks (2009) maintain, "*Modes of engagement* is a more useful term for the task of analyzing the creation, placement, and circulation of cultural works" (italics in original, p. 148). This is especially true in the case of Abramović's performance, 'The Artist is Present'.

More importantly, Abramović's performance is not concerned with the production of a tangible, physical object or a representational form; rather, the performance is concerned with the production of relations and/or the reconfiguration of existing ones. Her performance deals with the interhuman sphere – with a relationship with oneself and the space of relationships between individuals (Bourriaud, 2005). In a city where people learn to avoid eye contact with strangers, Abramović's performance force individuals to stare back, to engage her through their eyes, and to search for connection and participate in meaning making processes in that moment. During the time that I spent at the performance, I noticed that individuals who sat opposite Abramović reacted in different ways. Of the three men who participated in the performance while I was present, one sat quietly and tears rolled down his face; another sat staring intently afraid of losing the intensity of the moment; while, a third, found it difficult to hold the stare and looked away. During that time, many individuals circulated the bounded space that was framed within a large rectangle of light, while others sat on the floor, and some

stood against the wall and looked on quietly. Following a sitting with Abramović, one young man, Dan Visel, reflected, "Time was passing, but I couldn't tell. The overwhelming feeling I had was that you think you can understand a person just by looking at them, but when you look at them over a long period of time, you understand how impossible that is. I felt connected, but I don't know how far the connection goes."[5] As Visel's testament makes clear, the viewer is drawn into a silent exchange requiring an engagement and oftentimes an emotional investment that renders him or her both a subject and object of the work. In the work, the self is always in a process of becoming, is always emergent, and continually in the making (Ellsworth 2005).

One could say that Abramović's performance, in addressing, and even perhaps demystifying, the awkwardness of making eye contact with a stranger (an awkwardness that leads to certain forms of alienation and anonymity) and holding it, offers new ways of being with the other – new forms of sociability – and new ways of understanding the self. Contrast this with the scenario where for the past several decades art education in schools has been primarily concerned with the production of the tangible, physical object that the producer – the student – produces, presents for assessment, and later takes home (or leaves in the art room to be thrown out at the end of school year) after it has been displayed in the classroom or in another public area in the school. As Dipti Desai and Graeme Chalmers (2007) remind us, "Art educators have traditionally rewarded technically talented individuals" (p. 9). In addition, Abramović's performance demonstrates that art isn't purely visual but rather multi sensory. As an artwork, it is just as absorbing because of the space in which it is performed with all its associated sounds, smells, interactions, expectations and histories. Furthermore, Abramović's performance challenges the very notion of the artist as a single producer of an artwork. Her performance relies on the participation of audience members in order for it to function as intended. Given how participants engaged in the work, Abramović's performance demonstrates that "looking is inherently framed, framing, interpreting, affect-laden, cognitive and intellectual" (Bal 2003, p. 9).

What challenges does Abramović's performance pose for the teacher who is planning art education learning experiences for his or her students for the time of the now? What opportunities do this work, and the many other examples of work artists are currently producing, offer to the teacher who wants to educate his or her students for the time of the now? Thirty years ago, Stan Madeja (1980) wrote, "In the majority of programs now in our secondary and elementary schools, we do not treat the visual arts as a discipline with a history, a level of quality, and a knowledge base that must be learned" (p. 24). Madeja (1980) argued, "We do not emphasize enough the importance of the art form or of the artist. Art in the schools is not taught as a discipline but becomes what Arthur Efland has called 'school art'" (24). For him, the most pressing issue for art education at that time was to find ways to make meaningful connections with the field and its parent discipline: Art. Thirty years later, this issue continues to be a pressing issue in art education, and one that needs to be addressed. In the past, I have found that teachers are not always quite sure where to start when it comes to introducing their students to art works made in the now, or encouraging and assisting students to take up making practices of contemporary artists. The teacher candidates and practicing teachers I have worked with over the years have taught me that the best place to start is with the artists' work; asking questions about the work, how it is conceived, worked out, made, shown disseminated, written

about, and taken up by the public is a good place to begin. Oftentimes, these questions were asked in the act of encountering a work. Other times, new and different questions were asked as a result of reading artists statements and their writings, as well as the writings of curators and critics. These questions led to new questions being asked about art learning and teaching at the elementary level, which suggested new instructional, interpretative, and pedagogical approaches to art teaching and learning. Following the French sociologist, Pierre Bourdieu (1993), we approach this work by taking into account everything that helps to constitute the artwork as it is experienced and understood. Bourdieu (1993) argues that a sociological analysis of art should examine the symbolic production of art (that is, the value ascribed to art or an artwork and by implication the artist) as well as the material production of the artwork. What this entails then is taking into account the role (and actions) of the artist in addition to that of artistic mediators such as critics, gallery directors, academies and the education system as well as the agents within the system who "produce consumers capable of knowing and recognizing works of art" (p. 37) – everybody who contributes to the work's meaning and value and sustain the "universe of belief".

It is reported that teachers continue to teach content in their art classes that is outdated and at odds with how contemporary artists make work, convey ideas, tackle issues, and invite others to engage in the meaning of their works. In her article, *Postmodern Principles: In search of a 21st Century Art Education*, Olivia Gude claimed that the elements and principles of art are presented as the "essence of artmaking" and "are proffered as universal and foundational" (Gude 2004, p. 6). Research in the field of art education demonstrates the nature of art teaching in schools is at odds with the nature of art currently being produced. As Dennis Atkinson (2005) and others have pointed out, when "we turn to art education in schools we find a rather different picture of practice" than we find in the contemporary artworld (p. 23). It could be said that teachers are reluctant to incorporate contemporary art practices and contemporary methods of representation and meaning making into their classrooms. For a host of reasons, teachers are deeply attached to teaching students realistic representational strategies such as landscape painting, still life paintings, figure drawings etc. when artists of our time, especially those who are shaping and informing the artworld, are no longer interested in producing art of this nature. Rather as suggested in and by the work that is produced and shown in the time of the now, artists of our time are interested in artistic practices that promote interactivity,

As I stood in the Atrium of MoMA observing a group of high school students observe Abramović observe participants who sat opposite her, and participants observe her, and museum-goers observe the performance, I wondered what this performance might mean to them, and moreover what it might mean for their teacher, as an educator, who had brought them to the performance, and, indeed, for all the teachers who create art learning experiences for their students in schools across the country and across the world. Elizabeth Ellsworth makes the argument that "Pedagogy is seldom engaged as an *event* in which the *materiality* of a time and place of learning impinges on the *materiality* of the learning self" (italics in original, Ellsworth 2005, p. 24). Abramović's

For a host of reasons, teachers are deeply attached... such as landscape, painting, still life paintings,... especially those who are shaping and informing the artworld,...

connectivity, collaboration, and participation (Bishop 2007). Spectator participation, as Claire Bishop reminded us, has become a common feature of recent work: Abramović's performance demonstrates how this occurs in the case of one artwork. And, as Nicolas Bourriaud (2002) claimed, the 'new' is no longer a criterion for making, judging, or is interpreting artworks. Nancy Spector (2008) maintained "For the artists of the 1990s, in reaction to this new culture of temporal simultaneity, time became a malleable material, a medium unto itself" (p. 22). Moreover, Olivia Gude (2007) pointed out, "it is difficult to find support in serious academic writing (as opposed to commercial textbooks) for using the elements and principles of design as a curriculum structure" (p. 7).

performance provides an opportunity to think about pedagogy as an event in, as Ellsworth (2005) puts it, "the *materiality* of a time and place of learning impinges on the *materiality* of the learning self". A collaborative art project that I conducted with a group of 17 elementary school boys who attended a single sex school in Ireland is an example of how elementary teachers might begin to think about exploring Ellsworth's idea that "the *materiality* of a time and place of learning impinges on the *materiality* of the learning self", as Abramović's performance does. Working over a three-week period, we explored how school space and place informs and shapes a sense of oneself as a boy, a learner, a student, a community member, a passer, an achiever, a non-achiever, a skipper, a team-player, a loner, and a host of other categorizing categories. We undertook this project, which emerged from a series of consultative sessions with students at the school, because boys wanted to better understand as well as influence and change how places were produced, organized and managed in their school. Students in the school wanted to create a platform where they could communicate and participate with their teachers and the school management in creating spaces and places that respected difference, recognized diversity, fostered meaningful peer relationships and provided a sense of belonging. Investigating how various school spaces were perceived, experienced, read, and interpreted by boys, and how those readings impacted and shaped boys' subjectivities provided data that enabled teachers and school management in this school

used moving and still images together with text in their work). During and following these inquiry sessions, the 17 boys created still and moving images of the school places that they encountered, hung out, avoided, produced, felt part of, or estranged from. They followed other students and their teachers in order to get a sense of how others navigated school space and produced places through attachment. They later edited their video footage into short movies that addressed several themes including, but not limited to the following: inclusion; exclusion; discrimination; belonging; freedom; responsibility; learning; surveillance; intimacy; estrangement. In addition, this group of boys recorded and edited sound pieces that captured the sounds of various places in the school. They interviewed their fellow students and

...to teaching students realistic representational strategies
...figure drawings etc. when artists of our time,
...are no longer interested in producing art of this nature.

to establish safe, equitable, and inclusive places for all students. While these boys produced a number of different art forms (photographs, short films, posters, soundscapes, and booklets), which are described in the following paragraph, these works generated and contributed to debate and discussion about school space, and initiated and informed policy change within the school.

Using cameras and sound recording devices we began the project by inquiring into how artists of our time convey certain ideas or create conditions for certain understandings and meanings to emerge from their work. We examined the work of performance artists, installation artists, video artists, sound artists and mixed media artists (including those who

wove the narratives of their classmates with the sound recordings they had made. They distributed their short films and exhibited their photographs, and produced visual booklets that drew attention to the material and social aspects of school spaces. With the permission of the school principal, every morning for an entire month they broadcasted a sound piece over the school's intercom system.

This project succeeded because of a number of factors, not least its interdisciplinary nature, and its commitment to inquiry. It created spaces for dialogue and critical self-reflection. It embraced chance and uncertainty. While the topic of inquiry in this collaborative project was school space and place, there are many other productive themes that could generate new and different understandings about students' experiences in school. For example, what new types of understandings about schooling and education might a project that took education as a medium for art making generate? In what ways might such an art project question, inquire into, and problematize how knowledge is organized and produced in schools? How might art projects trouble and make visible the ways in which certain knowledges are legitimated, while others are sidelined? Sociologists of education and curriculum scholars such as Jean Anyon, Michael Apple, Madeline Arnot, Michelle Fine, Kathleen Lynch, and several others have for the past three decades been researching the connections between and among knowledge, teaching, and power in education. In what ways might these ideas be taken up in an art project about school in school? Such a project might, for example, inquire into the nature of schooling focusing on what students and others understand as school, while paying attention to how it has been constructed in the minds and representations of others, as well as how it finds visual form in school books, children's books, popular media representations and so on. The Raqs Media Collective (2008) posed several interesting questions that might be taken up in such a project – "Is school a place, an institution, a set of facilities, a situation, a circumstance, an attitude, or a constellation of relationships of the transfer of acquired, invented, and accumulated knowledge, experience, and insight from one generation to another? Perhaps a school or the idea of a school as a condition of learning, of being open to discourse and discovery, can also be seen as something that we might carry with us wherever we go, whatever we do." (p. 74).

In what ways might a project that attempted to address some or all of these questions serve to provide multiple readings of a phenomena that affects the lives of all students, and indeed teachers, parents and others? For example, in 1997, working with Barb Clausen and a core group of 30 high school female students and 15 adult women, the American artist, educator and social activist Suzanne Lacy produced a large scale public performance in downtown Vancouver that focused on the lives and experiences of young women in the city. The performance was performed in a construction site in the downtown core and had an audience of about 3,000 individuals. During the performance participants told stories to each other about their lives and lived experience. Sharing stories of loneliness, loss, anger, joy, inequality, and achievement, participants brought to the attention of others issues that were pervasive and oftentimes destructive in the lives of young women in Western Canada. These stories were recorded and broadcasted at the performance site on the day of the performance. The act of bringing together these young women to tell and share these stories and experiences of living and life, of being young and female in Western Canada created a platform for hearing about multiple and different ways of negotiating the world from a gendered, racial, and sexualized position. What did the students that I observed at MoMA who witnessed Abramović's 'The Artist is Present' learn by being present in a place set up for them by the artist? What memories did they recall while present, and what stories did they tell as a result of being present in the atrium at MoMA in the company of the artist? What new forms of understanding about self and other emerged for these students in this social and physical place – that served as a site of production and exhibition simultaneously?

Informed by bel hooks' (1994) notion of classrooms as "locations of possibilities", I believe that contemporary art practice, such as Abramović's practice, has much to offer for rearticulating and reforming art education pedagogical practices and curriculum content of the future. Elsewhere, I have developed and presented seven lessons that artists and artist practice of the present can teach us about designing art education curriculum and pedagogical practices for the time of the now. Space doesn't permit me to elaborate here. These seven lessons – more appropriately called commitments – are not to be viewed as definitive or finite. Rather, they ought to be viewed as principles that support teachers in developing art education curriculum for the twenty-first century.

An art education curriculum that is designed in accordance with principles and practices of contemporary art – art of the twenty first century – is one that values and promotes inquiry practices that arouse curiosity, that heighten students' senses, evoke and provoke memories, invite questions, and fosters debate and dialogue. It keeps certain things in suspension, produces doubt and uncertainty, and model forms of exchange for students to come to know in relation. Such a curriculum requires attention to social spaces as learning spaces. Providing a space for presentation and discussion is as important as providing a space for creation and production. In addition, pedagogical practices are not confined to the production of artworks but also involve setting the conditions and initiating contacts and connections that enable the work to be produced. This curriculum advances a team-based approach to production rather than the more traditional individualized approach. It too promotes project-based learning. Schnapp and Shanks (2009) observed: "project-based learning implies an emphasis on both process and output. Process involves a focus on the ways in which different forms of work (leading to the creation of objects, textual artifacts, soundscapes, constructions, and so on) are carried out, and it assumes the form of iterative trials: create, monitor process, test reaction, and adapt, and repeated the standard pattern" (p. 153).

> An art education curriculum that is designed in accordance with principles and practices of contemporary art – art of the twenty first century – is one that values and promotes inquiry practices that arouse curiosity, that heighten students' senses, evoke and provoke memories, invite questions, and fosters debate and dialogue.

Conclusion

In this chapter I hope to invite future teachers to think about developing a new form of art education curriculum that requires new and different forms of pedagogies. This is not necessarily an art education curriculum that is better than the ones we currently have, but, rather, one that is different and attentive to the art practices and processes of our time. Deborah Britzman (2003) argues that "part of the work of the teacher consists in creating the conditions for the young to learn traditions and histories that are not of their own making but that they are expected to continue", which, she claims, leaves "little room for the new generation to create their own sense of life's becoming" (p. 9). Creating one's "own sense of life's becoming" is essential if we hope to educate citizens of the future to be affective, effective, critical, fair, honorable, respectful, principled, flexible, and adaptive. The students that we encounter in our classrooms on a daily basis have the right to explore, understand, and engage with issues and processes of meaning making of their time. It is negligent not to attend to art and art practices of our students' time. It too is negligent not to explore visual meaning making processes that are likely to assist them as they negotiate their way through life. It is no longer acceptable to teach outdated processes of artmaking, while ignoring new practices of visual production, new ways of showing and disseminating artworks and new ways of talking about and understanding these works.

While the content of art education programs in schools is affected by many factors, and while curriculum must be shaped in accordance with how learning occurs, I argue that teachers and teacher educators need to continue to present alternative models of art education to their students and teacher candidates – future teachers – that are firmly located in the art practices of our time. These models ought to be informed by the shift, flow, and tensions in the art field. Attention ought to be paid to the nature of artworks that are currently being produced and to the artmaking practices of artists of our time, especially given that in the field of art, as Robertson and McDaniel (2010) suggest, "Old hierarchies and categories are fracturing; new technologies are offering different ways of conceptualizing, producing, and showing visual art; established art forms are under scrutiny and revision; an awareness of heritages from around the world is fostering cross fertilizations; and everyday culture is providing both inspiration for art and competing visual stimulation" (p. 11). Attending to art of our time will enable us to imagine different and more relevant types of art learning experiences for students in our schools, different types of pedagogical and instructional practices, and a different language to evaluate and communicate student learning. In this chapter, I am not suggesting that Abramović's performance ought to be viewed or considered a prototype for art education curriculum. I don't think there is anything much to be gained by simply replicating Abramović's performance, or similar such performances by artists of our time. This practice would be no different from recreating a Cezanne Still Life, a Picasso Portrait, or a Monet Landscape. Rather, I believe that her work and the work of others suggest ways of thinking about creating learning situations and learning events that reflects the fact that our students grow up in the contemporary artworld; that artists are producing work that deals with issues that are important to students; and that students are using and interacting with 'globalizing technologies', media, and thought processes that contemporary artists are using in the production and dissemination of their artworks. What would it mean to develop curriculum and pedagogical approaches alongside and with artists and their practices?

As educators, we do not need to continue teaching outmoded practices of visualization and representation. To do so would not be education but rather, conservation. As art educators it is essential that we take up and address issues of our time using forms and media of the now because artists and cultural workers in the 21st century are not making art about line, shape, texture, tone, balance, etc. Rather, they are engaging in questions and issues about living, life and the world.

Through their practice and works, artists have drawn attention to social and culture issues and inequalities that have not always found their way into the public consciousness through more mainstream means.

As we move forward together in this uncertain world, it is important that we create learning opportunities that amplify the practice of paying attention; that engage in effortful observation; that embrace uncertainty and court ambiguity; that are open to chance encounters; and that value the act of being awakened by situations and seduced and cajoled by them. It is necessary that our students know that it is important to be unafraid of not knowing; to being curious about knowing differently; and, to being open to using meaning making strategies employed by others who have focused on similar ideas. To do so would draw attention to the usefulness of wonderment, and particularly to the value of wondering, especially for the type of questions or actions that it might call forth.

References

Atkinson, D. (2005). Approaching the Future in School Art Education: Learning How to Swim. In. D. Atkinson & P. Dash (Ed.), *Social and critical practices in art education*, (pp. 21-30). Stroke on Trent, UK: Trentham Books.

Bal, M. (2003). Visual essentialism and the object of visual culture. *Journal of Visual Culture, 2*(2), 5-32.

Birnbaum, D. (2009). *Venice Biennale 2009: 53rd International Art Exhibition*. Retrieved August 10, 2009 from http://universes-in-universe.org/eng/bien/venice_biennale/2009

Bishop, C. (2007). The Social turn: Collaboration and its discontents. In M. Schavemaker & M. Rakier (Eds.) *Right about now: Art and theory since 1990s* (pp. 58-68). Amsterdam: Valiz Publishers.

Bourdieu, P. (1993). *The field of cultural production: Essays on Art and Literature*. (R. Johnson, Intro & Ed.) Cambridge: Polity Press.

Bourdieu, P. (1996). *Rules of art: Genesis and structure of the literary field* (Translated by S. Emanuel). Stanford, CA: Stanford University Press.

Bourriaud, N. (2002). *Relational aesthetics*. Les Presses du Réel.

Bourriaud, N. (2005). *Postproduction*. New York: Lukas and Steinberg.

Britzman, D. P. (2003). *Practice makes practice: A critical study of learning to teach. Revised edition*. Albany, NY: State University of New York Press.

Crosby, M. (2008). Humble materials and powerful signs: Remembering the suffering of others. In D. Augaitis & K. Ritter (Eds.), *Rebecca Belmore: Rising to the occasion* (pp. 77-92). Vancouver, BC: Vancouver Art Gallery.

Desai, D. & Chalmers, F. G. (2007). Notes for a dialogue on art education in critical times. *Art Education, 60*(5), 6-12

Ellsworth, E. (2005). *Places of learning: Media, architecture, and pedagogy*. London: Routledge.

Gross, J. R. (2000). Osmosis. In J.R. Gross & L. Hyde (Ed.), *Lee Mingwei, The Living Room* (pp. 1-13). Boston, MA: Isabella Stewart Gardner Museum.

Gude, O. (2004). Postmodern principles: In search of a 21st century art education. *Art Education, 57*(1), 6-14.

Gude, O. (2007). Principles of possibility: Considerations for a 21st-century art and culture curriculum. *Art Education, 60*(1), 6-17.

hooks, b. (1994). *Teaching to transgress: Education as the practice of freedom*, London: Routledge.

Madeja, S. S. (1980). The Art curriculum: Sins of omission. *Art Education, 33*(6), 24-26.

Raqs Media Collective. (2009). How to be an artist by night. In S. H. Madoff (Ed.), *Art school: Propositions for the 21st century* (pp. 71-81). Boston, MA: MIT Press.

Robertson, J., & McDaniel, C. (2010). *Themes of contemporary art: Visual art after 1980*. New York: Oxford University Press.

Schnapp, J. T.& Shanks, M. (2009). 'Artereality (Rethinking craft in a knowledge economy)'. In S. H. Madoff (Ed.). *Art school: Propositions for the 21st century* (pp. 141-158). Boston, MA: MIT Press.

Spector, N. (2008). Theanyspacewhatever: An exhibition in ten parts. In N. Spector (Ed.). *Theanyspacewhatever* (pp.13-29). New York: The Guggenheim Museum.

Sullivan, G. (2006). Research acts in art practice. *Studies in Art Education, 48*(1), 19-35.

Endnotes

1 The retrospective, curated by Klaus Biesenbach and shown primarily in the Joan and Preston Robert Tisch Gallery on the sixth floor of the Museum, includes approximately 50 works that span four decades. Five of the approximately ninety performance pieces that Abramović created since 1969, including three that were originally performed with the German artist Ulay (Frank Uwe Laysiepen), her former lover and collaborator, are being reenacted by others – artists and dancers selected by Abramović.

2 On May 1st, 2010, the wooden table was removed.

3 "There are three dresses in total, one per month: A red dress, a blue dress, and a white dress. Marina's choices are based on energy. For the opening of the exhibition, she chose the bright red dress. For the rest of March, the first month, she wore the meditative, deep blue dress. In April to gain new energy because of the increasing difficulty of the performance, she has chosen the red dress. For May, Marina will wear a white dress to achieve a calm state for her final month of performing" FROM: http://webp2.moma.org/explore/inside_out/2010/03/29/visitor-viewpoint-marina-abramovic#comments.

4 She does not move from her chair, she does not eat, drink, or speak. Members of the audience, one at a time, can sit silently and engage through eye contact with the artist by being present. While audience members are allowed to sit across from the artist, they can stay as long as they wish. It has been reported that members of the public have sat silently with the artist from as little as 10 minutes and as long as 7 hours.

5 In his article, *Confronting a Stranger, for Art*, published on April 2, 2010 in the New York Times, Jim Dwyer reports this interview with Dan Visel.

CHAPTER 19

Art Education and Social Justice: An Elementary Perspective

Graeme Chalmers

Art involvement can become particularly meaningful in the lives of elementary students when we find ways to connect art learning and production to important social issues. Even small children can learn to see that art, in many different places and settings, can be used to perpetuate and to challenge the values of a society. And, children can use their own art making in the same ways. Where do they find injustice? What do they want to change? What should be affirmed?

In North America, education as social reconstruction can be traced back to George Counts (1932) who in his book *Dare the Schools Build a New Social Order?* argued that schools cannot be morally neutral and that educators need to collaborate with other groups to effect social change. Too often in elementary education, art simply serves as 'recreation.' Little or no attention is given to art-making as a political process. Students rarely talk about why art is made and displayed. Schools, even elementary schools, and the communities they represent, need to engage in this process; to see, feel, experience, and commit to the politics of art making. Artists make art to both sustain and challenge the status-quo. A world, a school, without art, needs to be unimaginable -- not just because the arts enrich our lives -- but also because we need art for social critique, cultural survival, and communal identity. Art education and arts involvement can encourage self-esteem when students know that they are dealing with really important issues and that, through their work, they too can make a difference.

Even small children can learn to see that art, in many different places and settings, can be used to perpetuate and to challenge the values of a society.

More than 30 years ago, educator Vincent Lanier (1969) proclaimed that "Almost all that we presently do in teaching art in . . . schools is useless" (p.314). He believed that students needed to examine "the gut issues of [their] day" - war, sex, race, drugs and poverty, and argued that

what we need . . . are new conceptions of modes of artistic behavior, new ideas of what might constitute the curricula of the art class. These new curricula must be meaningful and relevant to pupils . . . These new ideas must engage the "guts and hopes" of the youngsters and through these excitements provoke intellectual effort and growth. These new ideas must give the art class a share in the process of exploring social relationships and developing alternative models of human behavior in a quickly changing and, at this point in time quickly worsening social environment. (p.314)

Lanier was not just addressing secondary schools. Social responsibility begins in the home and then in pre-school and kindergarten. A look at current curriculum documents in many different jurisdictions indicates that teachers, at all levels, are now encouraged to give more attention to the social and personal contexts of art. In British Columbia there are teachers who have developed art 'units' focusing on identity and ethnicity, hunger, AIDS, making dolls for children in war-torn parts of the world, racism, and homelessness. A new cross-curricular initiative termed "social responsibility" is providing some great starting points for elementary education. The arts can be harnessed as schools address issues such as bullying

Social justice themes provide avenues for cooperation between elementary and secondary school art programs. More than 10 years ago, an article in a local BC newspaper claimed that at least 40% of Canadians had racist attitudes.

This claim, coupled with observed racist behavior within local schools, prompted some Burnaby, BC teachers to develop a unit "Art Against Racism" (Scarr & Paul, 1992). An exhibition "Fear of Others: Art Against Racism" had been held in Vancouver and a related slide set, video, and guide were produced. The visual arts part of the unit required students to respond to a variety of visual materials on issues of racism, to compose their own statement about racism, and to develop an original image suitable for an edition of linocut prints. Students developed complementary written statements and were required to critique their own work and the work of others attending to both the formal and the contextual qualities of the prints. Language arts classes produced poems and short stories and a drama class wrote and staged a play about racist behavior and attitudes. A large 6 by 30 foot mural was created as a joint celebration of the awareness that had been developed. With additional funding from the school district, the students went on tour to present their work to students in other schools, and some of their work was used for the cover and illustrations in a "multiculturalism issue" of the British Columbia Art Teachers' Association Journal for Art Teachers.

There are very few published curriculum projects that encourage students to explore the arts for social change. Such work must start with a deeply felt need; one that can be experienced locally.

Some elementary schools have become the sites for citizenship ceremonies. Recently Dunsmuir Middle School (Sooke, BC), used the results of an intensive week of "Celebrating Diversity Through the Arts" to decorate the gymnasium for a culminating event of the week: a Canadian Citizenship Ceremony. It is valuable when art can be used for such a purpose.

Founded in 1996 in Vancouver, ArtStarts in Schools is a unique not-for-profit organization offering educators, artists, parents and students a broad range of programs, services and resources to promote art and creativity among young people. Their many activities include: innovative arts programs, services and resources for teachers and artists, funding resources, etc. Of particular interest to those wishing to promote anti-racist education is the Art as a Catalyst for Change program which brings important social and community issues into the art class. In an innovative series of artist-led workshops and residencies, Art as a Catalyst for Change brings artists and elementary classroom teachers together to present art-based programs on curricular themes focused on social concerns including human rights, anti-racism, media education, and the environment.

ArtStarts has many services including an Artists' Directory which provides marketing and program information on over 225 artists and groups who work with young people throughout Western Canada. At the time of writing ArtStarts' booking service coordinates, schedules, negotiates and contracts 1800 arts events annually in schools and communities throughout British Columbia.

Teachers working with Vancouver's Holocaust Centre, which has produced a number of school programs and resources, including some very popular Discovery Kits, has also facilitated some innovative arts-based anti-racist projects. A project, which could be adapted for elementary students, was called Building Bridges: Visual Stories and Perceptions of the Holocaust. Other projects suitable for upper elementary grades include the Suitcase Project and I never Saw Another Butterfly. The Centre encourages teachers to submit a proposal to show work done by their students on Holocaust related, social justice themes, for their summer exhibition schedule. Similarly the Westcoast Coalition for Human Dignity has produced an excellent kit for educators entitled Choose Dignity, and many activities are suggested that could be developed through art.

If art education is to be meaningful, we must not shy away from controversial themes.

A number of theatre arts companies work with anti-racist themes in school and community centres and encourage teachers to actively explore links between drama and social justice. Often schools choose to perform plays with anti-racist themes. These experiences can be followed with related work in the visual arts.

We can also learn from what has happened elsewhere. At The New Museum of Contemporary Art in New York City, educators Susan Cahan and Zoya Kocur (1996) show that when the goals of multicultural art education include inquiry into current social conditions, contemporary art is an indispensable resource that should be brought in to the classroom. Their school art resource guide, includes themes (many related to social studies curricula) that could and should be explored in elementary education: immigration; changing definitions of the family; discrimination, racism and homophobia; mass media; war; and the roles of public art in society.

A group in New York City "Artists/Teachers Concerned" (n.d.) states:

> For many of our students real choices and opportunities are few or nonexistent. In this context, the need for a meaningful art education curriculum . . . is clear. Through socially motivated art education programs and exhibits we give our students a chance to actively voice their opinions and be recognized for caring about themselves and their future. As educators, if we are going to honestly tell our students that they have the power to criticize and change their situation in society, then we have to believe that our educational system can reinforce those objectives and facilitate the atmosphere in which such changes can occur." (n.p.)

There are very few published curriculum projects that encourage students to explore the arts for social change. Such work must start with a deeply felt need; one that can be experienced locally. Among the few published resources are Art and Development Education and the Art as Social Action video materials (Oxfam, 1990) piloted in inner London (UK) schools. This project focused on addressing racism and apartheid through art-based approaches. Another London-based group, Art and Society, working with Amnesty International (1991) produced an art education teaching pack titled Free Expression.

Sharing the Vision, (National Symposium on Arts Education, 2001) a national framework for arts education in Canadian schools, begins with the statement that "Any parent or grandparent will tell you that from an early age, children naturally immerse themselves in drama, dance, music, and the visual arts: to play, to learn, to communicate, to celebrate, and to find out who they are." The arts are valued because they express and engage the human spirit in profound and powerful ways. Sharing the Vision goes on to state "We . . live at a time when violence and misunderstandings seem to be spreading in our society. The arts can be a direct way of vicariously but meaningfully encountering sensitive issues and values."

If art education is to be meaningful, we must not shy away from controversial themes. The literature in art education is increasingly addressing such issues (e.g. Albers, 1999; Bolin, 1999; Heath, 2001; Jeffers and Parth, 1996; Milbrandt, 2001). In an essay in the New Art Examiner, Henry Giroux (1996) pleads for pedagogical practices that help young people learn about and "understand their personal stake in struggling for a future in which social justice and political integrity become the defining principles of their lives" (p.21). Arts teachers can help, and schools, and community-based programs can dare, to build a new social order.

References

Albers, P.M. (1999). Art education and the possibility of social change. *Art Education*, *52*(4), 6-11.

Amnesty International. (1991). *Free expressions: the Amnesty International art education pack*. London, UK: Amnesty International British Section.

Artists/Teachers Concerned. (n.d.). *Brochure*. New York: Artists/Teachers Concerned.

Bolin, P. (1999). Editorial: Teaching art as if the world mattered. *Art Education*, *52*(4), 4-5.

Cahan, S. & Kocur, Z. (1966). *Contemporary art and multicultural education*. New York: The New Museum of Contemporary Art and Routledge Press.

Counts, G. (1932). *Dare the schools build a new social order?* New York: Day.

Giroux, H. (1996). What comes between kids and their Calvins: Youthful bodies, pedagogy, and commercialized pleasures. *The New Art Examiner*, (February), 16-21.

Heath, S.B. (2001). Three's not a crowd: Plans, roles, and focus in the arts. *Educational Researcher*, *30*(7), 10-17.

Jeffers, C. & Parth, P. (1996). Relating contemporary art and school art: A problem-position. *Studies in Art Education*, *38*(1), 21-33.

Lanier, V. (1969). The teaching of art as social revolution. *Phi Delta Kappan*, 50(6), 314-319.

Milbrandt, M. (2001). Addressing contemporary social issues in art education: a survey of public school art educators in Georgia. *Studies in Art Education*, 43(2), 141-152.

National Symposium on Arts and Education. (2001). *Sharing the vision*. Ottawa: NSAE.

Oxfam. (1990). *Art against apartheid and antiracism and art in Britain and South Africa*. Oxford, UK: Oxfam Education and Publications.

Scarr, M. & Paul, D. (1992). Art against racism. *British Columbia Art Teachers' Association Journal for Art Teachers*, *32*(1), 32-37.

CONNECTIONS, REFLECTIONS AND CREATIONS

CHAPTER 20

First Nations Art and Culture
Tradition and Innovation

Bill Zuk and Robert Dalton

First Nations

Most Canadians are relative newcomers to the land called Canada. Some are first generation Canadians and many others have parents or grandparents who came here from other countries. As Canadians, we often describe ourselves as a young country and while this may be true in one sense of the term – as a political entity – there are people who have lived here for thousands of years. The indigenous peoples or First Nations hold a special importance to Canada, our history and collective identity. When we want to tell others what makes us distinctive as a country we often turn to First Nations art. For example, the Canadian embassy in Washington D.C. features a large sculpture by Haida artist Bill Reid (1991). Visitors to Canada arriving at such places as the Vancouver airport terminal see aboriginal art prominently displayed. When the eyes of the world turned toward us during the 1994 Commonwealth Games in Victoria, the 1988 Calgary Winter Olympic Games or the 2010 Vancouver Winter Olympic Games, opening ceremonies proudly represented First Nations cultures through costume, dance, music, and art. First Nations cultures are rich and diverse with over fifty different languages still spoken in Canada. The Inuit of Nunavut, the Coast Salish of British Columbia, the Cree of Saskatchewan, the Mohawk of Quebec, and the Mi'kmaq of the Maritimes – nearly every region of this vast land has indigenous peoples with unique histories, languages, and cultures.

Traditional and Contemporary First Nations Art

Traditional art served a practical purpose. A kayak is a marvel of design; a painted buffalo hide offers visual history in narrative form – daring exploits or warfare; medicine wheels, masks, woven baskets, snow shoes, and other utilitarian articles are further examples of art's role in meeting the economic, political, social, and spiritual needs of individuals and their communities. However there are some who question whether or not this is *art*. Ellen Dissanayake (1988) provides compelling reasons why utilitarian objects should be considered as such. She took the unusual approach of looking at the function and purposes of art, finding that especially in small-scale pre-industrial societies they accomplish similar purposes to that of fine arts in contemporary western society.

Traditional arts can still be found in First Nations cultures though many examples are retained for ceremonial purposes today; items used in everyday life are generally not made by local people from local materials but have been replaced by manufactured goods. Contemporary artists, however, often make reference to these traditions in work intended for museums, galleries, and other places where fine art is displayed (Irwin, Rogers & Wan, 1998). Where traditional art tended to remain within the community and was used in daily life, fine art today is more often sold or shown outside the community to a much wider audience; it also tends to be more overtly pedagogical, a form of communication and teaching. In an era where indigenous cultures throughout the world are at risk of being eliminated through globalization, it is all the more important for artists to play a leading role in preserving key aspects of traditional life. Artists can often teach members of the dominant culture something of the beauty and wisdom of indigenous ways; reaching even further, artists may garner support for cultural preservation.

What is taught or conveyed through traditional art? Viewers may come to appreciate the genius of First Nations adaptation and survival in the harsh climate of Canada and gain insight into traditional values such as reverence for, and spiritual connection to the land, respect for the wisdom of elders, and so forth. Viewers will likely recognize the skilful working of materials evident in much of the work. In contemporary art there can also be very positive aspects but some of what is presented represents difficulties and struggle. Viewers may become more keenly aware of common concerns such as poverty, discrimination, and environmental concerns. Colonialism resulted in mistreatment of Natives. Acting in a paternalistic manner, the Canadian government authorized residential schools to remove children from their families. This action and others like it tore the social fabric of many communities. The results of these unfortunate events continue to surface in healing ceremonies and political arenas today. Through art, First Nations people often reach out to make connections with their past, reclaiming their cultural identities. They use art to communicate with one another, and they communicate with non-Natives, teaching them about their proud heritage while revealing their perspectives and concerns. First Nations were the first inhabitants of this continent, they shared their knowledge and through their art they continue to build bridges of understanding and respect.

Learning through Study and Discussion of First Nations Art

Like all living organisms, cultures adapt and change. A culture deeply rooted in the past is able to draw nourishment from its history – a sense of purpose and wisdom gained from experiences that enable it to grow and flourish. This is why many First Nations artists are helping their communities recover a past that in some instances has largely been lost due to disregard and policies of cultural assimilation. As aspects of culture are recovered, they are made relevant for the 21st century. In this respect, First Nations artists may serve as historians, elders, shamans, or others in leadership capacities, speaking *to* their people and speaking *on behalf of* their people. Tradition and innovation provide a means for understanding the past and the present. First Nations artists are normally aware of the traditions passed down to them. Studying traditional art forms and the contemporary interpretations of those forms enables viewers to recognize some of the changes that have occurred. Those changes might represent a relatively brief period of perhaps twenty years or a vast span of time involving many thousands of years. Teachers can search through books to find exemplars and after reading about the artist/culture and the work, make decisions to pair them for student study as tradition and innovation. There is great merit in examining artwork involving what the writers term a comparative picture approach (Zuk & Dalton, 2003). Learning resources are available (Zuk & Bergland, 1992; Zuk & Dalton, 1999) where research information and large format reproductions are provided, illustrating how traditions function and how they are being revitalized.

There are two principal approaches to begin understanding how tradition and innovation relate to one another. One uses a process of seeing or perceiving while the other engages the student in creating or producing innovative artwork. Perceiving can be accomplished in various ways; one commonly accepted method proposed by Feldman (1987) recommends starting with the work(s) of art and describing what can be observed. This simple and very concrete beginning teaches students to look carefully and to take account of the subject matter and media/materials used by the artist in creating it. Also included are observations about colour, form, texture, and other elements of art. Comparing the traditional and innovative works encourages careful examination and facilitates discovery. Formal analysis follows description, considering how the work is composed. Students should be guided to note relationships of scale and format, for example, or subject matter and colour. How is the viewer's eye led about the composition and what feelings are evoked by emphasis, contrast, rhythm, pattern, and balance? Description and analysis *fund* interpretation but more information is needed before students can put forward a theory about its meaning. The cultural/historical context must be considered and this requires looking outside the artwork. Information external to the work is needed to understand something of the events, beliefs, and cultural practices that may have influenced the artist in creating the work. Biographical information about the artist is often very helpful as well. From the wealth of observed and gathered information, students are then in a position to develop a theory – an explanation that seems to adequately account for the contents and organization of the artwork. Agreement is not always necessary among students in a classroom; a lively exchange of reasoned argument is a natural and welcome part of perceiving. This prepares students for the next step, to speculate on cultural change based on the differences between the historical and contemporary works of art. Appropriately matched pairs of traditional and innovative artworks showing *old* and *new* can be very revealing.

Learning through Studio Activities

Creating is a special and significant way of knowing. Through hands-on studio activities, students benefit in ways that are different from *seeing* or *perceiving*. Those who have participated in life drawing classes know how wholly absorbing the process of creating art can be, especially when one attends to every nuance of light and shadow, and through empathy *feels* the model's energy, muscle tension, or the distribution of weight and balance of a pose or stance. Concentration on the task can be considerable, even exhausting, and at the same time deeply satisfying. When students work with their hands to create, they invest themselves physically and emotionally in a task, often entering into a metaphysical union with their artwork that leads to new ways of knowing. In some art activities, the principal aim may be to discover and record as realistically as possible but the power of creative expression adds another dimension of significance when we engage in an act of interpretation. Drawing inspiration from a masterwork, students can be encouraged to make a personal connection with the fundamental ideas embodied in an exemplar that results in a new and unique response.

Sydney Roberts Walker (1996) took a critical look at school art projects and concluded that if the goal of art education is to develop understanding, then some of our studio projects remain at a level of skill building or experimentation and stop short of moving students to applying what they've learned. Using three hypothetical projects based on Deborah Butterfield's sculptures, she pointed to common problems.

Chiefly they concern *distance* and *transfer*. A project that copies or mimics an artwork can be *too close*, failing to draw students into expressing their own ideas. It remains primarily an act of appreciation. Alternatively a project may be *too distant* or different from the exemplar with the result that there is no real transfer of knowledge; what is learned from the exemplar cannot be used or applied to the studio project. Even projects that involve the right *distance* can still fail to fulfill their potential if they involve a transfer of knowledge that is solely technical and opportunities for individual meaning making are lost.

It is relatively easy to cite examples of superficial responses to First Nations art that result in copying or appropriation. It is more productive to refer to exemplary responses. Cree artist George Littlechild worked with students in Vancouver's George T. Cunningham Elementary School; artist-in-residence Alison Diesvelt continued that initiative to create a body of artworks that were exhibited in the Surrey Art Gallery. *We are All Related: A Celebration of Our Cultural Heritage* (1996), reveals the personal connections children were able to make. Walker concluded that for understanding to emerge, key ideas must be identified so that students recognize what the master artwork is really about. Knowledge transfer must provide opportunities to extend those ideas. Personal connections must be made and problem finding or problem solving must be involved. For this, teacher guidance is invaluable.

Figure 1
Drum Dance, Luke Iksiktaaryuk, 1971.
Bone, antler, wood. 27.8 x 40 x 42.5 cm.
Photograph courtesy of Art Image
Publications, Montreal, PQ.

These ingredients can be found in the Cunningham Elementary project. Students spoke with their elders – parents and grandparents – asking them to share the family photo album as a means of recalling experiences reaching back to their own childhood. Copies of the photos were arranged to create a central composition. Students also asked family members to tell them about their cultural heritage. Colourful motifs or designs from their country or countries of origin were used to develop borders. In gathering information and creating these artworks, children discovered and expressed personal and cultural identities developed from knowledge passed down to them from elders. These values can be found in the work of First Nations artists like George Littlechild. The learning experiences in this project were substantive, not superficial, and the imagery was personal, not appropriated.

2 Examples from Inuit Art

Canada's far north was the last area to be settled by non-Natives. In the twentieth century change came quickly and dramatically to the culture and art of the Inuit (Zuk & Dalton, 1996). Oil and gas exploration, pipeline construction, mining, and the recent discovery of diamonds in the north brought industry and a southern way of Canadian life to the people of the Arctic. Permanent settlements were established throughout the vast region and with it, all the advantages and problems of modern culture. Along with missionaries, trading posts, R.C.M.P. stations, schools, and modern medicine came rapid transportation, mass media, fast food, and alcohol. The Inuit struggled to deal with massive changes to their way of life but like their ancestors, they have proven to be remarkably adaptive as evidenced by the formation of Nunavut, a huge semi-autonomous territory created in the eastern Arctic in 1999 (Sinclair, 1999). Some of this change can be discovered through an examination of artwork produced in communities across the Canada's far north. To illustrate how cultural change and adaptation work, we have chosen to use a traditional work and an innovative one separated by a mere twenty years. Both works deal with traditional community life and have a drum as their focal point, representing cultural continuity and leadership.

The traditional work is *Drum Dance* (Figure 1) by artist Luke Iksiktaaryuk. Knowing the approximate size of caribou antlers, viewers have a sense of how large the sculpture is. Bone and wood are the other materials used in the carving. There is a circular grouping of figures, perhaps seated and small in relation to the standing drummer whose pegged arm allows the stick to be moved up and down imitating the action of playing the drum. All figures face inward, women differentiated from men by the longer tails of their parkas. Cutting and carving these hard materials with stone tools or more recently steel or power tools often meant that traditional artists tended not to include complex details. The figures are relatively simplified; drawing by means of scratching or incising lines is a technique that has been used. The

Figure 2
Northern Myth, Northern Legend, Abraham Anghik Ruben, 1991. Limestone, bone, stone, and precious stones. 490 x 120 cm. Photograph courtesy of Art Image Publications, Montreal. PQ.

miniaturized drum is especially faithful to actual drums used by community leaders. A typical Inuit drum consists of a shallow rim with hide stretched tightly. A short handle is attached so the sound will not be dampened as it would if it were held directly by hand. Where the articulated figure would be rather stiff in its drumming action, an actual drummer uses coordinated steps and a swaying motion, turning the drum to strike the broad surfaces and also the rim. In traditional Inuit society, songs were used for many occasions including ceremonies, contests, and entertainment. If the drummer were a shaman, the booming tones would have been used to create an atmosphere conducive for summoning spirits.

The innovative sculpture is *Northern Myth, Northern Legend*, by Abraham Anghik Ruben (Figure 2). Probably the most striking aspect of the work is its scale; this limestone carving is almost five meters high. Traditional Inuit carving is generally quite small; nomadic people carried their possessions from place to place and many examples from past centuries are the size of amulets that would fit in the palm of the hand. Now living in permanent homes and having power tools available, Inuit artists are able to work on a larger scale than ever before. Unlike some types of soft soapstone commonly used in the north, limestone is a harder material to carve and this too, calls for tools available in the modern world. Anghik's work is organized very differently from Iksiktaaryuk's being compact and columnar with figures fused together. At the base of the sculpture are animals: a dolphin, seal, and polar bear. Among the animals is Sedna, a mermaid-like goddess. Above and supported by these creatures are humans, young and old, male and female. The viewer's eye is directed by gesturing figures and flowing lines to the top where a drummer holds his instrument aloft, stick poised to strike. The smoothly rounded and somewhat simplified figures have eyes of inlaid semi-precious stones that make them more lifelike and perhaps magical.

Context and Meaning

Abraham Anghik Ruben is uniquely qualified to speak through his art about Inuit culture and change. Born in Pauletuk in 1951, his early childhood in the western Arctic introduced him to living off the land – hunting, trapping, and other aspects of a nomadic life. His grandmother and grandfather were both shamans of renown. At the age of eight he attended a residential school, like so many Inuit youths, and this separated him from his family and community for much of the year, turning his world upside down. However through his art he hopes to pass on his knowledge of customs and community life. "Individuals like ourselves have a responsibility to be the culture bearers, to carry on the stories, the legends and certain belief systems" (Schrager, 1994, p.9). In traditional Inuit society, cultural history was conveyed through song. The drummer related the myths and legends of the people, an interpretation that is supported by the title of the work. A related but slightly different interpretation grows out of another aspect of its creation. A large pharmaceutical company commissioned the huge sculpture; the drummer may well be a shaman who serves as spiritual leader of the community and practices the healing arts. Many of our modern day remedies for illness have come from folk medicines of indigenous people. This sculpture may pay tribute to that fact. Its towering scale ensures that the artwork will have a *presence* in a large commercial building but there is more to its size. In the film *Spirit of the Arctic* (1994), the artist indicated he works on a monumental scale to give viewers a lasting impression of the vastness of the Arctic. In *Northern Myth, Northern Legend*, Abraham Anghik Ruben represents the close link his people have to the land, the animals, mythological creatures that inhabit it, and perhaps ancestors who walked there before.

There are many ways in which the two sculptures are similar. Both involve carved and somewhat simplified figures; both have a drummer as the focal point. Each represents an aspect of community life in traditional Inuit culture. There are notable differences as well: The traditional work has its figures arranged in a circle while the innovative one places figures one above the other in a vertical column. The dramatic change of scale is quite apparent. Viewers might also notice the change from local materials such as caribou antler to imported materials such as Indiana limestone. But more significant than any of this is the meaning of the works. Luke Iksiktaaryuk's *Drum Dance* appears to describe a moment of time, a ceremonial event in Inuit culture. The articulated arm invites viewers to imagine the rhythmic beat of the music in a community gathering. In contrast with this, Abraham Anghik Ruben's *Northern Myth, Northern Legend*, seems to include all living things, animals, mythological beings, community members, and perhaps ancestors – a universe bound in a block of stone. The work suggests a wide span of time and cosmology. The drummer is upheld by a throng and on their behalf, leads and mediates with the spirit world. The drum is not so much a sound as a portal – an instrument of communication from past to present, and from this world to another. Perhaps this work shows a greater sense of the passage of time because the pace of change was so evident to the artist. And perhaps the myths and legends of the Inuit should be shared with the outside world to foster respect, cultivate appreciation, and encourage cultural sensitivity. Retaining something of the past is a key to cultural survival.

Having gained a level of understanding of the works, it is possible to devise meaningful studio activities, ones in which students are encouraged to apply those perspectives to their own lives. Questions can be raised about the nature of one's own community gatherings: The role of music in focusing attention, arousing emotions, creating a sense of shared identity and purpose; our relationships with the land, animals, and ancestors; and the specialized roles of historian, politician, physician, musician, and religious leader in our own society as compared with the multiple roles of a leader in a small community. And from the sculptural methods employed by the artists, students can assemble or join natural materials, use inlaid objects, make moveable parts, incise and polish soft carving materials. They can experiment with scale and format to better understand how a visual idea changes through such important adjustments. Space does not permit a fuller discussion here but the principles, we hope, have been established for designing studio activities that enable students to make meaningful connections and enter into new understandings of themselves and their world

A Matter of Respect

Art educators must be sensitive to the need to proceed carefully where matters of cultural appropriation are concerned. Canada's First Nations have experienced challenges in holding onto their traditional forms of art. The challenge has occurred in two opposing ways. Since first contact with Europeans, there has been misunderstanding that led to the destruction of much of the material culture and practices of the indigenous peoples of Canada. Working for museums, anthropologists, Indian Affairs agents, and others carried away many culturally significant items in order to advance knowledge and make them accessible to others. Missionaries often encouraged the destruction of items thought to be pagan. And governments banned such practices as the potlatch on the northwest coast of British Columbia in the mistaken view that they were protecting Native people from themselves. Residential schools took children away from their parents and communities, creating numerous dysfunctions in the family and community. Such paternalistic attitudes left First Nations people dissociated from their past.

More recently, there has been a cultural renaissance and reclaiming of the past. But with it a new danger has emerged, that of appropriation. With the growing popularity of the unique and beautiful creations of First Nations artists, corporations, and individuals have copied or *adopted* the style, imagery, and design motifs. This has led to revenue loss for Native artists. But more than that, imagery and visual forms of family history are sometimes blatantly used and changed in ways that are offensive and hurtful. The financial loss does not begin to compare with the harmful effects of losing control of cultural ownership.

Guidelines (Irwin, 1997) have been drawn up to assist teachers in this sensitive area. The Canadian Society for Education through Art (CSEA) has reprinted *Arts Education: A Curriculum Guide for Grade 5*, 1991, *Saskatchewan Education*. In those guidelines teachers are urged to contact a local First Nation, Metis, or Inuit Elder in their community. Elders are leaders and often well versed in their culture and history; asking them to recommend someone who might be willing to share their knowledge, shows respect for them as leaders. Locating an Elder is best done through a letter sent to a local Band Council, District Chief's Office, Tribal Council Office, or Friendship Centre. The letter should also indicate the particular interests and curricular needs of the students to insure that suitable candidates are chosen. Teachers and students should be aware of cultural etiquette, completing the cycle of giving and receiving through an appropriate offering that shows appreciation for the knowledge shared by the Elder or First Nations artist. The Band Council could suggest an appropriate gift. If the School Board or its representative division normally provides an honorarium and/or expense reimbursement, this should also be offered to the guest. Richly rewarding experiences are possible through classroom activities focused upon First Nations art and culture. And where local resources are unavailable, there are films, videos, texts, and learning resources kits developed for classroom use.

References

Brown, H. (Producer). (1994). *Spirit of the Arctic*. [video]. (Available from The Canadian Broadcasting Corporation, P.O. Box 4600, Vancouver, B.C.)

Feldman, E. B. (1987). *Varieties of visual experience* (3rd Ed.). Englewood Cliffs, NJ: Prentice-Hall.

Dissanayake, E. (1988). *What is art for?* Seattle, WA: University of Washington.

George. T. Cunningham Elementary School (1996). *We are all related: A celebration of our cultural heritage.* Vancouver, BC: Author.

Irwin, R. L. (Ed.). (1997). *The CSEA national policy and supporting perspectives for practice guidelines.* Boucherville, QC: Canadian Society for Education through Art.

Irwin, R. L. Rogers, T., & Wan, Y. Y. (1998). Reclamation, reconciliation and reconstruction: Art practices of contemporary Aboriginal artists from Canada, Australia, and Taiwan. *Journal of Cultural and Cross-Cultural Research in Art Education*, 16, 93-101.

Reid, B. (1991). *Spirit of the Haida Gwaii: The black canoe.* Retrieved March 4, 2003, from http://www.civilization.ca/aborig/reid04e.html.

Schrager, R. (1994). Three cousins in two worlds. *Inuit Art Quarterly*, 9(1), 4-12.

Sinclair, L. (1998). *Charting new territories.* CBC Ideas. Toronto, ON: The Canadian Broadcasting Corporation.

Walker, S. R. (1996). Designing studio instruction: Why have students make artwork? *Art Education*, 49(5), 11-17.

Zuk, W., & Bergland, D. (1992). *Art First Nations: Tradition and innovation.* Montreal, QC: Art Image Publications.

Zuk, B., & Dalton, R. (1996). Cross-currents: Tradition and innovation in circumpolar art. *Journal of Multicultural and Cross-Cultural Research in Art Education*, 14, 104-113.

Zuk, W., & Dalton, R. (1999). *Art First Nations: Tradition and innovation in the circumpolar world.* Laval, QC: Art Image.

Zuk, W., & Dalton, R. (2003). Comparative picture approach enriches study of art and culture. *BCATA Journal for Art Teachers*, 42(2), 24-27.

CONNECTIONS, REFLECTIONS AND CREATIONS

CHAPTER 21

Starting with...

...Visual Culture

Photo By: Andrew Purtell

Photo By: Andy Bahn

EVERYTHING $15 OR LESS

Lorrie Blair

Starting in the 1980s and continuing through the 1990s, Discipline Based Art Education (DBAE) dominated the field of art education in North America. At its conception, DBAE proponents asked art teachers to start their lessons with a work of art "drawn from landmark works recognized by experts as worthy of study" (Delacruz & Dunn, 1996, p. 72). Early on, many opposed DBAE because of what the canon included (dead, white European males) and omitted (art made by artists of colour, women, and marginalized groups, among others). Delacruz and Dunn noted that shifts in the DBAE approach became evident after teachers adapted it to meet the specific needs of their students. Teachers drew imagery from a wide range of areas including popular art. Although proponents of DBAE expanded the canon to include this imagery, critics argued that the DBAE approach to teaching art was inherently flawed in that it served to "devalue the everyday cultural production of young people by limiting notions of creativity to the sphere of 'art'" (Trend, 1992, p. 40).

In the early 1990s, Visual Culture Art Education (VCAE) began to gain prominence in the field and, by the end of the decade it replaced DBAE in importance. VCAE differed substantially from DBAE in both the exemplars teachers were asked to start with and how they were expected to teach them. Duncum (1990, 1999) advocated that teachers start their art lessons with students' everyday experiences in order to make art relevant and to better engage students. Others followed by suggesting that teachers start with any number of visual culture examples, such as a doll, an advertisement, an article of clothing, or a work of art and, importantly, to adopt a critical inquiry approach to teaching. This approach starts with the premise that cultural objects and activities are political, ideological, and often problematic.

VCAE lessons start with the assumption that visual culture tacitly transmits values that help shape our collective behaviour. Tavin and Anderson (2003) write: "As critical art educators, we should investigate how corporations produce knowledge about the world, distribute and regulate information, help construct identity, and promote consumption in visual culture" (p. 34). They borrow from Henry Giroux's (1999) book, *The Mouse that Roared: Disney and the End of Innocence*, to create lessons that question Disney's role in shaping childhood values, national identity, and gender roles. Following their lead, I investigated Mattel's Art Teacher Barbie. I asked what happens when corporations create and distribute representations that help construct the social reality of teaching art (Blair, 2006). By reading audit reports on factories in China and Mexico, I was better able to understand the working conditions of the women who make the dolls. My investigation also made me aware of the approaches marketing agencies use to sell products and services to children.

Photos of student work courtesy of: Karina McGrath.

Critiquing VCAE: The good, the bad, and the ugly

The good: Art educators, such as Barrett (2003), Chung (2005, 2007), and others posit that studying visual culture helps students develop critical thinking skills, which make them more informed consumers. They agree that children are surrounded and influenced by media images. Chung (2005) states: "Through visual and textual manipulation, media advertising not only persuades people to buy the advertised product but it also constructs false or questionable realities, beliefs, and values in relation to that product" (p. 19). One of the main goals of VCAE is to help students critically examine mediated messages. Examples drawn from visual culture provide teachers with starting points to discuss stereotyping, representations of "other" in media, racism, sexism, and a host of other concerns that confront their students. A VCAE lesson plan asks students to consider how media carries meaning and how they can subvert ads in playful and thoughtful ways. Chung and Kirby's (2009) article entitled *Media literacy art education: Logos, culture jamming and activism* and Darts' (2004) article entitled *Visual Culture Jam: Art, Pedagogy, and Creative Resistance* provide the rationale and some student examples.

As a proponent of VCAE, I witnessed the positive aspects of teaching about popular visual culture. One of the best experiences I had in my teaching career happened during a lesson on tattoos given to a class of over 100 students. Half of the students in the class had one or wanted one, and everyone had an opinion they wanted to express. The students were engaged and I learned from them. The lively spirit of that lesson continued throughout the semester. Through written comments in my teaching evaluations and emails I received at the end of the semester, students told me they enjoyed the course because they felt they had a voice and that they found the subjects covered in class to be relevant.

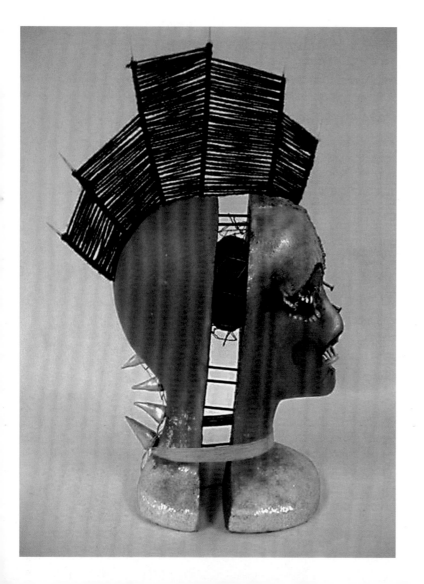

The bad: Like DBAE before it, VCAE has its detractors. A key criticism leveled against a VCAE approach is that it is more talk than action. Dorn (2005) writes: "What some consider most radical about the VCAE approach is its attempt to shift the Art Education field from its traditional emphasis on studio art into a dialog about art as a socially constructed object, devoid of expressive meaning" (p. 47). Herrman (2005) also characterizes many of the studio activities suggested by authors of articles dealing with teaching visual culture as "teacher directed activities" (p. 42). She states, "Students are told how they should react to the images and what forms their visual response should take" (p. 42). Maya Shalmon and I discovered the difficulties of incorporating studio activities into our investigation of cosmetic surgery and the cultural construction of beauty (Blair & Shalmon, 2005). Although we enjoyed learning and teaching about how fairy tales, movies, dolls, and other forms of visual culture transmit notions of beauty, we were remiss in that we did not produce a studio component for the lesson.

With so little time allotted for teaching art, critics see VCAE as usurping the time students have for making and viewing the fine arts. Although the fine arts are part of visual culture, the emphasis of VCAE is on the social and political context of the cultural artifact, not on any aesthetic quality. This stance has caused some to criticize VCAE as being more about sociology than art. Efland (2004) sums up this argument when he writes: "If the sociology of art helps students understand the connections between art and the social world, we may have taught something quite valuable, but we have not taught art" (p. 243).

The ugly: The worst criticism leveled at VCAE is that it harshly judges students' culture. Herrman (2005) explains, "Some teachers are presenting ideas, even if more socially aware, multicultural, and politically correct, as truths to be handed down to students. This dogmatic instruction can result in either outright rejection of ideas or compliant acceptance by students without real learning taking place" (p. 46). Critique can seem like dismissal. Lessons that critically examine the magazines our students read, the ads for products they use, or the toys with which they play can inadvertently make students feel guilty for enjoying their culture. Deconstructing Disney is not a fun lesson for the student whose family saved money for an

entire year to be able to provide memorable vacation. Moreover, such approaches tend to see visual culture as something from which children need protection and deny that they have agency to reject or subvert any intended meaning on their own.

Successful VCAE: Three examples

Just as DBAE was adapted to the realities of the classroom, teachers have also altered VCAE. In this section, I will describe three examples of how art teachers tailored VCAE to their needs. They start with aspects of their students' culture and use it as momentum to teach art.

Nancy Long (2009) started with jellybeans to motivate students to make quality watercolours and to take pride in their work. Rather than lecture students on bad eating habits, Long explored childhood memories of candy. She considered, "If everyday food and taste are capable of eliciting an aesthetic experience defined by meaningful learning, through memory and/or emotional response, then students engaged in a taste experience in art class can possibly be motivated to use and capture those memories in a piece of art, and in turn, feel a personal and meaningful connection to the work" (p. 17). Long teaches at a private girls' school and understands that art making, particularly the finished product, is important to parents, administrators, and students.

Melissa Ledo (2009), who teaches at a public school, tapped into her students' interest in tattooing to teach principles of harmony, balance, and repetition. She also taught lessons on the history of tattooing across various cultures, and covered health and safety issues. Ledo knew that some of her students would get tattoos so her lessons provided information, not judgment. She states: "…the results of this lesson were something that students were proud of. Attendance of students who were often absent was remarkably improved. Students were engaged throughout the whole process, and one year later students are still talking about the project!" (p. 51).

Karina McGrath took a playful approach to studying visual culture. According to Richard (2005), this approach "allows one to examine the practices of youth as consumers of mass media who also produce their own artifacts, that reflect their common interests and values, all the while creating a playful community of shared practices" (p. 34). McGrath started with the fantastical characters of the Cirque du Soleil's Alegría to encourage students to consider how outward appearance communicates identity (http://www.cirquedusoleil.com/en/shows/alegria/show/characters.aspx). Rather than deconstruct the motives of Cirque du Soleil, McGrath's lessons relied the fact this successful Québec company employs hundreds artists, performers, designers, and craftspeople. McGrath's students created new characters for future shows and imbued their characters with complex identities.

Long, Ledo, and McGrath's lessons start with positive aspects of student culture and an emphasis on student production. They consider why their students value candy, tattoos, and circus characters without rejecting or judging their values. For example, the dolls that we may disapprove of as being sexist might hold very different meanings to our students. These objects can hold authentic memories of childhood. They might represent playing with friends or a gift from a loved one. By starting with students' visual culture and a willingness to explore a range of meanings with our students, teachers can provide meaningful and enjoyable art lessons.

References

Barrett, T. (2003). Interpreting visual culture. *Art Education, 56*(2), 6-12.

Blair, L. (2006). Art Teacher Barbie: Friend or foe? *Canadian Journal of Education, 29*(1). Retrieved February 24, 2010 from: http://www.csse.ca/ CJE/Articles/FullText/CJE29-1/CJE29-1-blair.pdf

Blair, L. & Shalmon, M. (2005). Cosmetic surgery and the cultural construction of beauty. *Art Education, 58*(2), 14-18.

Chung, S. (2007). Media/visual literacy art education: Sexism in hip-hop music videos. *Art Education, 60*(3), 33-38.

Chung, S. (2005). Media/visual literacy art education: Cigarette ad deconstruction. *Art Education, 58*(2), 19-24.

Chung, S. K. & Kirby, M. (2009). Media literacy art education: Logos, cultural jamming and activism. *Art Education, 62*(1), 34-41.

Cirque du Soleil. (1995). *Alegría*. Retrieved March 17, 2010 from http://www.cirquedusoleil.com/en/shows/alegria/show/characters.

Darts, D. (2004). Visual culture jam: Art, pedagogy, and creative resistance *Studies in An Education, 45*(4), 313-327.

Delacruz, E. & Dunn, P. (1996). The evolution of discipline-based art education. *Journal of Aesthetic Education, 30*(3), 67-82.

Dorn, C. (2005). The end of art in education. *Art Education, 58*(6), 47-51.

Duncum, P. (1990). Clearing the decks for dominant culture: Some first principle for a contemporary art education. *Studies in Art Education, 31*(4), 207-215.

Duncum, P. (1999). A case for an art education of everyday aesthetic experiences. *Studies in Art Education, 40*(4), 295-311.

Efland, A. (2004). The entwined nature of the aesthetic: A discourse on visual culture. *Studies in Art Education, 45*(3), 234-251.

Giroux, H. (1999). *The mouse that roared: Disney and the end of innocence.* Oxford: Rowman & Littlefield Publishers.

Herrman, R. (2005). The disconnect between theory and practice in a visual culture approach to art education. *Art Education, 58*(5), 41-46.

Ledo, M. (2009). Art education through tattoo culture: Taboo or just tattoo? *Canadian Art Teacher/Enseigner les arts au Canada, 8*(1), 48-51.

Long, N. (2009). Meaningful art through taste and smell. *Canadian Art Teacher/Enseigner les arts au Canada, 8*(1), 16-19.

Richard, M. (2005). *Engaging youth through popular culture: Engaging looking glass youth in art through the visual narratives of the transforming self in popular culture.* Retrieved March 17, 2010 from: www.cultuurnetwerk.nl/producten_en_diensten/.../cpluse15overig.pdf

Tavin, K. & Anderson, D. (2003). Teaching (popular) visual culture: Deconstructing Disney in the elementary art classroom. *Art Education, 56*(3) 21- 24, 33-35.

Trend, D. (1992). *Critical pedagogy: Art/education/politics.* New York: Bergin & Garvey.

CONNECTIONS, REFLECTIONS AND CREATIONS

CHAPTER 22

Digital Technology in Art Classrooms

Connecting the Earliest 'Flicks' to Digital Video

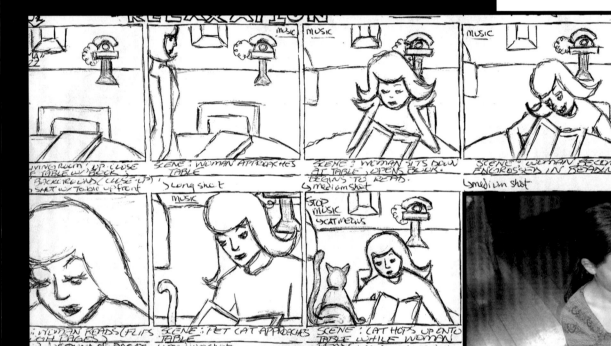

Joanna Black

Why bring technology into visual art classrooms? Why not continue to do what we have always done by teaching painting, drawing, sculpture and other traditional art media?

Visual art is fundamental to media production: just examine the significant function of pictures in ubiquitous modern day new media such as websites, videopodcasts, video production, Facebook sites, blogs, and wikis. You will find they play an instrumental role. Without visual images the media site looks empty.

In our Digital Age, with the supremacy of the written text being superseded by multimodal literacies (including images, sounds, words, music and oral language), the visual image is becoming more dominant (Duncum. 2004; Jewitt, 2008). Digital pictures now form an integral part of and form interrelationships with other multimodal texts[1].

The relationship between young people and technology is extremely important and as art educators we should pay attention. Technology is playing an increasingly more significant role in our children's lives. Our youths are plugged-in, "wired" multitaskers: it is common to see them doing homework, e-mailing, and listening to iPod music simultaneously. Additionally youths are using technology for social networking and co-creating purposes (making works through on-line collaboration) through use of such free software like Twitter, Facebook, MySpace, YouTube and Flickr. They enjoy using media: it is highly motivating. Moreover, the relationship between our children and their technology usage is changing. From the turn of the century until the 1990's children used to have one-way communication with media, either listening to music, watching television, or hearing the radio. Now in our Web 2.0 culture youths are becoming not just consumers but creators (or in technology terms, "*prosumers*") in ways their parents had not even imagined (Jenkins, 2009; Tapscott, 2009). For example, they make their own videos and post them on sites such as *YouTube*. Children produce other media such as mash-ups, remixing of sound, website design, recordings, and advertising, like culture jam imagery which they post on the Internet. In the past, students' creations would most often gather dust on their bedroom shelves after they had shown it to their peers, teachers, and parents. Now, by posting their work on the Internet they can reach an international audience.

Technology is part of our often tech-savvy, computer dexterous youth culture. It is part of their day-to-day experience, and when children encounter it creatively taught in classrooms, in my experience they enthusiastically and whole-heartedly embrace it. The final and very crucial reason is that visuals can provide significant meanings to multimodal, new media texts (Duncum, 2004). Technology without content is empty. Duncum (2004) writes that the notion of multiliteracy and multimodality is directed related to visual culture in which images are a part of communications. The "… study of visual imagery is concerned with more than images; it is concerned with the whole context of images, their production and the lived experience of those who view and interpret…" (p.254). Visual culture extends into cultural, economic, social, and political contexts. The well thought-out and designed image provides significant meaning. In fact, because of all these reasons, more visual art educators are now incorporating digital technologies into their art curricula. Art teachers have done this successfully through incorporating technology creatively in art lessons (Black, 2009; Delacruz, 2004, 2009; Gregory, 2009). I will recount my own introduction to integrating technologies in a visual art classroom context.

Video in the Art Classroom: My Personal Experience

Almost twenty years ago, I first became involved with teaching art and technology. I was hired to teach visual art to at-risk students at a high school in inner city Metropolitan Toronto. Within this school I worked in a special program addressing students' needs called, *"Communities in Schools."* The students were at risk of dropping out for a variety of reasons: disillusionment with education, troubled lives, difficult private relationships with family and friends, trouble with the law, and tumultuous pasts affecting their present lives. In my first year of teaching I planned with my students to create a half hour documentary dealing with the special program they were in and the ways it was affecting them personally. During this time video cameras were analogue (electronic), costly, enormous, rare, heavy 'monsters.' Consequently, they were rarely used in teaching, and boards owned few. To obtain these 'beasts,' my colleagues and I had to endure copious paperwork, long waiting periods, and short time periods for filming. But, it was worth it! As soon as I put a video camera into the hands of my at-risk students they changed and with it, the class dynamic: they were excited, actively engaged, and highly motivated. They planned to interview each other, their family members, their teachers, and administrators in the program including the then Superintendent of the North York Board of Education. They fulfilled these intentions and successfully completed the project. Finally, they proceeded to screen their work for the community at large. The students were 'hooked' on video and were extraordinarily proud of the documentary they created.

The consequence for me as an Art Educator was that I was likewise 'hooked' on teaching video production in my visual art class. I am still 'hooked'.

Since 1992 there have been significant advances in video production. In 1998 the firewire was invented by Michael Teener, formerly of Apple, (Smith, 2002), and Steve Jobs incorporated this invention into the Mac framework. As a result, digital video technologies were made accessible, easy to use, and inexpensive for educational purposes. Consequently, in the last decade, digital video has become accessible, popular and video usage has proliferated in schools. When I first began teaching video there were few educators using video cameras and few schools with programs in film or video or television. Almost all video/film programs were designed for high school students. Increasingly, over the last ten years, middle year educators and even early year art educators have begun to bring cameras and editing hardware and software into their art classrooms.

Next, I will outline how I have introduced the teaching of video in my classes. The inspiration came from the work of the Lumière brothers, famous for their technological invention of the modern camera/film developer/projector in one unit, and creating the first modern day film. I have taught the following approach to students ranging from teacher candidates at the university level to children in the earlier grades. For the description of the project I draw not only upon film history but also film theory, and hands-on production.

The Art Video Project:

Film History: The Lumière Brothers

Sometimes key inventions occur from a frenzied race between innovators from a variety of countries in a grueling, fast paced competition. Such was the case with the invention of modern film. Exactly who made the first movie has often been debated as it was indeed a pursuit between Thomas Edison (yes, the inventor of the light bulb!) the little known, Max and Emil Skladanowksy from Germany, and the now famous Lumière brothers from France. Edison's invention, the Kinetograph, had drawbacks: it was limited to one person as viewer and weighed in at several hundred pounds. The Skladanowsky brothers developed the "Bioskop." Unfortunately they lacked business acumen and advertising 'smarts' and even though they screened their film two months before Auguste and Louis Lumière, they remain virtually unknown. During pre-Hollywood times, it was French film producers who had the greatest influence in the emerging days of the film industry much because of the Lumière brothers. They owned a factory in Lyon, France, where they produced photographic equipment. Prompted by their father, they worked on creating a camera. In 1894, their father showed them Edison's Kinetescope and implored them to create a version of their own. The elder Lumière told his sons: "This is what you have to make, because Edison sells this at crazy prices and the concessionaires are trying to make films here in France to have them cheaper" (as cited in Robinson, 1996, p.61). The brothers far surpassed Edison. They invented something greatly superior, naming their invention the Lumière Cinématographe. In March 1895 the Lumière brothers began to demonstrate its usage and by December 28th of that year they screened their most famous and influential projection of ten films in Paris at the Salon Indien du Grand Café in Paris. Even though they are often inaccurately attributed with projecting the first modern moving picture, their work was certainly the most influential. They became internationally famous as a result of their well-designed, light, and efficient invention: the lightweight camera (only 16 pounds!), which was a film camera, developer, and projector all in one. The Lumière Cinématographe had other advantages as well, relying on hand power rather than electricity, allowing people to film in any location however exotic; it was extremely portable, and illuminated by limelight. In the early days of the 'moving pictures' camera, the Lumière brothers hired and trained twenty-one camera operators/projectionists who showed the marvelous, then radical, practical capabilities of their invention to the public. By July 1896, Lumière camera/projectionists had reached outside of France to other parts of Europe including London, and New York and by the end of that year Asia, Africa and even Canada (Cook, 1996; Ellis, 1990; Nowell-Smith, 1997; Robinson, 1996). By the very next year camera men/projectionists were bringing back films shots in hitherto remote locations, showing glamorous, exotic scenery from around the world.

The most famous, early films created by the Lumière brothers are primarily documentaries running approximating 50 seconds. They could not be longer because of the technology at that time in which the film base strength was weak and if the film was long, when pulled through the filmgate, broke as a result of high tension (Nowell-Smith, 1997, p. 7). The brothers filmed using a stationary camera, with no scene changes, no cuts, no edits, at eye level, using one shot. The first film ever made by them was called *La Sortie de l'usine (The Workers Leaving the Lumière Factory)*[2] and was shown at the initial Grand Café screening. Quite simply, it was an extreme long shot staged at the Lumière factory depicting workers departing from a hard days work walking both right and left out of the camera frame. Another film shown at the café was *L'arrivé du train à la gare de la ciotat (The Train Arriving at a Station)*. The brothers had excellent composition skills: the camera was set up so that the train appeared to arrive at the train station at an oblique angle. Audience members at that time, unused to the film medium, read the visuals literary: consequently, to save themselves, many hid under their seats, terrified of the train running over them (Cook, 1996; Nowell-Smith, 1996). Audience members during this period were utterly fascinated by the recording of day-to-day realistic events like a leaf fluttering and a baby eating food. Film as a new medium was embedded in realism. Another well-known film was called *Le Déjeuner de Bébé (Baby's Lunch)*. This is set up as a medium shot and is a recording of Auguste Lumière feeding his baby daughter at a table in the presence of his wife. The baby is dressed in the cotton-frilled finery of the period, a marvelous depiction of life in France for the upper middle class. Another early film called *L'Arroseur arrosé (Watering the Garden)* deviates from the documentary genre. It is the world's first comedy (Nowell-Smith, 1996) in which a boy steps on a garden hose, preventing water from coming out of it until the most opportune moment: exactly when the gardener peers into the hose to see what's blocking it. A chase between the gardener and boy ensues, ending with the adult spanking the rambunctious youth. All of the famous Lumière films previously discussed can be found on YouTube at : www.youtube.com/watch?v=NrhVvp2IfYA [3] Another interesting resource I have found helpful to show students is a DVD entitled, *Lumière and Company* (original title "*Lumière et Cie*")(Angelopoulos & Aranda,1995) commemorating the 100 anniversary of the Lumière brothers invention. It is comprised of films from forty international film directors who were provided with a Lumière camera and given a 52 second film time to produce a Lumière style film.

Setting up the Project: Hands-On Production

For the making of a Lumière video, I ask students to create footage replicating the style of a Lumière film. The Lumière format is an excellent way in which to begin teaching video to students, from young children to adults, who have little experience making videos. As with the Lumière brothers, the running time of the video is 50 seconds, using one-shot and no scene changes, camera cuts, or edits. They can film inside or outside in any location providing there is age appropriate teacher supervision. Like the Lumière brothers, students can use either documentary depicting everyday life, or comedy genres. They can select people, animals, and objects which are frequently moved toward and away from the camera. Students are asked to find drama within a real life situation. I point out that as a result of the subjects and method, Lumière brothers have provided us with a fascinating surface perspective of the people and their world at the turn of the century. (Ellis, 1990, p.6) I ask them to do the same with our world today.

I provide students with the following written description of the project:

Back in 1895 the Lumière brothers set the world on fire with their cinematic classics as *The Train Arriving at a Station*. These short films made the world look at itself with new eyes: the eye of the motion picture camera. This was a radical assault on the perceptions of the day. The world had never seen itself in such a way. In the spirit of the Lumière brothers show us the world we normally don't see or pay attention to: everyday things in our everyday life that we normally take for granted. Show us the banal, the mundane, and through doing this, make us pause to see something we haven't seen or wouldn't or don't think is worthy of our attention. Make us "stop and smell the roses" with your camera. Open our eyes to see something interesting in something simple. Show us visually a new perspective, through your keen observation. Produce a 50 second video short using the style of the Lumière brothers (Field and Black, 2001).

Visual Style and Theory

Key to a successful Lumière style film is the careful selection of (1) camera placement, (2) camera distance and (3) composition. In 1895 there was no camera movement, thus no panning, arcing, dollying, tilting or trucking.

As a result of the camera being stationary, camera placement was crucial. The filmmaker treated the unfolding events being filmed as a theatrical event where there were neither cuts nor edits. The viewer remains in the same position as though viewing a play in the theatre. Thus camera location is key because this is the area in which the filmmaker has control. The Lumière brothers carefully planned the camera position and I ask students to similarly think about this as well. The location affects the perspective the viewer obtains: will it be above eye level, below eye level, or at eye level? The Lumière Brothers often chose the latter. Will the objects or people being filmed be placed in the middle of the viewfinder? Will the movement appear to be coming at the viewer at an oblique angle?

The camera distance from the subject of the film also becomes important. They range from the extreme long shot to the extreme close-up[4]. There are seven basic shots:

Photo By: Dimitri Castrique

Figure 1:
Camera Distance
to Subject Filmed

Shot Types

1. **Extreme Close Up (ECU)** Top of the head to the chin
2. **Close Up (CU)** Top of the head to the shoulders
3. **Medium Close Up (MCU)** Top of the head to the chest
4. **Medium Shot (MS)** Top of the head to the waist
5. **Medium Long Shot (MLS)** Top of the head to the knees
6. **Long Shot (LS)** Tip of the head to the toes
7. **Extreme Long Shot (ELS or XLS)** Many people and settings including backgrounds indicating what season, date, time of day, and location of the shot.

Will students choose what the brothers often preferred: an extreme long shot or a medium shot? If the camera is placed far away from the subject, creating an extreme long shot, the location, setting, and action are important. However if the camera shot is a medium shot, then the expressions of the people or details of the object being filmed are significant. If students select a close-up, then the camera catches minute facial expressions. Students plan what is essential for them to pictorially depict whether action or setting or expressions or minute details.

Good composition is an arrangement of separate, disparate parts of the picture to create a unified, congruous, well-balanced completed image[5]. A film shot is closely akin to a painting or a drawing. Addressing the issue of balance is just as important in the hand created image as it is in the film shot. Thus, well-planned and well-executed compositions are important in Lumière style films. Paying attention to this will create a better video image.

The film frame is a horizontal rectangle in which the film director often balances the right and left side (Bordwell & Thompson, 2010). Teachers can show students unbalanced shots that have a variety of points of interest spread unevenly throughout the film frame. Compare unbalanced shots to points of interests spread evenly throughout the film frame and discuss the difference. Educators can discuss the simplest way to balance the composition which is by centering the person or people in the middle of the frame while eliminating any distracting images out of the shot. At a higher grade level than early years, teachers can discuss the effectiveness of unbalanced shots and more sophisticated compositions, including the rule of thirds (Bordwell & Thomspon, 2010, pp. 148-155). One of the key aspects of producing strong composition is to prevent too much headspace: space between the uppermost part of the frame and the top of a person's head.

Process from Working out Ideas to Screening the Students' Videos

It is not a good practice to simply place a camera in a student's hand and ask her/him to film without first planning the video: this is comparable to asking pupils to complete an elaborate painting without prior preliminary sketches. As in any visual art project, time must be provided for students to develop their own ideas. Additionally, and again as with any visual art project, it is at this initial stage in the process that students require a thoughtful approach to the project. In order to work out ideas for the 50-second video, students are asked to write up a description in one simple paragraph. Typically, at this stage, I ask questions in order to stimulate videographers to plan the video well.

**Figure 2:
Guiding Questions
Ask of Students**

1. What or whom will you videotape?
2. What is the setting/location of the video?
3. Describe the scene of the "everyday occurrence" you will record.
4. What camera shot will you use and why?
5. What camera height will you use?
6. Where will you place the camera in relation to the people, animals or objects filmed?
7. Will you use any special effects that were used in the days of the Lumière brothers?
8. Explain why this will be a good video using the Lumière brothers' style.

I then ask students to write out what costumes or props they will need. Next they proceed to describe the roles they will take from camera operator to actors and director.

The next step is for students to create a simple storyboard[6]. Storyboarding is the process of creating a visual record in drawing form of the planned video shots. They should consider what has been taught: subject matter, camera placement, camera distance, and composition. The storyboard should provide images of the pictorial movement. Art educators should require their students to plan extensively and work out ideas using traditional art media like sketchbooks and pencils. Once ideas have been solidified, description written, storyboard accepted, the students are ready to film. Provide time for students to make mistakes, experiment, reshoot and select the best film footage to use. Once they have filmed, are happy with the video footage, they are ready to edit.

The art of editing did not exist in the time of the Lumière brothers: it had not been invented. Art teachers who do not have computers for editing can leave the video as unedited footage. The other option is to use an in-camera edit process if the camera has this capability. The third option, and the one I use, is to edit the film using a computer and video software including the popular iMovie (for Apple computers) or Movie Maker (for PC computers)[7]. Almost all editing software allows students to:

(1) change the coloured video to black and white;
(2) add an old style effect to it so it looks like a "flick" running with a sped up, flickering effect of 16 to 20 frames per second (rather than the current 24 frames per second);
(3) add an aged crackling film effect;
(4) delete the filming soundtrack;
(5) add copyright free classical music to the moving image; and
(6) add written text.

The student Lumière looks complete if a title and credits are added. I ask students to add the title at the beginning of the film and to add the credits at the end of the film. The credits should include text indicating cameraperson, actors and director; the school in which the video was produced, and the year it was created. Adding text and music to the visual creates the multimodal work.

Marking, as with any visual art project, includes process and product. Initially I give students a camera test on how well they know their camera equipment. Also I mark students' descriptions of their projects, their storyboards, and their editing process. Finally, I mark their final video production in terms of what I have taught. Examining the following components have proved effective: (1) visual ideas; (2) composition; (3) how well pupils have followed the format of the Lumière film (including fifty second time limit, black and white footage, stationary camera usage, effective camera height; and picking a certain shot type that makes sense in regard to the subject matter depicted). I also mark for the effective choice of matching the music to the visuals.

I have found it effective to conduct a final screening of students' works in class or for the entire school. I remember one student, who notoriously missed most classes but did manage to make an innovative Lumière film. His peers were supportive and surprised at the school screening that he had actually become 'hooked' on the video process. Billy not only completed the video but had done it well: loud clapping, hooting, and cheers were heard in support of his achievement! Students take pride in their work and compiling a class Lumière film festival has always been successful. During class screenings I ask my students to discuss their visual ideas, their filming and their editing processes, thus sharing with their peers their own struggles and successes. Moreover, it is valuable for students to hear feedback about their final Lumière video from their peers through verbal critiques

Conclusion

Even though digital technologies can be used for a variety of purposes in art education, from using computers for research, for communicating, for use as art tools, I have concentrated in this chapter on its use in creative production. How is making Lumière style films beneficial for students? By outlining the process of creating videos in the style of the Lumière brothers, I have provided an example of a project that can engage students with multimodal literacies, including sound, texts, with the visual image, and their interrelationships. Additionally, making Lumière videos connects the earliest modern day films created by the Lumière Brothers to the making of digital video in art classrooms of today. Students can connect our rich art traditions of the past to the exciting present technologies that can be used in art. It also highly motivates and engages students in current digital technological processes.

With new software and hardware developing at a rapid pace, we need to ask questions such as, "Why use certain technologies?" "What value does it have for students?" "How do I approach using it in my class to enhance student learning?" "How does it interconnect to visual art?" I have found some people uncritically buy and adopt the latest 'sexy digital tools' with little thought, being enticed by marketing strategies and the desire to possess the latest digital gadgetries. Examine critically what software and hardware you should buy that will be beneficial for teaching and learning. Otherwise it may be relegated to becoming a toy that students become bored with extremely quickly. You may find that some technologies will be rejected and left by the wayside; others can be incorporated into classrooms to enhance teaching and learning, a few will be inspirational. Video making has been and remains inspirational for me and many of my students. I have found it promotes remarkable creativity, wonderful insights, and significant originality.

I believe that teaching technology in visual art without meaningful art content is empty. Through asking students to think about and plan the videotaping of a subject about everyday experiences using the Lumière film style, interesting content is developed. As well, throughout the Lumière project the visual arts are fundamental to media production, from storyboarding and filming, and planning the composition, to creating the final Lumière video. Students become creators through the making of Lumière videos. This project fosters knowledge building in art and technology, communication skills, and creative expression. I have found that through teaching the Lumière video project Leonardo da Vinci observations 'ring true' that, "Art lives from constraints and dies from freedom" (Genn, 2010). Through students returning to and working within the limitations of the past they create new, thoughtful, expressive, multimodal video art.

Reference

Angelopoulos, T & Aranda, V. (Directors). (1995) *Lumière et compagnie.* [DVD] Available from http://www.amazon.ca/s/?url=search-alias%3Daps&field-keywords=1572522119%7C%206304287356&tag=imdbca-20

Black, J. (2009). Necessity is the mother of invention: Changing power dynamics between teachers and students in wired art classrooms. *Canadian Review of Art Education, 36,* 99-117.

Bordwell, D. and Thompson, K. (2010). *Film art: An introduction.* Toronto: McGraw-Hill Companies, Inc.

Cook, D. (1996). *A history of narrative film.* New York: Norton & Company.

Delacruz, E. (2004). Teachers' working conditions and the unmet promise of technology. *Studies in Art Education, 46*(1), 6-19.

Delacruz, E. (2009). Art education aims in the Age of New Media: Moving toward global civil society. *Art Education 62*(5), 13-17.

Duncum, P. (2004). Visual culture isn't just visual: Multiliteracy, multimodality and meaning. *Studies in Art Education, 45*(3), 252-264.

Ellis, J. (1990). *A history film.* New Jersey, United States: Prentice Hall.

Field, D. & Black, J. (2001). *The Lumière challenge.* Unpublished manuscript. Toronto, Ontario.

Genn, R. [Editor]. *The painter's keys.* Retrieved May 8, 2010 from http://quote.robertgenn.com/auth_search.php?authid=243.

Gregory, D. (2009). Boxes with fire: Wisely integrating learning technologies into the art classroom. *Art Education, 62*(3), 47-54.

Hart, J. (1999). *The art of the storyboards: Storyboarding for film, TV, and animation.* Woburn, MA: Focal Press.

Jenkins, H. *(2009). Confronting the challenges of participatory culture: Media education for the 21st Century.* Cambridge, Massachusetts: MIT Press.

Jewitt, C. (2008). Multimodality and literacy in school classrooms. *Review of Research in Education, 32,* 241-267.

Mascelli (1965). *The five C's of cinematography: Motion picture filming techniques.* Beverley Hills, CA: Silman-James Press.

Nowell-Smith, G. (Ed.). (1997). *The Oxford history of world cinema.* New York: Oxford University Press Inc.

Robinson, D. (1996). *From peep show to palace: The birth of American film.* New York: Columbia University Press.

Smith, S. (2002). *Firewire filmmaking.* California, USA: Peachpit Press.

Tapscott, D. (2009). *Grown up digital: How the Net Generation is changing your world.* New York: McGraw-Hill Books.

Endnotes

[1] Multimodal is defined as meanings derived from language incorporating image, gesture, gaze, body posture, sound, writing, music, and speech (Jewitt, 2008, p.246).

[2] Names of the films appear differently in a variety of texts. For this chapter I am using the titles of the Lumière films used in The Oxford History of World Cinema (Nowell-Smith, 1996).

[3] To see the Lumière films individually which are discussed in the chapter refer to YouTube sites as follows: (a) Workers Leaving the Lumière Factory at http://www.youtube .com/watch? v=OYpKZx090UE; (b)The Train Arriving at a Station at http://www.you tube.com/watch?v=2cUEANKv964; (c) Baby's Lunch at http://www.youtube.com /watch?v=1WmimQd0qW8 (d) Watering the Garden at http: http://www.youtube.com/watch?v=watch?v=Ei6nJfXAuHQ

[4] There are numerous websites showing pictures of camera shots. One example is http://books.google.ca/books?id=XK4Bq45DM4oC&pg=PA12&lpg=PA12&dq=extreme+long+shot+to+close+u%5B&source=bl&ots=vKdPW7et58&sig=VtI3VC8_jfkHQ9Zl3H00Hcjlp5E&hl=en&ei=xnDtS4yIKsL88AbPp7H-Cg&sa=X&oi=book_result&ct= result&resnum=3&ved=0CBsQ6AEwAjgK#v=onepage&q&f=false

[5] For a thorough and superb discussion of composition in film refer to Mascelli (1965) pp. 197-244.

[6] There are many books written in which the author describes in detail how to create storyboards. One example is by John Hart (1999).

[7] If a teacher is unfamiliar with editing software there are excellent on-line tutorials obtained through Google.

CONNECTIONS, REFLECTIONS AND CREATIONS

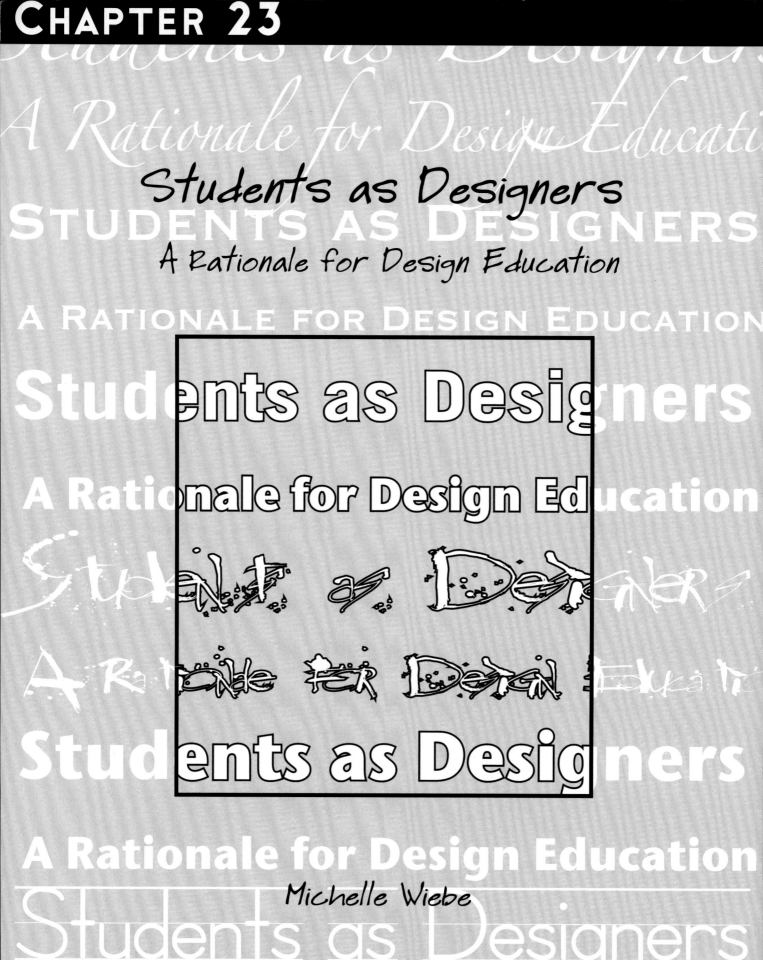

CHAPTER 23

Students as Designers

A Rationale for Design Education

Michelle Wiebe

By the time your students reach the classroom each day, they have already encountered countless examples of design because "*everything* that affects our lives was designed by *somebody*" (Brainard, 2006, p. 6). In our industrialized world, everything from the dwellings in which we live to the cars we drive began as a design concept. In fact, "designers are the largest group of artists in industrial societies and their work comprises some of the most public, most widely viewed, and most frequently consumed forms of art" (Marschalek, 1995, p. 20). Thus, the study of design in elementary schools should move beyond a contemplation of the elements and principles of design in relation to fine art to encompass application of design principles to the creation of meaningful communication and objects.

> Youth need the opportunity to learn more about design and human behavior so they can learn they have choices about how supportive their environments can be. Children can [determine] how design influences their behaviors; how design can be used to manipulate behavior; how design can encourage or discourage conversation, establish status, put people in power positions, increase or decrease anxiety. (Clemons, 2006, p. 279)

Additionally, including design training in art increases students' visual literacy and enhances their ability to understand the myriad of visual messages to which they are exposed (Nixon, 2003, p. 407). "By educating students to understand and communicate through visual modes, teachers empower their students with the necessary tools to thrive in increasingly media-varied environments" (Riesland, 2005, p.2).

Defining Design

The term design can suggest many things because "there are many kinds of design under the *Design Umbrella* (Brainard, 2006, p. 6). Students begin to understand design further when they see that it can be "classified into four categories: functional design, graphic design, environmental design, and nonfunctional design" (Brainard, 2006, p. 6). Functional design includes multiple categories. For instance, product, industrial, and architectural design are all functional design in three dimensions whereas graphic design and environmental design are more about the development of two-dimensional visual communication than about the design of objects. Nonfunctional design, however, has more to do with the decorative arts. "It is usually considered nonfunctional, because it satisfies more of an emotional or aesthetic need than a practical need" (Brainard, 2006, p. 7). Athough functional design is created to have purpose we tend to put emphasis on functional design that also appeals aesthetically.

The Act of Designing

Designing is often defined as problem solving and "problem solvers by definition are hunters engaged in a search for solutions" (Meggs cited in Landa, 2001, p.xiv). "Design activity is always grappling with the unknown.... It is a problem-centered activity..... The design act is one of discovering and elaborating and adapting requirements and provisions to match one another" (Archer & Roberts cited in Parkinson, 2007, p. 244). Design itself can be described as "the way you put everything together – how you arrange the elements" (Landa, 1998, p. 22).

Elementary students engaged in design activity are active problem solvers seeking to develop solutions to everyday problems. Student designers model, construct, layout, plan, and are involved in experiential learning. "The experiential learning cycle involves a concrete experience that leads to observations and reflections then to formation of abstract concepts and generalisations, before finally testing implications from concepts in new situations" (Clemons, 2006, p. 276).

Designers typically work and rework ideas to refine, polish and enhance them. Encouraging students to utilize the design process to produce their own designs helps them develop strong process skills. Additionally, gaining an understanding that concepts improve with revision helps student designers in all of their endeavors.

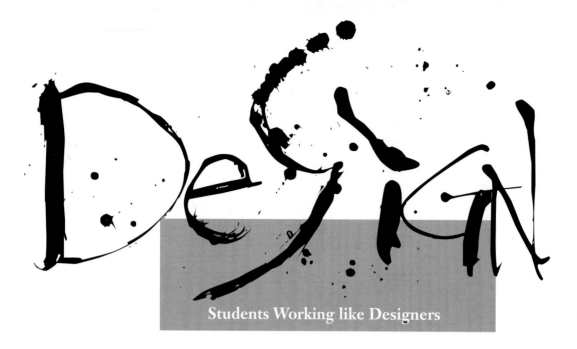

Students Working like Designers

When good design is concept driven, student designers develop the habit of beginning their designs by refining their ideas. "The design concept is the creative solution to the design problem" (Landa, 2001, p. 48). The design process typically begins with research and concept development. In terms of design, research can encompass manipulating existing products, looking at visuals, talking to viewers about their reactions, testing art materials, and brainstorming. Research should be guided by a clear understanding of the design problem and a crucial aspect of design education involves working with students to help them conceptualize the design challenge before they begin working. Students should be encouraged to write the problem in their own words or engage in a class discussion of the problem so that everyone clearly understands the challenge.

Research should generate potential solutions recorded in a series of thumbnail sketches. Producing two thumbnails may challenge young students whereas upper elementary students can competently produce multiple visual solutions. When the students are working on product or packaging design, some of their "thumbnails" may actually be mock-ups. Sketching multiple thumbnails is as much about refining ideas as it is about generating new ones. Thus, it is worthwhile to remind students that they don't need to come up with multiple ideas but that they do need to devise multiple ways to express their ideas in order to generate original concepts. Students who get stuck or who are stressed because they can't think of a great idea are sometimes able to push forward when they are encouraged to think of the wrong idea. Strangely enough, trying to think of the wrong idea often encourages original concepts because students begin to think of the design problem in different ways.

A working designer will take his or her best ideas and produce rough sketches. Likewise students should be encouraged to create a rough version of their chosen idea at close to actual size so that they can alter space relationships that worked in a small sketch but are not ideal when the work is larger. The process of producing rough sketches can allow students to experiment with materials and colours as well.

The final step in the design process is producing comprehensives. This finished work is usually referred to as the final comps. Student designers are able to produce excellent work in their comps because of all of the planning and refinement that has preceded the final work.

Since students are not working designers, the steps in the design process may be condensed depending on the design problem and the grade. The initial planning stages are important for all students, however, and the results of the process are readily apparent in the finished designs as well as in the students' ability to talk about their work.

The Challenge

Susan sits with her chin resting in her hands; her face a study in concentration. She is staring at the box of bandages on the corner of her desk. She scribbles something on the paper in front of her, then shakes her head and crosses it out. She thinks some more then appears to stare blankly ahead. Her eyes rest briefly on the tape dispenser sitting on the teacher's desk and suddenly she is drawing rapidly on her paper. She picks up the bandage box and removes a bandage so that she can measure it. Then she draws some more.

Susan is engaged in a package redesign exercise. She brought the bandage box from home because it was a product that frustrated her. As she has explained, "bandages are really silly because when you cut yourself and you are bleeding, you can't get them open." Thus, Susan is determined to figure out a new way to package bandages and the tape dispenser has given her an idea.

Each student in the class is working on the redesign of a package. Since beginning the project student are demonstrating a heightened awareness of the packaging that surrounds them. Their comments show that they are also paying close attention to the use of image, type and colour in packaging design.

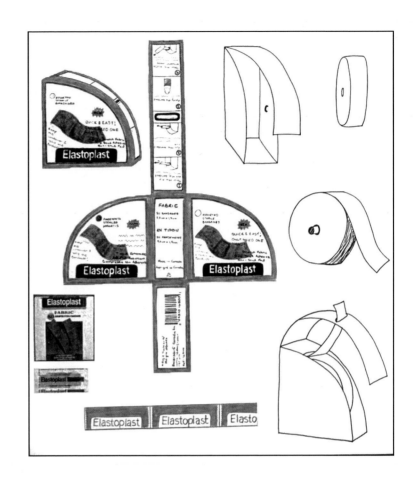

Design Activities for the Elementary Classroom

Being surrounded by design, it is simple to find many examples for class discussions, for product redesign and to provide examples to students. A class discussion of the use of colour in several product packages can be a great way to discuss colour and how it affects the viewer. Additionally, students can critique posters to see if they are able to gain all of the information that they should from the poster.

Beginning the following activities with a critique of existing designs gives students ideas about what to do and what not to do. Looking and thinking about what they see helps students to be aware of the designs in the world around them while it informs their own work.

Pictogram Design

A pictogram is simply defined as a "pictorial sign that depicts a simplified representation of a particular object or activity" (Livingston & Livingston, 1998, p. 156).

Activity: Discuss the use of pictograms and how often we rely on them. Have students do a series of sketches to design a pictogram of their own. A good starting point is to have students re-design washroom or no smoking pictograms. A more involved project would be one where students work in teams to create a signage system for the school wherein pictograms are designed as signage systems for an open house or sports event. This could be carried further into a project where students develop an information system for a park that is entirely composed of pictograms so that small children can understand them.

201

Typographic Design

Type surrounds us and having children study typefaces provides a strong grounding for many design activities. A great way to begin the consideration of type is to have students develop their own collection of typefaces. Depending on the age of the student, there are many possible sources for lettering. Very young children are exposed to letterforms in books teaching them the alphabet. Because of repeated exposure, "a child learns to recognize the shape of a letter and to associate it with sound and meaning" (Landa & Gonella, 2001, p. 18). Recognizing that children already have deeply ingrained perceptions about letters can be a good starting point for a class or group discussion of the nature of different typefaces. Encouraging students to realize that each letterform has particular characteristics that convey feelings can increase their understanding of printed communication.

Thus, spending time with type is an excellent way to get students to focus on imagery that has a subtle but direct impact upon them throughout their lives. The study of type is integral to design and encouraging students to focus on the form of letters early is valuable because as Landa & Gonnella (2001) point out, "a successful and creative designer intimately knows every curve, angle, and stroke of letters" (p. 20).

Typographic exercises provide students with the opportunity to work on their drawing and observational skills while they learn to focus on the manner in which type enhances meaning.

1) Illustrated word:

- Choose a word to illustrate. Do not use pictures or distort your letterforms into pictures to tell your story. Let the letterforms communicate their message visually through size, colour, value, shape, structure, texture, placement (Arnston, 2003, p. 75).

2) Replace a letter:

- Choose a word and replace one of the letters with an object that refers to that word.

- For example, replace the "p" in spoon with a spoon (Landa & Gonnella, 2001, p. 38).

3) Word and meaning:

- Design a word that imitates the sound or the action that the word expresses.

- Think about the fact that type can suggest sound as well as other sensations (Landa & Gonnella, 2001, p. 30).

4) Alter a letter:

- Students find a typeface that has characteristics they like and then work to subtly alter two of the letters so that they can write their initials in a type that they have re-designed

Consideration of type leads quite naturally into the creation of logos.

Logo Design

"The logo is a unique type of lettering that spells out the name of the company or product. It may be hand lettered, but is usually constructed out of variations on an existing typeface" (Arnston, 2003, p. 88).

Activity: Creating a successful logo is an involved activity because logos often involve both words and images. Logos can be just a name or they can be words cleverly combined with a symbol so that a clear idea about the object or company is conveyed. A good logo design project for young students involves creating a personal logo using the letters of their name combined with an image that says something about them.

Environmental Design/Wayfinding: Sign Design

Signs are "communication in the environment"

(Wheeler, 2006, p. 138).

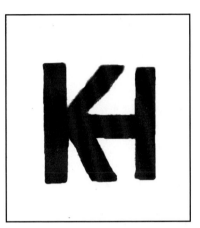

Activity: Creating a scenario where students not only think about the signs that they see regularly but also how type, scale, and colour contribute to communication is a worthwhile goal. Signage is often three-dimensional and sign design provides the opportunity to study sculptural issues. Students are to design a sign for their bedroom, the classroom, their desks, or any other appropriate venue (for instance, the activity could be tied to Language arts or to Social Studies if the students were to design signs for the places they were studying or for places in a novel they were reading). If materials such as play dough are used the students could make letters out of the play dough, if plaster is used it can be poured into a sturdy paper plate and the letters can be pushed into the surface when the plaster is almost set or carved into the surface after the plaster has set. Alternately, students can create the sign's message with found objects like rocks or sticks that have been arranged in a paper plate or a box lid and then pour the plaster carefully over the objects to create an inlaid sign. [* if using plaster be sure to put straws through or embed paper clips in the back for hanging]. It can be helpful to remember that the objectives of signage design are to:

- communicate information
  - be clear to potential users
  - be visible to the average user (designers must think about whether the viewer will be moving quickly, in dim light, or be far away)
  - use colour, scale, format, type, materials, placement to assist visibility
  - create signs that will be durable where they are placed
  - complement the surrounding environment. (Wheeler, 2006, p. 139)

Promotion/Information Design: Poster Design

"A poster is a two-dimensional, single-page format used to display information, data, schedules, or offerings, and to promote people, causes, places, products, companies, services or organizations" (Landa, 2001, p. 142).

Activity: Poster design can encourage students to think deeply about the visual message that they are trying to communicate. At any age designing a poster should begin with brainstorming to generate ideas about the poster's intended message. This activity encourages students both to synthesize information into a single visual and to extract information from the many posters that they see each day.

Successful posters may be designed using just words. Often, however, they are a combination of words and images. Any image can work in a poster from very abstract to photographic. When student designers work on posters they should be challenged to think carefully about the message that they wish to communicate. Designing a successful poster is a challenge because the poster format requires transmitting a message using design principles.

The objectives of poster design are to:

- transmit a clear message
- develop an easily read and understood design
- produce a design that is clear from a distance
- include all of the necessary information (and remove information that isn't necessary
- plan a design that emphasizes the most important information
- use the principles of design to guide the arrangement of the visual elements
- design appropriately for the subject, audience, and environment
- express the spirit of the subject. (Landa, 2001, p.148)

Poster design can be very involved and with young children it is best to stress one or two objectives at a time. For instance, primary students can focus on creating a design that is directed at their own age group. The benefit of this approach is that it encourages children to think about the messages in posters and helps them realize that the posters they like are probably aimed at them. Older students can grapple with issues of legibility and hierarchy of information.

204

Package Design: Shopping Bags

"Think of a shopping bag as a portable store display."   (Landa, 2001, p. 198).

Activity: Shopping bag design is the basis for a versatile project because shopping bags come in a range of sizes and styles. Part of the design challenge can be having students design the size and shape of the bag to suit its probable use. Shopping bags are often created using durable materials so that they can be re-used. This means that the design will endure. Primary – students may design and create a shopping bag for a particular shopping activity (i.e. groceries, clothes, pet food, etc.). The colours and pictures on the bag should be appropriate for the chosen activity. Upper elementary – students could create a community or cultural shopping bag. The graphics on the bag should reflect a chosen aspect of the community or cultural group upon which the student has chosen to focus. Media should be chosen to fit the theme.

Objectives to consider in shopping bag design.

- bag should be easy to fold and store
- bag should be sturdy so that it can be re-used
- bag is three-dimensional and students need to consider all sides
- graphics on the bag should reflect its use
- graphics could be promotional and this needs to be considered

Packaging

"Although packaging is essentially a three-dimensional design discipline, the two-dimensional design on the surfaces of a package is an integral part of the overall impact" (Landa, 2001, p. 186). Packaging design is a specialized field because it requires knowledge of a wide range of materials, technical information, construction issues, manufacturing, safety, display, recycling and packaging regulations (Landa, 2001, p. 186). Students working on package design projects can be engaged and challenged planning for format and graphics.

205

Package Design

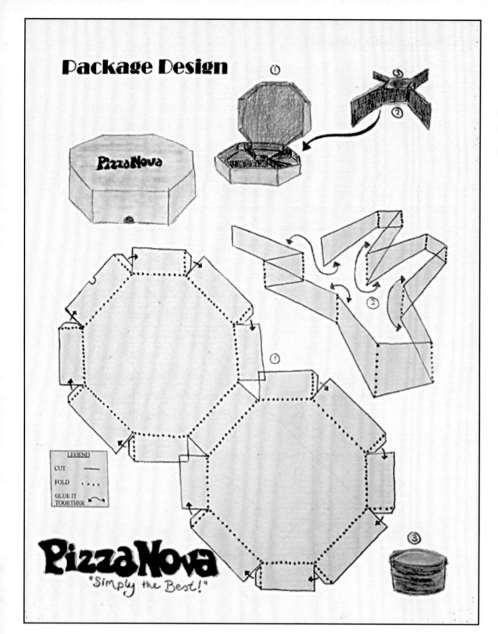

PizzaNova

Pizza Nova
"Simply the Best!"

LEGEND
CUT ——
FOLD · · · ·
GLUE IT TOGETHER

Packaging Re-design

Activity: Students are to choose an existing product/package then brainstorm to come up with words that describe the attributes of that product.

- Who is the target market for the product and how does the package reflect that?

- What does the product do?

- Is this a product that does the same thing it has always done but looks very different than it used to look?

- Students should consider the parts of the package that would be unlikely to change – for instance, a brand name is unlikely to be written differently.

- Once the students have decided on an approach they should begin sketching their solutions prior to building the mock-up of their redesigned product.

Your objectives when designing a product package are to:

- plan for functionality
- be able to make a mock-up
- research materials and construction
- be aware of recycling and wastefulness
- consider the package from all sides
- consider the impact of colour
- consider the *intended audience* and try to plan the design accordingly
- make it work with a larger visual identity system (if applicable)
- research the competition (optional for higher grades)
- make it stand out from the competition (optional for higher grades). (Landa, 2001, p. 197)

Remember, "in the average half-hour trip to the supermarket, 30,000 products vie for the shoppers attention" (Hine cited in Wheeler, 2006, p. 134). Packaging often makes the difference in terms of what you choose to buy.

Surface Design

Surface design is the field of design that is concerned with pattern. Surface designers create wall coverings, Kleenex boxes, dinnerware, and greeting cards. Surface design is often nonfunctional design in that the design of surface is focused on the aesthetics of an object.

Kleenex Box Cover

Activity: Each student should begin with an old Kleenex box that he or she covers with corrugated cardboard that is roughly taped or glued in place (this makes the box larger so that the papier-mâché box cover will fit easily over a new box of Kleenex). Once the Kleenex box is covered with corrugated cardboard, it should be placed in a plastic bag or covered with plastic so that the papier-mâché doesn't adhere to it. The upper surfaces are then covered with papier-mâché (the bottom must remain open so that the Kleenex box cover can be placed over a new Kleenex box). Once the papier-mâché has dried, students should decorate the surface with paint as if they were surface designers designing a Kleenex box. The older the students the more they should be encouraged to plan their design to match a room in their home. The finished product may be varnished for greater durability.

References

Arnston, A. E. (2003). *Graphic design basics* (4th edition). Toronto, ON: Thomson Wadsworth.

Brainard, S. (2006). *A design manual* (4th edition). Upper Saddle River, NJ: Pearson Prentice Hall.

Clemons, S. A. (2006). Interior design supports art education: A case study. *International Journal of Art and Design Education, 25(3)*, 275-285.

Landa, R. (2001). *Graphic design solutions* (2nd edition). Scarborough, ON: Onword Press – Thomson Learning.

Landa, R. (1998). *Thinking creatively: New ways to unlock your visual imagination*. Cincinnati, OH: North Light Books.

Landa, R. & Gonnella, R. (2001). *Visual creativity: Workout book*. Scarborough, ON: Delmar - Nelson Thompson.

Livingston A. & Livingston, I. (1998). *Dictionary of graphic design and designers*. London: Thames and Hudson.

Marschalek, D.G. (1995). A Guide to curriculum development in design education. *Art Education, 48(1)*, 14-20.

Nixon, H. (2003). New research literacies for contemporary research into literacy and new media? *Reading Research Quarterly, 38(3)*, 407 – 413.

Parkinson, E. (2007). Practical modelling and hypothesis testing in primary design and technology education. *International Journal of Technology & Design Education, 17*, 233–251.

Riesland, E. (2005). *Visual literacy and the classroom*. (on-line). Retrieved on 01/28/10 at: www.newhorizons.org/strategies/literacy/riesland.htm

Wheeler, A. (2006). *Designing brand identity* (2nd edition). Hoboken, NJ: John Wiley & Sons.

CHAPTER 24

Take it Outside!
A Place-Based Approach to Art Education

Hilary Inwood

It's a frigid February day, with the temperature hovering fifteen degrees below zero; the type of day that most teachers would expect to hear students' excuses to stay inside, even at recess. But down in the school garden, a class of grade five students is working on a collaborative ice sculpture. Having frozen leaves, pine cones and twigs into containers of water the night before, they work quickly, popping the works out of their molds and carefully considering the placement of their individual pieces in the creation of the whole. Inspired by the artwork of Scottish artist, Andy Goldsworthy, they remove their mittens as they freeze one piece to another with water, working quickly so their fingers don't get frostbite. After an hour of cooperative art making, they run back to their classroom to warm up, excited about their winter art adventure and confident that they have created something creative and unique.

What this class didn't realize was that their engagement with this project exemplifies an approach to learning called place-based art education. Inspired by the more general movement of place-based education, this approach encourages teachers to take students out of the confines of classrooms to experience the rich learning grounds of their communities. This is being used to great advantage by art teachers and generalist teachers alike to inspire their students to undertake art-based learning that connects and responds to the local environments that inform their daily lives. It results in students' increased involvement with physical, political, and cultural aspects of their communities, broadening and deepening their connections to and understanding of the places in which they live.

Place-based education *advocates* for the important roles local communities should play in learning at all levels, from primary through to higher education (Sobel, 2004). By rooting learning in the real world, students are able to experiment with how concepts and ideas from all subject areas have a value and application in the 'real world'. Typically used in conjunction with experiential and constructivist approaches to learning, place-based education encourages students to take an active role in their own learning and apply their new-found knowledge to solving social, economic or environmental problems faced by their communities. Working from these experiences in their own neighbourhoods and a strong connection to place, students are able to better relate their learning to the complexity of national or global issues as they get older.

One can argue that place-based education is nothing new, as indigenous cultures have utilized place-based learning for centuries as a way of connecting to the rhythms, resources and challenges of their locales. Certainly some communities have maintained a close connection to place through their schools, but in many more (particularly in industrialized nations) these connections have been greatly reduced, if not entirely lost, in the shift towards educational standardization and mass-produced curricular resources.

For many educators who teach art, place-based education is innovative as it offers a rationale to open the door of the classroom and take their students outside to use the local community as inspiration for their art lessons. They recognize that this runs counter to the approach taken by others who feed students a steady diet of art for art's sake, studio techniques, colour theory, and Old Masters artworks inside the 'blank canvas' of an art room. This misses an important opportunity for students to develop an appreciation of the ways in which the visual arts can be used to create connections in their lives or to bring about positive social change in their communities. But as educators are introduced to contemporary artists' creative solutions to social and environmental challenges, and to the extensive body of writing about place-based education, (Gruenewald, 2003; Orr, 1992; Sanger, 1997; Sobel, 2004), more and more teachers are considering the benefits of a place-based approach.

This is creating an important integration, as art education brings its own strengths to place-based education: it has proven to be fertile soil in which to grow creative approaches to problem-solving, critical thinking and self-reflexive learning, all necessary for making our communities healthier and happier places. It achieves this by making learning personal, in part through developing learners' visual, spatial, emotional and embodied forms of intelligence, and by giving them communicative tools to share their individual perspectives. It is this ability to feed learners' minds yet also touch their spirits that makes art education a strong ally in fostering place-based learning.

I am not the first art educator to recognize the potential for integrating a place-based approach with art education. Almost two decades ago Blandy and Hoffman (1993) called for "an art education of place" in content and pedagogy (p. 23). They encouraged learners to use their local communities as a source of imagery and inspiration for all aspects of art education – art making, art history, art criticism and aesthetics. In this they demonstrated their support for a bioregionalist stance, one that takes the realities and needs of learners' surrounding communities into consideration and sees the possibility of enlarging the range of activities typically found in art class:

210

Exploring and conveying relationships with the Earth; performing acts that cleanse the land, air, and water; and empowering people to act for a healthier environment are important and credible tasks for the artist and important and credible acts to be studied as art. (p. 30)

Along with other art educators like Graham (2007) and Gradle (2007), I have also been inspired by this seminal article to further develop ideas about place-based art education (Inwood, 2008). Graham advocates linking art education to a critical pedagogy of place, defined as moving beyond the physicality of natural environments to include the social, cultural, ecological and political dimensions of place. I wholeheartedly agree with his assessment of the advantages of intersecting these models of learning:

> Art asks us to resist habits of conventional thinking and to consider what we live for. Art education seeks divergent responses to important personal, environmental, and social problems that require creative, imaginative solutions. Art education framed by a critical pedagogy of place creates opportunities for students to engage in thinking and artmaking that considers vital questions about nature, place, culture and ecology. (Graham, 2007, p. 387)

Taking a place-based approach to art education offers an unexpected advantage by connecting to other theories in the field. One of these is community-based art education; one it strongest advocates, London (1994), called for a "curriculum more responsive to the world of the child [by] broadening the arena of education to include the people, places, and events of the entire community" (p. xi). He noted the positive attributes of this by writing that "the world outside the classroom is far grander, more compelling, and ultimately more instructive than the world inside the classroom" (p. xiii). Urban art education proponents (Asher,

2000; Holloway & Krensky, 2001; Thurber, 1997) are also supportive, as a place-based approach better supports urban learners in seeing the positive qualities of their own communities, as well as having them work actively towards making them better places to live aesthetically, physically and environmentally. There is also a connection to built environment education in its increased attention to learners' local surroundings, to the influences that shape built and natural spaces, and for the need to participate in shaping our places in the future (Adams, 1999).

While its theoretical connections are important, what does place-based art education look like? As evidenced in the literature, it can manifest in a variety of ways, depending on the community in which it is conducted. For example, Birt, Krug and Sheridan (1997) described the artistic and scientific investigations of a local pond by students at Pickerington Elementary School in Ohio, resulting in a mosaic installed on site to share their learning with other visitors. Anderson (2000) outlined an interdisciplinary program that has adolescent learners drawing, painting and sculpting as a means to explore the ecology of a local river. Eco-artist Lynn Hull led a program in West Texas that involved observations, research and artworks made specifically for the wildlife of the Playa Lake area by college students (Keifer-Boyd, 2002).

I am happy to report that place-based art education is also putting down deep roots in Canada and appearing in a variety of school and community-based contexts. In the *Neighbourhoods* program, the Toronto District School Board has funded residencies for visual artists to work with elementary students to examine their sense of place in their local communities. These explorations result in large-scale children's art projects, often permanently installed in schools, which investigate and celebrate aspects of their own communities and cultures. These programs involve students going on walking tours of their neighbourhoods, researching their local history and cultural traditions, talking with community elders, and sharing stories of their own experiences. The results have been as unique as the communities themselves: mixed media murals on school walls; paintings collaged with photos and remnants of the students' own clothing; large, hand-drawn aerial maps of their communities; and multi-layered quilts that symbolize aspects of community life.

At Runnymede Public School, the site of the ice sculpture project mentioned at the outset, students have been using their own place-based art to ameliorate environmental problems in the schoolyard (Inwood, 2006). Three primary classes created 'art gardens' of artworks and plantings in the raised beds near the school's front door; the presence of their art solved a school problem by keeping children from trampling the plants in these same beds. In another part of the yard, the grade eights cast large concrete garden stones with environmental images to create pathways to reduce soil compaction around tree roots. Grade five students wove a giant grapevine basket around a Medicine Wheel garden for protection, and then installed a knit bombing project on a tree trunk to signify its special status in the garden. These projects have resulted in a dynamic schoolyard that can be used as a learning resource for other classes, and have taught the young artists involved that they can use their creativity to find solutions to local environmental problems; they understand that they can make a difference.

A further example of place-based art education that casts a wider net can be found in two community-based art projects focused on the health of local fish and their watersheds. In the FishNet project [www.projectfishnet.org], artists worked alongside school children to study the challenges faced by indigenous fish species in the Great Lakes. After learning about and witnessing the detrimental effects of habitat destruction, pollution and invasive species on these fish, students worked with local artists to create over a thousand painted fish for a community exhibition. Strung from the ceiling of a lakefront gallery, viewers felt as if they were swimming in a school of fish themselves. The gallery sold symbolic fishing licenses to viewers, with the proceeds going to local fish-friendly charities and enabling the permanent installation of the artistic fish in the participating schools as a reminder of students' important learning. On the west coast, the *Stream of Dreams* project [www.streamofdreams.org] undertakes similar learning that results in schools of colourful wooden fish being created and installed on school fences as evidence of students' involvement in learning about local watersheds.

These place-based art education programs offer insight into the advantages and challenges of this approach. On the plus side, students are often more engaged when immersed in learning about their own communities, especially if their learning takes them outside. Their excitement can feed into the project at hand, and result in a higher quality of work as they see its purpose and connections to their own lives. Another advantage is that place-based projects are often interdisciplinary in nature, weaving together learning about art, history, science, language arts and geography, better emulating what many professional artists go through in creating their work. Because of this, students may also get more feedback from both inside and outside of the school; local community members will often more positively receive their art as they appreciate the connections being made to their lives as well.

But there are challenges to a place-based approach to teaching art that need to be taken into account by teachers at the outset. Moving outside the classroom with students requires permission forms from parents and support from administrators, as well as dealing with raised eyebrows from colleagues. Weather conditions, transportation issues, insects, animals and curious community members can all influence a project in unexpected ways, so flexibility and a sense of humour is required. But these are not insurmountable and become commonplace the more the class moves out into their community; both teachers and students learn to cope and quickly realize that the serendipity and excitement of working in the real world far outweighs the safety and security of the four walls of the classroom.

There are ways to circumvent these challenges and make a place-based approach to art education pleasurable for both teachers and students from the start. If possible, get one blanket permission form signed by parents early in the year covering all walking distance excursions, saving endless paperwork. Teach the class how to be prepared with clothing and footwear for the weather, but keep a supply of items (mittens, rubber boots, scarves from the lost and found) on hand for those who forget. Before starting out, ensure that your students have a firm grasp on the principles of outdoor class behaviour; for some groups this may take repeated small forays just in the school yard before they are ready for trips farther afield.

Certainly knowing about and incorporating your students' own community interests are a great way to keep them on task. For instance, start the year by getting to know aspects of the neighbourhood they love or want to improve. Introduce them to the work of other artists who respond to the needs and interests of their communities (refer to Lippard, 1997 for a terrific introduction). Ask for students' input in establishing the theme of a community-based project, and enlist their help in identifying useful resources, support people, or local places of interest. Put a constructivist approach to teaching and learning about art (Milbrandt et. al., 2004) into play by letting their interests and questions inform the development of the project, rather than dictating what you think is best. Listen to their ideas, hopes and dreams for their community, so they can learn how to take an active role in its improvement.

Finally, look to your community not just as a site for art making but also as a source for images, materials, exhibit venues and expertise. Keep a set of portable art tools (like drawing boards and digital cameras) on hand to capture aspects of the community firsthand. Have treasure hunts to look for natural and found materials in the community to integrate into artworks; these materials bring meaning by deepening connections to place. Bring local experts to talk to the class in and out of the school; hearing veterans' stories in front of a war memorial or architects talking about a building they designed while standing inside it is far more powerful than reading about these forms of art in a book. And search for community venues to display your students' art once completed; this strengthens the bonds they have started to develop and invites connections from a variety of community members who view it.

Ultimately place-based art education seeks to establish connections between learners and their own neighbourhoods, increasing the relevance of curriculum and making it directly applicable to their lives. If students develop strong bonds with their place and their community physically, politically, culturally, emotionally, and spiritually, they are more likely to care for it and seek to protect and improve it as they mature. So take your art program outside – not only will you develop your students' art skills and knowledge, but you will also contribute to their growing sense of place, empathy and respect, qualities they can take with them any place in future.

References

Adams, E. (1999). Art and the built environment: A framework for school programs. In Guilfoil, J. (Ed.), *Built environment education* (pp.184-193). Reston, VA: National Art Education Association.

Anderson, H. (2000). A river runs through it: art education and a river environment. *Art Education, 53*(6), 13-18.

Asher, R. (2000). The Bronx as art: Exploring the urban environment. *Art Education, 53*(4), 33-38.

Birt, D., Krug, D. & Sheridan, M. (1997). Earthly matters: learning occurs when you can hear the grass singing. *Art Education, 50*(6), 6-13.

Blandy, D. & Hoffman, E. (1993). Toward an art education of place. *Studies in Art Education, 35*(1), 22-33.

Gradle, S. (2007). Ecology of place: Art education in a relational world. *Studies in Art Education, 48*(4), 392-411.

Graham, M. (2007). Art, ecology, and art education: Locating art education in a critical place-based pedagogy. *Studies in Art Education 48*(4), 375-391.

Gruenewald, D. A. (2003). Foundations of place: A multidisciplinary framework for place-conscious education. *American Educational Research Journal, 40*(3), 619-654.

Holloway, D. & Krensky, B. (2001). The arts, urban education and social change. *Education and Urban Society, 33*(4), 354-365.

Inwood, H. (2006). Growing art in school gardens, *Green teacher, 80*, 39-42.

Inwood, H. (2008). At the crossroads: Situating place-based art education. *Canadian Journal of Environmental Education, 13*(1), 29-41.

Keifer-Boyd, K. (2002). Open spaces, open minds: Art in partnership with the earth. In Gaudelius, Y. & Spiers, P. (Eds.), *Contemporary issues in art education* (pp. 327-343.) Upper Saddle River, NJ: Prentice Hall.

Lippard, L. (1997). *The Lure of the local: Senses of place in a multicentered society.* New York: The New Press.

London, P. (1994). *Step outside: Community-based art education.* Portsmouth, NH: Heinemann.

Milbrandt, M., Felts, J., Richards, B., & Abghari, N. (2004). Teaching-to-learn: A constructivist approach to shared responsibility. *Art Education, 57(5),* 19-24, 33.

Orr, D. (1992). *Ecological literacy: Education and the transition to a postmodern world.* Albany: State University of New York Press.

Sanger, M. (1997). Sense of place in education. *Journal of Environmental Education, 29*(1), 4-8.

Sobel, D. (2004). *Place-based education: Connecting classrooms and communities.* Great Barrington, MA: The Orion Society.

Thurber, F. (1997). A site to behold: Creating curricula about local urban art. *Art Education, 50*(6), 33-39.

Contributors

Joanna Black is currently an Associate Professor of Art Education in the Faculty of Education and is cross-appointed as an Associate Professor in the School of Art at the University of Manitoba, Winnipeg, Manitoba, Canada. She teaches visual arts and new media education including video art. Her research interests and published works are on the subjects of the virtual visual arts classroom, new media in education, and digital visual arts pedagogy. She is currently curating a new media exhibition for the Canadian Society for Education through Art (CSEA). This show will be a representation of Canadian secondary students' art that will be held in Estonia. Previous to this, she has worked as an art director, curator, museum art educator, art consultant, and K-12 teacher for close to twenty years in public and alternative school settings.

Lorrie Blair is Associate Professor of Art Education at Concordia University. Her teaching and research interests are censorship, outsider and folk art, Irish popular culture, and popular visual culture, with a particular focus on the gendered meanings and practices of body modification. She is active as a supervisor of MA and PhD thesis students.

Mary Blatherwick is a professor in Art Education at the University of New Brunswick. She studied at the Nova Scotia College of Art and Design, University of British Columbia, and Roehampton University in London England. Mary is a strong advocate for both public school and community-based art education. Her accomplishments include: developing collaborative programs with public schools, arts centres, museums and galleries to increase critical awareness and learning through the arts, creating educational and cultural resources based on her research findings, and working with political interests to improve art education opportunities in this region of Canada. She has received several awards, which include the Award of Excellence in Arts Education from the province of New Brunswick and the Allen P. Stuart Award of Excellence in teaching given by the University of New Brunswick.

Mary is researching and documenting the creative practices of prominent New Brunswick visual artists. This series of films is used as an educational resource in schools and galleries of Atlantic Canada. Other research interests include: visual communication, art and cultural understanding, and the role of creativity in education. She presents her research regionally, nationally and internationally

In 2002 she established the New Brunswick Visual Art Education Association (NBVAEA). Mary chairs the Saint John Arts Centre, and is an executive member of the Canadian Society for Education through Art.

Juan Carlos Castro is Assistant Professor of Art Education at Concordia University. His research focuses on the dynamics and qualities of knowing, learning and teaching art through new and social media as understood through complexity thinking, network theory, hermeneuticsand phenomenology. He is also a practicing artist whose current inquiry explores place, ecology, and learning. Prior to joining the faculty at Concordia University, Juan has taught at the University of Illinois, University of British Columbia, Johns Hopkins University, Maryland Institute College of Art, and the Burren College of Art. Juan is a National Board Certified Teacher and taught at Towson High School in Maryland from 2000-2006. As a high school teacher, Juan's teaching and curriculum was awarded a Coca-Cola Foundation Distinguished Teacher in the Arts from the National Foundation for the Advancement in the Arts and twice awarded with a U.S. Presidential Scholars Teacher Recognition Award.

Aileen Pugliese Castro is a Visiting Assistant Professor of Art Education at Concordia University, and an exhibiting watercolour landscape painter. She has taught at University of Illinois in Urbana-Champaign and University of British Columbia. She has over thirteen years of experience teaching young artists (preschool and elementary) in Howard County Public Schools, Maryland and at Arts Umbrella in Vancouver, British Columbia. She has her BFA and MAT from the Maryland Institute College of Art, Baltimore, MD.

Graeme Chalmers is a Professor Emeritus of Art Education, University of British Columbia, where he also was the third holder of the David Lam Chair in Multicultural Education. He was born, attended school, university art school, teachers' college, and began teaching in Auckland, Aotearoa/New Zealand. A Fulbright Award enabled Graeme to earn graduate degrees in art education in the United States (Indiana and Oregon), and he came to Canada in 1972, first to Concordia University and then to UBC in 1975, retiring in 2008. With research areas in both art education history and the socio-cultural foundations of art education he has authored four books and many journal articles and reports. He has served as Senior Editor of Studies in Art Education and on several editorial boards. He is the recipient of awards from the Canadian Society for Education through Art, the National Art Education Association, INSEA, the British Columbia Art Teachers' Association, and Heritage Canada. A former Chief Examiner in Visual Arts, Graeme is still actively involved as Principal Examiner for Extended Essays in Visual Art with the International Baccalaureate Diploma Program.

Miriam Cooley, BFA, BEd, MA, PhD (Concordia) is an Associate professor of Art Education in the Faculty of Education at the University of Alberta. Her work in teacher education is grounded in her experience as a classroom art specialist and in teaching graduate and undergraduate art education and studio courses in Montreal, Nova Scotia, and now in Edmonton. Painting and drawing were her first passion, although her current artistic work is in photography, film, and video and photo installation. She researches visual culture, creativity and creative process(es), teacher inquiry, collaborative research practices, and the dynamics of artistic production as research.

Michael J. Emme is associate professor of Art Education at the University of Victoria in British Columbia. He has co-created comic books, gallery art, installations and performance works with elementary students, educators and fine arts graduate students alike in Canada and the U.S. His visual and academic research centers around the ways that 'lens media' and digital technology can support collaborative-creative inquiry. His current work focuses on the potential for Graphic novels to support multimodal academic inquiry. Previously Dr. Emme has served as faculty at the University of Alberta, Central Washington University and the Nova Scotia College of Art and Design. He has also served on committees developing the elementary curriculum guidelines in both Washington state and British Columbia and as editor of the *Journal of Social Theory and Art Education*. He is currently editor and art director for *The Canadian Art Teacher*.

Stephen Elliott is currently Dean and Associate Professor in the Faculty of Education at Queen's University in Kingston, Ontario. His major academic interests involve art education, aesthetics and art criticism. Prior to his appointment as Dean he has served as Associate Dean and Chair of the Faculty Board. Dr. Elliott is actively involved in the visual arts community and is currently the Co-Coordinator of the Artist in Community Education Program in the Faculty.

Dr. Elliott holds an Ontario Teachers Certificate, a BFA (Honours) and a B.Ed. From Queen's University, an M.Ed from Queen's University, and a Ph.D. in Art Education from Concordia University. He is a recognized painter and printmaker working from his studio in Gananoque Ontario. His artistic work, primarily still-life, explores the personal narratives we create in the domestic spaces where we live and work. He has a refereed portfolio of paintings and an extensive record of juried exhibitions and awards within the art community. He has worked as a custom printer for several notable artists including Andre Bieler. Dr. Elliott has publications, professional presentations, and has presented academic papers at conferences in the field of art education.

Kit Grauer is currently a professor of art education at the University of British Columbia and actively involved in art education organizations at the local, national, and international levels. Dr. Grauer's interests include arts-based and image-based research, international issues in art education, teacher education, museum education, digital media and art curriculum and instruction. She has taught art as a classroom teacher and an Art Supervisor of Instruction in classrooms from kindergarten to graduate school.

Hilary Inwood teaches Art Education in the Initial Teacher Education program at the Ontario Institute of Studies in Education at the University of Toronto. She holds degrees in education (M.Ed, University of Toronto), art history (MA, York University) and art education (Ph.D, Concordia University). Her research focuses on integrating art education with environmental education to develop learners' ecological literacy in school and community settings. Her work as an educator and artist extends beyond the classroom to include school gardens, outdoor education centres, parks and galleries.

Rita L. Irwin is a Professor of Art Education, and Associate Dean of Teacher Education, at the University of British Columbia, Vancouver, BC, Canada. Rita received her formal education at the University of Lethbridge (B. Ed.and Diploma), the University of Victoria (M.Ed.) and the University of British Columbia (Ed.D.). She has been an educational leader for a number of provincial, national and international organizations and her research interests have spanned in-service arts education, socio-cultural issues, and curriculum practices across K-12 and informal learning settings. Her most recent co-edited books include "Curriculum in a New Key: The Collected Works of Ted T. Aoki" (co-edited with William F. Pinar), "Revisions: Readings in Canadian Art Teacher Education" (co-edited with Kit Grauer and Mike Emme), and "Being with A/r/tography" (co-edited with Stephanie Springgay, Carl Leggo and Peter Gouzouasis). Rita is an artist, researcher, and teacher deeply committed to the arts and education.

Robert Kelly Artist and educator Robert Kelly is an associate professor in the Faculty of Arts and an adjunct associate professor in the Faculty of Education at the University of Calgary. His research focus is creativity and educational practice. He is co-editor (with Carl Leggo) of the book Creative Expression, Creative Education: Creativity As A Primary Rationale For Education. He is currently researching and developing two new volumes on creativity in education entitled The Creative Disposition: Developing Personal and Professional Creativity focused on professional development and Educating for Creativity focused on methodology. He is also associate editor of the volume Creative Arts In Interdisciplinary Practice: Inquiries For Hope and Change (Cheryl McLean, editor).

As artist, his most recent work is his conceptual Minutia installation exhibited across Canada consisting of eleven books of concrete poetry on lecterns, based on the sentence fragment "the first time I heard the sound of a page turning."

He has developed several courses on creativity and educational practice and is a regular presenter of keynotes, lectures and workshops across Canada on this topic. Robert is currently piloting a unique School of Creativity research project in a K to 6 public school in Calgary. rkelly@ucalgary.ca www.robertkelly.ca

Sharon McCoubrey is the Associate Dean of the Faulty of Education at UBC Okanagan. She is Past-President of the Canadian Society for Education through Art and has been on the British Columbia Art Teachers' Association Executive for over 20 years. She is currently President of the Arts Council of the Central Okanagan, serves on the UBC Okanagan Senate, Chairs the Lake Country Public Art Commission, is President of the Lake Country Art Gallery Society, and is in her 13th year as Chairperson of Lake Country ArtWalk Festival.

Dr. McCoubrey obtained her Bachelor of Education and Master of Education Degrees from the University of Victoria and her Doctorate Degree from UBC, all in art education. She has been the recipient of several Excellence in Art Education Awards, and has also been presented with the Order of Lake Country for her work in Public Art, a BC Achievement Award, and the UBC Outstanding Faculty Award for excellence in professional and community work. When possible, Sharon spends treasured time in her painting studio, or in the peaceful gardens on their organic orchard in Lake Country, BC.

Dónal O'Donoghue is an Associate Professor in the Faculty of Education at the University of British Columbia (UBC), Vancouver, where he serves as Chair of Art Education. His research interests are in art education, arts-based research methodologies, curriculum theory, and masculinities. He has published widely in these areas, and received the 2010 Manuel Barkan Memorial Award from the National Art Education Association (United States) for his scholarly writing. Prior to his appointment at UBC, he taught at the University of Limerick, Mary Immaculate College, Ireland. He was a secondary school art and design teacher for many years before becoming a university professor. He has extensive experience in curriculum design and assessment, having worked with the National Council for Curriculum and Assessment, Ireland as an art education consultant. Currently, he serves as a member of The NAEA Council for Policy Studies Art Education, The NAEA Higher Education Division Research Steering Committee, IVSA Executive Board, and Studies in Art Education Editorial Board. Previously, he served as the Honorary Secretary of the Arts Based Educational Research SIG of AERA and the Educational Studies Association of Ireland. As an artist, he has exhibited his work in Europe and North America.

Heather Pastro is a professor of Art Education at Vancouver Island University, where she is also the coordinator for the Post Baccalaureate Degree Program. Heather supervises pre-service teachers while simultaneously teaching art education methodology courses. Heather holds a master's degree from San Diego State University and a B. Ed. from the University of British Columbia.

Highlights in her career as an art educator have included coordinating children's art exhibitions at local galleries, hosting the BC Art Teacher's Association annual provincial conference, and working with teachers as she conducts workshops on a variety of topics in art education. For four years Heather has worked with Binney and Smith, makers of Crayola products, as a site coordinator for the Western Pacific region of Canada. She has delivered scholarly papers at international conferences and taught art lessons to children in her community, always mindful of the depth and breadth of art education.

Currently, Heather is an active executive member of the B.C. Art Teacher's Association as well as a member of both the Canadian Society for Education through Art and National Art Education Association. She has received recognition awards from the NAEA and the CSEA for her contributions to art education. Her recent research is in the area of visual literacy, as Heather strongly believes that creativity and literacy are very important in education.

Although teaching art requires much of her energy, Heather tries to make time to work in her own studio with a variety of media and feels that through teaching art and making art, she is in her element.

Harold Pearse resides in Edmonton, Alberta with his wife, cat and two dogs. Educated at the University of British Columbia, Vancouver BC (BEd), Sir George Williams University (Concordia), Montreal, Que. (MA in Art Education) and the Atlantic Institute of Education at Dalhousie University, Halifax, NS (PhD), he has over forty years experience teaching art at the public school and post secondary levels. Formerly a Professor of Art Education at the Nova Scotia College of Art and Design, he is currently an Adjunct Professor in the Faculty of Education at the University of Alberta and a Sessional Instructor in the Department of Elementary Education. Dr. Pearse has delivered presentations, lectures and workshops to art and education groups at the local, national and international levels and has held office in a variety of professional associations and organizations – most recently as Past President of the CSEA. He has authored or edited books, chapters and articles on various aspects of art education for Canadian and American professional publications. As a practicing artist he has had numerous solo and group exhibitions, commissions for art in public buildings and art work (paintings, drawings, prints, photomontages) in public and private collections.

Patti Pente is an artist and scholar working at the University of Alberta, Edmonton, AB. Her interests include aspects of continental philosophy, visual art, and curriculum theory. She has taught in elementary, secondary, and post-secondary institutions and is a parent of two young children. She continues to investigate her interests through painting, poetry, video, and/or site-specific work.

Anita Sinner is an Assistant Professor of Art Education at Concordia University. Her research interests include preservice and inservice teacher education, community-based art education, arts-based methods, relational aesthetics, life and light writing and digital media. As an artist, researcher and teacher, Anita brings interdisciplinary perspectives to research involving qualitative approaches and many forms of arts research in relation to curriculum studies and social and cultural issues in education. Anita publishes widely, exhibits her artworks and has secured a range of research grants, including a SSHRC Post-Doctoral Fellowship to support her historical research into the lives of teachers in Canada and England. In recognition of her commitment to art education, she has received a number of awards for her scholarship and teaching.

Karen Taylor is a nearly completed undergraduate student at the University of Victoria with special interests in History, Art, cartooning, education and dogs. (Not necessarily in that order.)

Boyd White (Ph. D. Concordia University) is Associate Professor in the Department of Integrated Studies in Education, Faculty of Education, McGill University. Early in his career White was a printmaker, painter, and art educator. Currently his key teaching and research interests are in the areas of philosophy and art education, particularly on the topic of aesthetics and art criticism. Dr. White is the author of numerous journal articles, has chapters in various texts, among them, Readings in Canadian Art Teacher Education and this edition of Starting with…. Recently, he has published two texts: Aesthetics Primer (2009), Peter Lang Publishers, and Aesthetics Education for the 21st Century, co-edited with Tracie Costantino, (2010), Sense Publishers. For a number of years he was editor of Canadian Review of Art Education: Research and Issues. He serves as a reviewer for a number of journals and educational research organizations.

Michelle Wiebe, Ed.D., RGD, is an art educator and a Registered Graphic Designer with many years of experience in the classroom. She has taught in Alberta, British Columbia and Ontario. She taught graphic design in Toronto for 7 years before moving to Victoria to teach at the University of Victoria. At U Vic she has the pleasure of teaching both studio courses and art education methods courses.

Bill Zuk is Professor Emeritus and **Bob Dalton** is an Associate Professor in art education at the University of Victoria. They have a longstanding interest in the art and culture of indigenous people, particularly in the Pacific Northwest. Bill's teaching career began among the Inuit of the Canadian Arctic and then a remote Tsimshian village on coastal British Columbia. They have written numerous articles and published a series of texts with large-scale reproductions for teachers – "Art First Nations: Tradition and Innovation in the Circumpolar World". Their description and interpretation of the work compares traditional and contemporary art forms, and incorporates the lens of image development strategies to analyze the art, moving towards an understanding of the power of the imagery. Prior to the release of this series, Bill collaborated with another colleague to create a series focused on the traditional and contemporary art of aboriginal peoples from various geographic regions of Canada and the United States. Consultation with aboriginal elders and artists respecting their role as rightful guardians of knowledge insured that appropriation and inaccuracy was avoided. As well, both authors are dedicated to their own studio development and exhibit and co-curate exhibitions with students and fellow instructors.

notes & sketches